University City

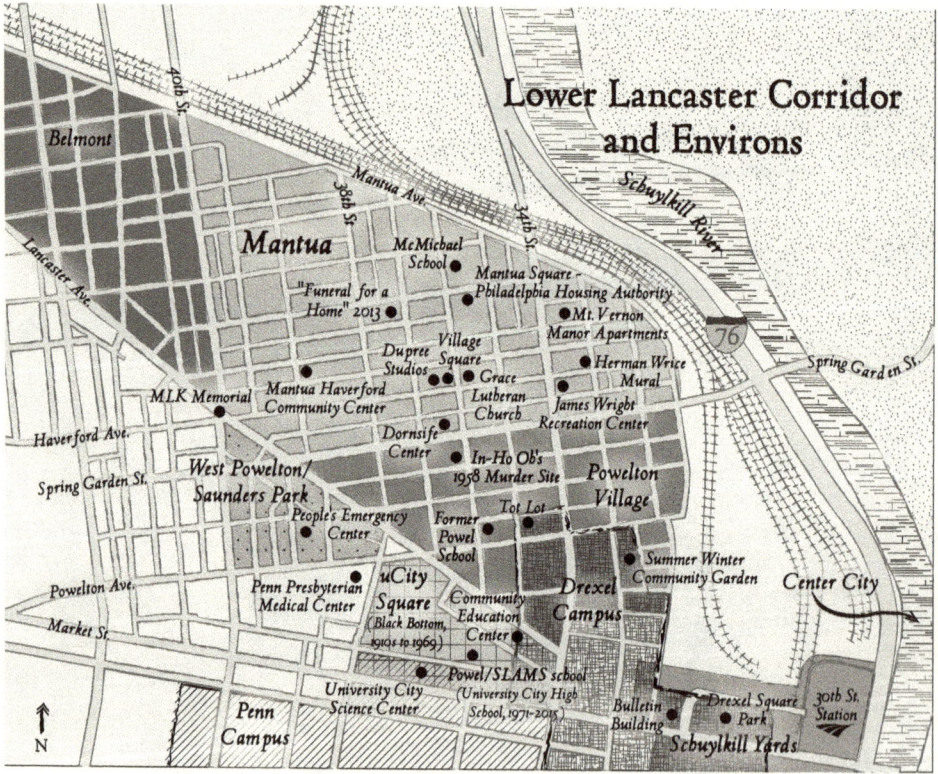

Lower Lancaster Corridor and Environs

Belmont

40th St.

Mantua Ave.

38th St.

34th St.

Schuylkill River

Mantua

McMichael School

Mantua Square
Philadelphia Housing Authority

Lancaster Ave.

"Funeral for a Home" 2013

Mt. Vernon
Manor Apartments

76

Spring Garden St.

Dupree Studios

Village Square

Herman Wrice Mural

MLK Memorial

Mantua Haverford Community Center

Grace Lutheran Church

James Wright Recreation Center

Haverford Ave.

Dornsife Center

Spring Garden St.

In-Ho Oh's 1958 Murder Site

Powelton Village

West Powelton/ Saunders Park

Tot Lot

People's Emergency Center

Former Powel School

Summer Winter Community Garden

Center City

Powelton Ave.

Penn Presbyterian Medical Center

uCity Square

Drexel Campus

Market St.

(Black Bottom, 1910s to 1969)

Community Education Center

University City Science Center

Powel/SLAMS school
(University City High School, 1971–2015)

Bulletin Building

Drexel Square Park

30th St. Station

N

Penn Campus

Schuylkill Yards

UNIVERSITY CITY

History, Race, and Community in the Era of the
Innovation District

Laura Wolf-Powers

PENN

UNIVERSITY OF PENNSYLVANIA PRESS

PHILADELPHIA

Published by
University of Pennsylvania Press
Philadelphia, Pennsylvania 19104-4112
www.upenn.edu/pennpress

Printed in the United States of America on acid-free paper
10 9 8 7 6 5 4 3 2 1

A Cataloging-in-Publication record is available
from the Library of Congress
Hardcover ISBN 9781512822731
eBook ISBN 9781512822717

Frontispiece. Mantua, Powelton Village,
and Environs, 2022. Image by Elizabeth Rose.

This book is dedicated to Josh and to Sasha.

CONTENTS

A Twice-Cleared Place

In 1967, with the blessing and financial support of the federal Urban Renewal Administration, the Redevelopment Authority of the City of Philadelphia began its long-planned demolition of the Black Bottom, a predominantly Black neighborhood north and south of Market Street between 34th and 40th Streets in West Philadelphia.[1] Part of a an expansive 82.6-acre tract that government officials and academic administrators referred to as University City Urban Renewal Area Unit 3, the Black Bottom had been home, six years prior, to 69 businesses, 1,407 homes, and 3,423 people, many of them first-generation migrants from the southern United States.[2] Of the 1,407 homes, 1,153 had been rental units (most in poorly maintained subdivided row houses), while 254, or 18 percent of the total, had been owner-occupied.

In 1965, a residents' organization, the Citizens Committee of University City Redevelopment Area Unit 3, had presented redevelopment officials with a strong case for preserving or reconstructing housing in Unit 3. The group's members had asserted that the area offered stable living options for people who faced both marginality in the city's labor markets and a real estate color line that profoundly constrained their housing choices. "Negroes caught up in the relocation process currently are forced by a limited open housing market into ghettoes and slums," the committee wrote. "Should [the neighborhood] be designated for total clearance extraordinary pressure would be placed upon the adjacent areas to house the families which would be displaced. This would re-open the threat of overcrowding and rent gouging."[3] Despite the astuteness of this argument for neighborhood preservation and against displacement, the Redevelopment Authority would go on to demolish all sixty-nine of the Black Bottom's businesses and all but eight of its 1,407 homes.

City officials cleared Unit 3 primarily for the University City Science Center, a research complex that embodied the intention of five prominent West Philadelphia academic institutions and hospitals to contribute to the economic modernization of their city by facilitating the growth of what present-day policymakers would call "knowledge-based businesses." The project was an effort on the part of the West Philadelphia Corporation, a multi-institutional consortium spearheaded by the University of Pennsylvania, to provide "an unusual opportunity for education and industry to find common cause through research and development,"[4] and it remains America's first and oldest urban technology park. The Science Center also formed the symbolic heart of a bid to reimagine the residential and commercial landscapes immediately adjacent to the universities' campuses. The Science Center would help to invent University City: a technologically advanced and economically prosperous "city of knowledge" on the ruins of what officials had considered a disposable neighborhood.[5]

In addition to the Science Center, another significant new landowner in the Black Bottom in 1967 was the Philadelphia Board of Education. School board officials, whose number included ex-mayor and noted liberal reformer Richardson Dilworth, were ready to begin site preparation for a science-specialized high school that the West Philadelphia Corporation's board and staff members had spent considerable political capital to bring into being. Activists had fiercely protested the siting of University City High School at 36th and Filbert Streets, because it was the precise location where the Redevelopment Authority had pledged, three years before, to build replacement housing for homeowners who stood to be displaced by the Science Center. But proponents of the high school beat back these efforts, ultimately persuading city officials to clear all but a sliver of the Black Bottom neighborhood for redevelopment. The school as an educational institution would never achieve for its students what its advocates had promoted: a rigorous alternative curriculum and close partnerships with Science Center companies. But the construction of the school's building had helped to realize the West Philadelphia Corporation's vision of a completely new neighborhood, rid of all traces of the homes and businesses that had previously existed there.

Almost fifty years later, in 2015, again in the name of technology-driven, university-led urban revitalization, the fourteen-acre site at 36th and Filbert Streets in University City became a *tabula rasa* once more. Constructed on land purchased by Drexel University from the Philadelphia School District the prior year, the uCity Square project—which demolished the fortress-like

University City High School and replaced it with offices, labs, housing, retail stores, public spaces, and another school—emanated from a partnership that consisted of Drexel, the Science Center, and the property developer BioMed Realty and its subsidiary Wexford Science + Technology.[6] "Both a brand and a place," according to one media account, the uCity Square development expanded on the Science Center's core infrastructure to create a live/work/ play neighborhood featuring consumer-focused development aligned with the market for offices and research labs.[7] Three years later, a few blocks to the east on fourteen acres of former parking lots and industrial buildings near the Schuylkill River, Drexel and its partner Brandywine Realty Trust began work on Schuylkill Yards, a five-million-square-foot master-planned project that, like uCity Square, represented itself as an innovation district— namely, a "knowledge neighborhood," "centered around human interaction and unique environments" destined to be a hub for commercial and residential activity.[8] In a place that five decades before had been the subject of a deeply contested struggle over the means and ends of urban policy, another round of real estate investment had begun. As before, city and university leaders were positioning campus-adjacent neighborhoods as locations for a resurgence of economic prosperity built on scientific knowledge and commercial ingenuity. And as before, longtime residents of nearby low-wealth neighborhoods were concerned about where they fit into the plan.

* * *

In some respects, the contemporary political milieu for university-sponsored, innovation-driven economic development in West Philadelphia could not be more different from the context that surrounded the Black Bottom's redevelopment in the 1960s. At that time, in the few neighborhoods where discriminatory norms did not prevent them from doing so, Black households that rented or owned property faced a constant threat that they might be displaced by publicly funded redevelopment.[9] Today, politicians no longer see the taking of land through eminent domain and the expulsion of marginal residents and businesses as acceptable.[10] The federal government, so significant an actor in an earlier era, has for many decades dedicated little attention, and even less funding, to urban projects. Legislative and cultural changes sparked by the civil rights and Black Power movements have produced a larger and more stable Black professional class, and elected officials, activists, and community organizations representing Black and brown neighborhoods have achieved influence and respect in Philadelphia and throughout the United States. Since the Black Bottom was demolished, Philadelphia has had three Black mayors. Though barriers and predatory behaviors persist, housing and labor markets in U.S. cities are less overtly discriminatory than they were in the 1960s.[11]

Urban planning practice has also pivoted. Planners today regard redevelopment projects like the one that resulted in the University City Science Center with contrition. The dispossession of poor households of color that accompanied many urban renewal projects in the mid-twentieth century persists in the political discourse largely as a subject for historians—an uncomfortable aftertaste left over from a less enlightened time. Moreover, cities that experienced precipitous decline at midcentury are themselves experiencing reinvestment. City officials and urban university administrators in Philadelphia, Pittsburgh, St. Louis, and Boston were once on the defensive, scrambling to assemble federal funding for projects aimed at stemming drastic employment and population attrition. Now these actors' successors point to emergent innovation district projects that they are pursuing in partnership with private firms. Hailing a growing body of research on the catalytic effects of urban agglomeration on economic productivity, academics, and industry associations tout the innovation district as an economic engine, generating jobs and revenue while offering amenities and novel experiences to knowledge workers with a preference for urban lifestyles.[12] Innovation-branded, live/work/play development involving anchor institutions as partners has become a common component of many cities' economic development toolkits, and a standard product in real estate investors' portfolios.

Nevertheless, there are two significant points of continuity between twenty-first-century university innovation district politics and its mid-twentieth-century antecedent. The first is that nonfinancial investments people have made in neighborhoods that stand to be transformed by adjacent redevelopment—especially investments of time, care, and engagement—are not considered valuable. "Think about when they tear down a house," a community informant told me. "The memories, the lives of the people who lived there—and we just tear stuff up."[13] As a store of memory, and as a potential home for a household of limited means, an old house in a poor community adjacent to an innovation district site has value. In financial terms, it is worthless—a structure that must be torn down to unlock the value of underlying land.[14] Materials published by university and public sector actors about urban innovation districts tout dollars of capital invested, advertise the details of building programs and the number of square feet to be constructed, and dwell on the global reputations of the architects engaged to design new neighborhoods. This conveys a strong message that transactions pursued by firms in the real estate sector are synonymous with development, and that this development intrinsically addresses public needs. Yet even as university and government officials vow to develop without displacement and to elevate neighborhood-based asset-building, the opportunity to preserve and build upon what existing residents value and care about remains under threat when the practice of innovation-driven redevelopment is accountable overwhelmingly to conceptions of worth and viability defined by actors and investors in the property market.[15]

A second—and related—point of continuity between the present and the past is residents' uncertainty that they or their children will have a secure place in the revitalized neighborhoods that universities and their development partners envision. Academics and policy commentators agree that a modern knowledge economy rests on the synergy of private for-profit companies in sectors like life sciences and bio-informatics with universities and hospitals—the so-called "eds and meds" sectors. This is why universities are indispensable partners in innovation district initiatives. But while universities, hospitals, and the corporate spinoffs that commercialize academic discoveries are major employers, many residents of low-income neighborhoods around them find it difficult to obtain decently waged work there, whether because of inadequate skills, arrest records, or endowments of social capital and network ties that are incompatible with participation in the primary labor market. To address this dilemma, universities have mounted economic inclusion efforts. As a Drexel University vice president asserted in 2016, "This is a 15- to 20-year vision. The vision is that the child going to school in Mantua today will grow up to get one of those innovation jobs."[16] Statements like this one reflect a hope that universities' investments in educational initiatives, and the outreach they initiate in distressed areas near their campuses, will create a future in which formerly disadvantaged community members are welcomed into innovation districts as employees, consumers, and tenants. But it can be difficult for incumbent residents—particularly those who remember and have experienced the effects of previous rounds of university-driven redevelopment—to have confidence in this promise. As a community-based informant observed, "We have generation after genera-tion of people who have not progressed."[17]

This book investigates the contemporary politics of the innovation dis-trict by reflecting on its departures from and enduring connections to the politics of urban renewal. It does this by examining five decades of land use and economic development planning in and around the neighborhoods of West Philadelphia's Lower Lancaster Corridor, which runs from Market Street on the south to the Schuylkill River and the Amtrak/Southeast Penn-sylvania Transportation Authority railyards on the north, and from 34th Street on the east to 40th Street on the west (see frontispiece). Lower Lan-caster's innovation district story—like the stories of the Central West End/Forest Park East neighborhoods in St. Louis (home to the Cortex Innova-tion Community), Midtown Atlanta (home to Tech Square), East Baltimore (home to Johns Hopkins University's East Side Bio-Park), and others—is unique and idiosyncratic. At the same time, it is bound to other innovation district stories by common threads: the publicly subsidized construction of places dedicated to the commercialization of innovation; the outsized po-litical power of urban universities; and property investors' zeal to benefit from mixed-used development on university-owned land. It is also con-nected to those stories through urban renewal history, as the sites chosen for innovation districts are in many cases the same areas that were targeted for slum clearance in the mid-twentieth century.

I argue that in the celebration of the innovation district as a new urban form there often lies a politically expedient—but practically problematic—conflation of property wealth accumulation with broadly beneficial economic development. I further argue that university administrators, city officials, and investors avoid acknowledging the structural racism (evident during urban renewal and persisting into the present) that poorly situates low-wealth resi-dents of color with respect to the economic and cultural opportunities that innovation districts offer. With these arguments, I aim to unsettle the admit-tedly appealing consensus among contemporary innovation-district boosters that progressive and inclusive urban redevelopment policies in the United States have decisively superseded harmful, racist ones.

*   *   *

The relationship between the neighborhoods and universities of West Philadel-phia goes back to the nineteenth century. Real estate entrepreneurs originally constructed the residential neighborhoods of Mantua, Powelton Village, Saunders Park, West Powelton, and Greenville (Greenville more familiarly called the Black Bottom) in the mid-1800s on what had been farm and estate land across the Schuylkill River from Philadelphia's downtown core, known as Center City. The influx of working-class households into these new neighborhoods became possible through the extension of streetcar lines to West Philadelphia in the late nineteenth century. The new transit-oriented communities were clustered around Lancaster Avenue, a commercial thoroughfare that dated back to Native American habitancy of the Lower Schuylkill region. The University of Pennsylvania moved from Center City to the immediate south of Lower Lancaster Corridor in 1872, and the Drexel Institute of Art, Science and Industry—the forerunner of the institution that would sponsor the twenty-first-century innovation districts featured in this book—opened at 32nd and Chestnut Streets in 1891.

In the 1950s, faced with the postwar transformation of the Philadelphia metropolitan region and its manufacturing-based economy, both Penn and Drexel—like many urban universities—drew on the tools of the post–New Deal state to purge their immediate surroundings of people and buildings they saw as incompatible with their institutional aspirations. Adopting the name "University City" to claim the diverse neighborhood geographies surrounding their campuses, the universities—with the cooperation of municipal and federal officials—crafted and implemented multiple plans between 1950 and 1970 that demolished old neighborhoods and constructed new ones. As I elaborate in Chapter 1, one of these plans, the plan for University City Urban Renewal Area Unit 3, involved replacing the households and enterprises of the Black Bottom with three new facilities: the University City Science Center, the Penn Presbyterian Medical Center, and University City High School. In spearheading the Unit 3 clearance plan and in squashing opposition to it, the West Philadelphia Corporation, a consortium of universities in which Penn was first among equals, engineered a significant displacement event affecting hundreds of Black households.

Aside from the demolition of the Black Bottom, most of the University of Pennsylvania's urban renewal-era redevelopment projects took place south of Market Street. Thus, the bulk of the Lower Lancaster Corridor was minimally touched by university-led redevelopment in the urban renewal period, although residents of the Powelton Village neighborhood clashed with Drexel over its redevelopment agenda throughout the 1970s. More influential in the Lower Lancaster area at the time were the ideologies, programs, funding streams,

and discourses of the War on Poverty and Great Society, along with the narratives of the civil rights movement, the peace movement, and Black Power.
As I describe in Chapter 2, during the 1960s and 1970s, residents of Mantua,
the northernmost Lower Lancaster Corridor community, experimented
with social and political formations that offered alternatives to the universities' hegemonic idea of what a prosperous city ought to look like. For a time,
Mantua residents operated two powerful and resource-rich organizations:
the Young Great Society (YGS) and the Mantua Community Planners (whose
motto was "Plan or Be Planned For"). The efforts were led by local leaders
Herman Wrice and Andrew Jenkins, and by less visible actors (many of them
women) who got their start in the early 1960s working with neighborhood
young people to prevent and stem gang-related violence. As an outgrowth of
this work, and often in cooperation with residents of adjacent Powelton
Village (known for its middle-class progressivism), YGS and MCP sponsored a variety of self-help projects: community schools and tutoring projects; neighborhood play streets; a health clinic; a credit union; home repair;
sports leagues; a comprehensive neighborhood planning process, and the
construction of a HUD-sponsored low-income apartment complex, Mount
Vernon Manor. While the Young Great Society and Mantua Community
Planners existed, their efforts created employment, fostered social connections, and, according to informants interviewed for this book, changed lives.
For a variety of reasons, however, the groups lost political legitimacy and
financial viability in the mid-1970s, fading in stature as their leaders assimi-
lated themselves into the complex post–Great Society political landscapes of
Philadelphia and the nation.

By 1980, Penn and Drexel had largely completed the projects that early
plans for the University City Urban Renewal Area had mapped out. But their
interventions had transformed University City neither into a hive of science-
oriented employment nor into a harmonious collection of middle-class communities (though several neighborhoods west of Penn, such as Spruce Hill
and Cedar Park, retained university-affiliated households). In the subsequent decades, both universities turned their institutional gaze inward as
the city's continued economic decline, combined with the crack cocaine
epidemic, reduced decently remunerative employment, curtailed public services, and elevated the crime rate across West Philadelphia. Since the early
1970s, the federal government had gradually defunded urban antipoverty
initiatives while placing increasing resources into the criminal-legal system,[18]

and the results were evident in the neighborhoods adjacent to Penn and Drexel.

So universities again ventured into the communities beyond their campuses. Starting in 1996, during the presidency of Judith Rodin, the University of Pennsylvania spearheaded a new urban revitalization program, the West Philadelphia Initiatives (WPI), which targeted crime reduction and aesthetic improvements in Penn-adjacent neighborhoods and initiated major new real estate development in the form of university-serving housing and retail on "soft sites" that had been in Penn's portfolio since the urban renewal period.[19] Significantly, John A. Fry, who became Drexel's president in 2010, was a key implementer of the WPI while serving as an executive vice president at Penn. His experience exerted a clear influence on the redevelopment approach that Drexel took in the 2010s.

Because the Lower Lancaster Corridor neighborhoods fell into Drexel's ambit rather than Penn's, they were not a focus of the West Philadelphia Initiatives. Mantua, in fact, fell completely outside the boundaries of the University City District, a special services district established under the auspices of the WPI in 1997. Like much of the rest of West Philadelphia, the Lower Lancaster neighborhoods had grown progressively poorer and less populous since the late 1970s; aside from Powelton Village, which directly abutted Drexel and was home to many students and faculty, the Lower Lancaster neighborhoods were characterized by vacant land and buildings and by significant material poverty. Lancaster Avenue was a struggling business corridor. Closer in, toward the major thoroughfare of Market Street, University City High School was struggling, and the University City Science Center was not only an economic disappointment but also, according to historians of Penn, a "visual failure" flanked on the north by acres of surface parking.[20] Shortly after Fry ascended to the presidency of Drexel, areas around that institution's campus—including the very territories that had been epicenters of controversy in the 1960s—again became the subject of planning studies. As I show in Chapter 3, Drexel's 2012 Campus Master Plan and Strategic Plan constituted the start of an innovation-themed campus expansion.

Chapter 3 also discusses plans formed in the same period by civic organizations in Mantua and Powelton Village. The Powelton Village Directions Plan and the Mantua Transformation Plan documented existing conditions in those neighborhoods and asserted the civic groups' interest in shaping their futures according to the needs and aspirations of incumbent residents.

But as the decade proceeded, Drexel and its partners moved forward with two large-scale developments prefigured by its 2012 plans—uCity Square and Schuylkill Yards—that potentially threatened the visions articulated by the civic groups. While Drexel's projects benefited nearby neighborhoods in many respects, they also unleashed changes that increased pressure on economically insecure households, as the market's anticipation of uCity Square and Schuylkill Yards pushed up land values and accelerated property speculation.

As innovation districts emerged adjacent to the Lower Lancaster communities in the latter part of the 2010s, civic organizations faced a classic dilemma of neighborhood reinvestment. Drexel's Office of University and Community Partnerships was dedicating resources to a variety of programs designed to position children and adults in Mantua—as well as other low-wealth West Philadelphia neighborhoods—to succeed in the knowledge economy that they hoped would bloom nearby. Meanwhile, the university's real estate development arm was targeting startup firms and college-educated workers in partnership with investors who were betting on property price appreciation. Responding to these dynamics, civic groups drew on tactics of community mobilization honed decades earlier. Mantua-based groups, again working in a tense alliance with counterparts in the more affluent Powelton Village, mounted initiatives to preserve the neighborhood fabric and to ensure that low-income residents would be able to continue to live there if they chose, despite ominous trends in rents and property tax assessments. In 2017, a coalition called the Mantua-Powelton Alliance negotiated a historic Community Benefits Agreement (CBA) with Brandywine Investment Trust, the firm that had entered into partnership with Drexel to develop the Schuylkill Yards site. Chapter 4 describes the dynamics surrounding the CBA negotiation and sheds light on the achievements and limitations of the civic groups' approach.

*   *   *

This study, in drawing connections between the urban renewal-era development of a Science Center in West Philadelphia and the construction of innovation districts there in the 2010s, has several goals. The first is to point out how profoundly the governance of urban redevelopment—and university-led urban redevelopment in particular—has changed in fifty years. At midcentury, in such cities as New York, Chicago, Buffalo, Pittsburgh, and Columbus as well as Philadelphia, redevelopment authorities deemed university-adjacent dwellings and commercial establishments blighted and used federal urban renewal dollars to clear them and replace them with new academic facilities. These facilities not only expanded the universities' physical domains; they also shored up the reputations of the cities they inhabited, symbolizing and to an extent helping to realize cities' aspirations to economic centrality in a time when cities' relevance and utility were being called into question.

Since the turn of the twenty-first century, by contrast, new kinds of public and private partnerships have prevailed. The condemnation and destruction of existing city fabric still occurs, but much more rarely than in the 1960s. In the wake of the controversial 2005 Supreme Court case *Kelo v. City of New London*, new development in cities typically avoids using the power of eminent domain to take property; instead, redevelopment occurs on municipally owned land or on utility infrastructure like railyards.[21] The federal government's role in urban redevelopment has shrunk, and local governments no longer offer direct cash investment. Yet there are many ways of fashioning the grooves into which real estate capital flows. State and local governments are politically and administratively key to the establishment of mechanisms such as tax-increment financing, payments in lieu of taxes (PILOTs), and other exemptions and abatements that facilitate private development on university land. Financing comes from organized groups of investors who understand university-adjacent mixed-use development as a standard real estate product. This product's investment value is established through its association with the innovative, technologically advanced, economically generative aura of the university, and through its association with the wealth and disposable income of the consumers in the university orbit.[22] The new possibilities that university-adjacent master-planned development offers to real estate investors sit against a backdrop of central cities' resurgence as desirable destinations for coveted empty-nesters and young professionals—an inversion of the population and job flight that characterized the 1960s.

Since midcentury urban renewal, then, the terms of investment in and control over university-sponsored development have shifted in ways that are consequential. But the stigmatization of territory associated with communities of color remains an essential part of the urban redevelopment playbook. The second goal of this book is to shed light on the stubborn persistence of policies, habits, and narratives that delegitimize the spatial and social claims of people of color in the local political arenas that redevelopment creates. This devaluation, in West Philadelphia and beyond, occurs because discourses around real estate value and land redevelopment remain inseparable in American urban politics from ideologies of race and social caste. Wherever residential and commercial areas identified with minority groups (and particularly with Black communities) are implicated in redevelopment planning, stigma creeps into the discourse. Sometimes it works as an overt strategy and sometimes as lazily accepted received wisdom. Either way, dislocation, both physical and symbolic, results. When the redeveloper is a university, the rhetoric of stigmatization takes on an added significance because academic institutions lay special claim to qualities such as ingenuity, knowledge, and creativity that are purportedly central to the success of innovation districts. By implication, these qualities are seen to be absent from areas inhabited by low-wealth Black people.

Another apparent contrast between today's redevelopment politics and those of five decades ago has to do with the participation and influence of affected residents. During the protracted struggle over the Black Bottom neighborhood, the West Philadelphia Corporation assiduously ignored the main civic group attempting to assert a voice in the process, the Citizens Committee of University City Redevelopment Area Unit 3, and actively discredited its leaders. By the 2010s, in contrast, inclusion had become a mantra. Drexel's Office of University and Community Partnerships was in frequent contact with the civic groups and nonprofit service providers of the Lower Lancaster Corridor—collaborating with them on funding applications, making regular appearances at their meetings, and sponsoring forums at which the future of their neighborhoods came under discussion. Drexel was responsible for a significant flow into the neighborhoods of federal, city, and philanthropic resources for affordable housing, education, and crime prevention. In addition, the university raised money from alumni to establish two new institutions: the Dornsife Center for Neighborhood Partnerships (a university extension service physically located in Mantua), and a center for civic engagement on the school's campus. President Fry rarely missed an opportunity to highlight equitable, inclusive development as a core goal of "the most civically engaged university in the nation."[23]

Drexel's public pronouncements, though, masked a more complex reality. While the Office of University and Community Partnerships had one mandate, the Department of Real Estate and Facilities had another. The part of the university that managed relationships with third-party development partners responded to a different set of incentives and imperatives than the part of the institution that dealt with neighborhood representatives (as neighborhood representatives were well aware). Drexel officials kept the details of innovation district development projects embargoed until releasing them, fully formed, to the media. They resisted, or absented themselves from, the community benefits discussions that civic groups regarded as pivotal in advancing an anti-displacement agenda.

These stances on a university's part are not particularly surprising, despite officials' statements embracing development without displacement.[24] Municipalities, universities, and real estate professionals habitually deploy the language of equitable development and social inclusion when they speak about innovation districts' economic promise.[25] Activists are rightly skeptical, however, because the ability of low-income households to remain in rapidly redeveloping neighborhoods requires interventions that remove some land from the marketplace to keep it affordable, and policies that would decommodify real property remain anathema in contemporary policy discourse. In Philadelphia and elsewhere, officials consistently reject proposals advocating the commitment of publicly owned land adjacent to major redevelopment projects for deeply, permanently affordable residential or commercial development.

In tracing West Philadelphia activists' efforts to unpack the rhetoric versus the reality of equitable development in the era of the innovation district, I arrive at the third goal of the book: to consider the strategies that Lower Lancaster residents, acting through organizations past and present, have employed to contest the delegitimization of what they value. Recent work in sociology, history, and social psychology has cast new light on the way the stigma of racial inferiority operates politically. Drawing on the writing of W. E. B. Du Bois, Harry Haywood, and Oliver Cox, scholars have pointed to the attributions of pathology, criminality, and incapability that have functioned as forms of social control and normalized Blacks' exclusion from economic and political citizenship. Geographers have brought to the study of urban race politics the insight that stigma attaches recursively to individuals subject to discrimination *and* to the places in which they live. Places become "distinctive anchors of social discredit."[26] Territorial stigmatization serves a critical role in government-supported redevelopment, as policy makers reject landscapes inhabited by disfavored people as blighted and in need of fixing, even to the point of denying that they are places at all.[27] Then, at a later point in time, devaluation operates in reverse. The public sector participates in "fixing" or "improving" a stigmatized territory by making public investments (or forgoing government revenue) in ways that support the dislocation of low-income people from that territory while delivering property into the hands of investors. In the case of innovation districts constructed in formerly discredited spaces, social elites and private sector real estate investment become associated with skill, knowledge, and vitality, and with the economic promise of urbanity. The elevation of these associations, and their affirmation in public policy, normalizes the marginalization of residents of low socioeconomic status and devalues the nonfinancial investments they have made in neighborhoods. I do not argue that this is a conscious or deliberate strategy on the part of city planners or university officials. It is, however, what happens.

Scholars have also pointed out that in resisting stigma, people build identity and power.[28] Research on territorial stigma has noted that residents of denigrated places value them, despite poor-quality housing, inadequate municipal services, crime, and the pain of stigma itself. Reasons cited by research informants for valuing stigmatized places include friendships, proximity to public and third sector amenities, and social solidarity.[29] These findings are borne out by my research in West Philadelphia. Many contemporary informants in Mantua had either witnessed the demolition of the Black Bottom or had grown up hearing about it. Informants who were alive in the 1960s offered precise geographic coordinates for the Black Bottom, distinguishing it from Mantua and from an area to the west known as "the Top" and offering details about the architectural styles and interior décor of the neighborhood's homes. They remembered particular people who had lived there—people who gave dancing and piano lessons ("Anyone who was anyone had a piano in their home," said one informant), people who cooked for one another and looked out for each other's children in addition to the disreputable characters associated with "bottom" neighborhoods in popular culture.[30] They were proud of a previous generation of leaders and organizers who had fought racism in the city's redevelopment policies, offered social solidarity and economic opportunities to children and youth, and engaged residents in planning for their own neighborhoods.

Fifty years on in the Lower Lancaster Corridor, residents coalesced again, in formations they understood as carrying on the legacy of previous work. In rehabilitating distressed HUD Section 236 housing in Mantua in the 2010s, a local community development organization headed by a Young Great

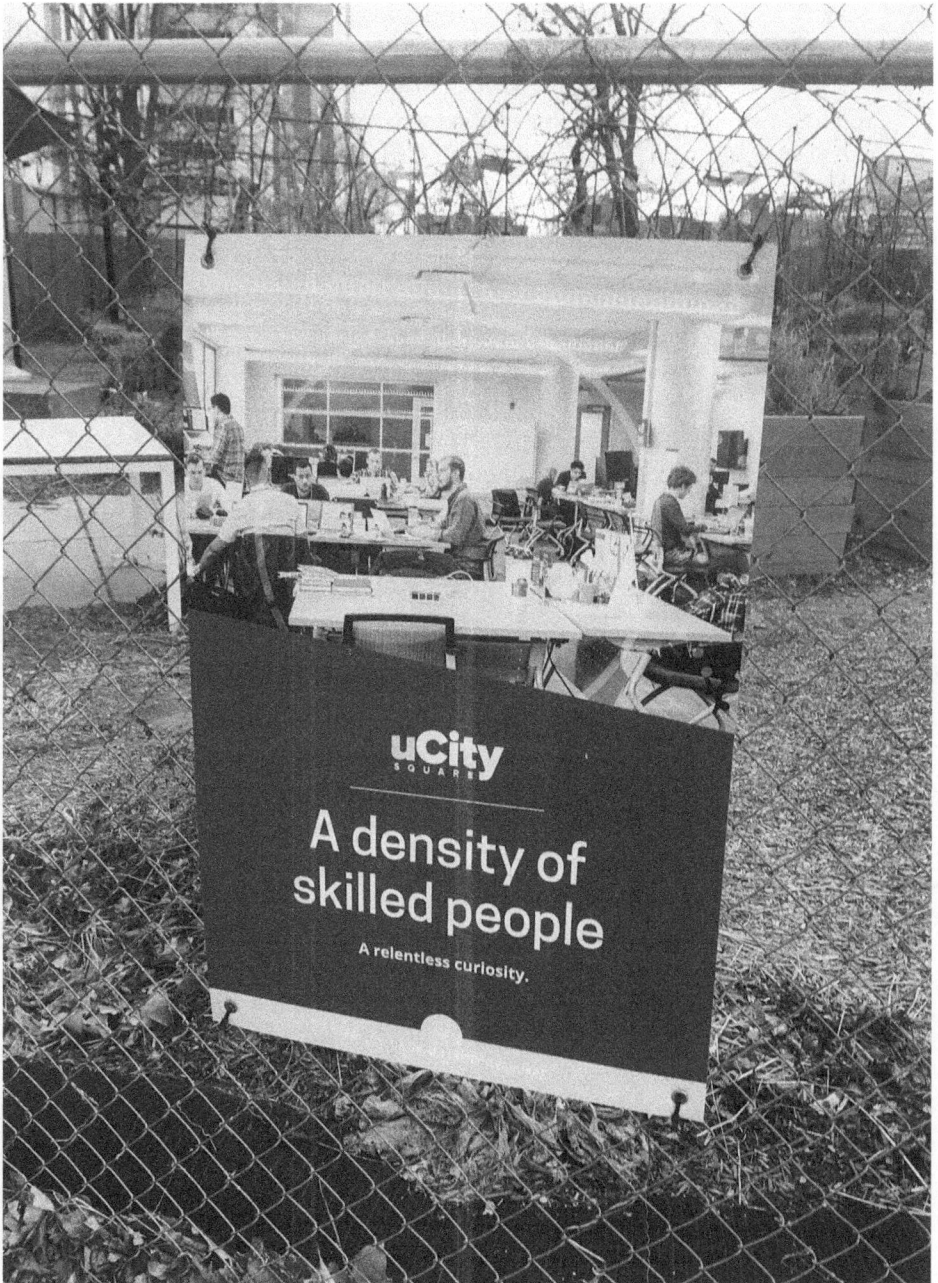

Figure 1. Promotional photo for uCity Square, 36th Street and Lancaster Avenue, 2020. Photo by author.

Society alumnus revived an asset that the Mantua Community Planners organization had built in its heyday. At meetings of a new civic association, Mantua residents strategized to keep homeowners from experiencing devastating increases to their property taxes as real estate values rose. They monitored the quality of social services for the elderly and evaluated the efficacy of efforts to help young people at risk of lifelong involvement with the criminal-legal system. They asserted the need for economic opportunities and the hope that redevelopment would bring jobs (or pathways to jobs) for members of their community. And they anxiously articulated the imperative to preserve Mantua as a place they recognized as theirs. Mantua leaders and their allies fiercely pushed cultural preservation and displacement concerns into the public discourse through their participation in the forging of the Schuylkill Yards Community Benefits Agreement in 2017. In a negotiation with representatives of the developer Brandywine Realty Trust, they won a community-controlled fund dedicated in part to ensuring that economically insecure families could keep a foothold in Mantua and surrounding low-income neighborhoods even as innovation district development changed local property market dynamics.

An undercurrent of resignation, however, pervaded my conversations with community-based informants. They were not typically optimistic that—CBA or not—things would work out well for them and their neighbors as development activity at uCity Square and Schuylkill Yards proceeded. As much as their recollections of the high-stakes redevelopment politics of the 1960s and 1970s informed their response to their current situation, they also were aware that past efforts to build political influence and capacity had resulted in relatively little in the way of enduring institutional power. They were fighting hard for legitimation and resources, but they harbored no illusions; the concessions they achieved might address some of the symptoms of economic and social marginalization, but they would not repair its causes. This was true for two reasons. First, the intergovernmental funding and administrative infrastructure that had briefly supported a War on Poverty in this country during the 1960s and 1970s were now utterly absent.[31] Second, the institutions controlling reinvestment in University City in the 2010s had extremely low capacity to recognize the structural, race- and class-inflected factors that were producing persistent marginality in the Black communities near the areas they had designated for redevelopment. Personnel at these institutions, even as they adopted the language of equity and inclusion, took a fundamentally philanthropic and mitigative—rather than reparative—approach to neighborhood distress.[32] The treatment of low-income Lower Lancaster residents as "stakeholders" in discussions about the uCity Square and Schuylkill Yards projects did not account for power imbalances, nor did it account for history.[33]

Methodologically, this book is a variation on an ethnographic revisit, which, in the words of sociologist Michael Burawoy, occurs when a researcher studies people in place "with a view to comparing his or her site with the same one studied at an earlier point in time."[34] Conceptualizing the ethnographic revisit in his 2009 book *The Extended Case Method*, Burawoy highlights Mitch Duneier's 1999 study of Greenwich Village street vendors, which draws on Jane Jacobs's observations of the same neighborhood forty years earlier. He similarly cites Mary Pattillo, who relates her observations of Black middle-class gentrification in Chicago's Kenwood-Oakland neighborhood in the late 1990s to classic writings by St. Clair Drake, Horace Cayton, and E. Franklin Frazier in the 1940s and 50s.[35] In many cases, researchers perform ethnographic revisits to build on (or to refute) the work of predecessors, but I do not revisit a prior ethnography here. Rather, I assemble an interpretive account of a crucial aspect of University City's planning and development history—drawing extensively on both primary and secondary sources—and combine that account with contemporary interview and observational data to shed light on the area's current dynamics. While not strictly an ethnographic revisit, then, this method deepens the understanding of the current politics of University City's redevelopment by situating them in a historical context. Specifically, I "excavate historical terrain" in a way that "gives meaning to the ethnographic present."[36]

What I find by means of this method is that the market-based, real estate-led approach to innovation-oriented economic development that the City of Philadelphia and its anchor institutions have chosen in the 2010s limits even well-meaning efforts to achieve equitable outcomes for adjacent economically insecure communities. And Philadelphia's anchors are not alone. Despite their contrition about urban renewal, universities across the United States continue to enact, in a contemporary context, many of the assumptions and valuation practices that made urban renewal so destructive for people of color. Planners and policy makers can achieve more equitable outcomes in the present, however, if we are willing to work to effect changes to the context in which redevelopment occurs. First and foremost, this requires that we attend more deliberately to history—to the ways that territorial stigmatization has operated and continues to operate in urban redevelopment processes. It also entails opening political space in which to give voice to heterodox definitions of what it means to be invested in places. And it means operationalizing these definitions in the form of policies—policies that remove land from the market for real property to ensure its long-lived economic accessibility for longtime incumbent residents. A central assertion of this book is that these things are possible, and that they are overdue.

CHAPTER 1

The Black Bottom and the Birth of University City

At 11:00 a.m. on Tuesday February 18, 1969, roughly four hundred people assembled on the green in front of the University of Pennsylvania's College Hall. Largely students from Penn and other area universities, carrying "brightly-colored flags and hand-lettered signs,"[1] they were responding to a call from the university's chapter of Students for a Democratic Society (SDS), an activist group whose leaders were determined to cast light on the devastating consequences of university-led expansion a few blocks from campus.

The demonstrators' destination was a muddy, snowbound construction site at 36th and Market Streets where a laboratory building was soon to rise under the auspices of a five-year-old nonprofit, the University City Science Center Corporation. Before they walked the two blocks in the "toe-curling weather,"[2] and again at the building site itself, speakers addressed the crowd. In an unusual turn for a campus demonstration at Penn, a Black activist from West Philadelphia, the Reverend Edward Sims, exhorted the students to advocate the interests of the community members outside the university gates. "This is your day," Sims intoned. "The university has taken some thirty acres of land from the blacks of this community. Are you good enough to get one acre of it back for us?" "The administrators of the University City Science Center think that we students are a bunch of children," asserted Steven Fraser, an SDS member from Temple University. "We will force them to use their wealth to help this community."[3]

After staging a theatrical performance designed to dramatize the Science Center's dispossession of households in a predominantly Black neighborhood known as the Bottom (as well as the organization's sponsorship of controversial military research), the shivering demonstrators returned to College Hall, where they intercepted University President Gaylord Harnwell on his way back from lunch. In addition to being Penn's president, Harnwell was also the president of the West Philadelphia Corporation, a multilateral organization (dominated by Penn), which constituted the main source of power behind the Science Center and other university expansion in West Philadelphia. Aggrieved students proceeded to "sit in" in the university building for the next five days, as they negotiated a set of demands, first amongst themselves and then with the university trustees.

On the evening of Sunday, February 23, the trustees and the students, with the support of the Faculty Senate and a delegation of West Philadelphia Black leaders, released a six-point agreement that ended the students' occupation of the building. The trustees had agreed two days previously that the Science Center would expressly agree not to "accept secret, classified, or military-related research contracts,"[4] extending to the Science Center Corporation a commitment that student protestors had extracted from the university itself two years prior. More tense and more complicated had been negotiations around a separate slate of demands related to the university's relationship with former residents of the Black Bottom and the inhabitants of Black-majority neighborhoods nearby. The trustees had agreed to form an inclusive multilateral group to set the terms of the university's activities in West Philadelphia going forward. They had also agreed to "raise $10 million for community renewal programs" while rebuilding housing demolished by university construction.[5] A jubilant member of the student negotiating team announced, "We changed the decision-making processes and priorities of this institution. Nothing was destroyed, but we built a hell of a lot."[6] A March 1969 article in Penn's alumni magazine presciently noted, "What was 'built' will be further determined . . . over the next months and years."[7]

The University City Science Center's emerging presence north of Penn's campus in the second half of the 1960s furnished a symbolic link between the university's support for wartime research and its perpetuation of racial injustice. This "perfect storm," as one historian has termed it,[8] made the Science Center a target for student activists in 1969 and briefly brought neighborhood representatives and student radicals together to demand alternatives to the status quo. As ecstatic students left College Hall on the night of February 23, there was reason to be optimistic that Black residents of West Philadelphia north of Market Street would (after years of fractious advocacy efforts) secure economic and political benefits from the area's redevelopment; the

Figure 2. UPenn President Gaylord Harnwell speaking with students at the February 1969 College Hall sit-in. University Archives and Records Center, University of Pennsylvania.

university administration had recognized them in a written statement as a consequential constituency with some claim on the future of the area. The gains won by the protestors in the College Hall sit-in, however, ultimately would do little to interrupt the momentum of an "interlocking directorate"[9] of city and university officials dedicated to a different vision for West Philadelphia. These officials exercised power and controlled resources on behalf of institutions whose rhetoric and actions, by 1969, had succeeded in creating a new West Philadelphia neighborhood called University City.[10] Redevelopment Authority personnel were already working to relocate over one thousand households displaced from the Black Bottom; the interests and claims of the residents who remained in the area were at best an irritant.

A New Name

The term *University City* first occurred in a public document as part of the Philadelphia City Planning Commission's annual report of 1958. While the Commission's 1957 annual report had referred separately to the "Powelton Redevelopment Area" (north of Market Street) and "University Redevelopment Area" (south of Market Street),[11] in 1958 parts of each had been amalgamated into the "University City Redevelopment Area," which contained five distinct subunits.[12] The term *University City* referred (and continues to refer) to the multiple areas of West Philadelphia into which Penn, Drexel, and affiliated medical institutions expanded their footprints during the 1960s and 1970s. University City Urban Renewal Area Unit 3, an 82.3-acre tract of land stretching north from Market Street to Lancaster and Powelton Avenues and east to west from 36th to 38th Streets, is of primary interest here.

The Planning Commission's adoption of the University City moniker occurred as Philadelphia's planning and urban renewal politics underwent a reorientation. The 1951 election of Democrat Joseph Clark as Philadelphia's first reform mayor in generations had aligned the city with a liberal urban consensus that tied big-city mayors and other municipal elected officials to the national Democratic Party and the post–New Deal administrative state.[13] Clark and the highly educated professionals he recruited to his administration had eagerly used the tools and funding provided by the 1949 Housing Act to pursue physical renewal in central Philadelphia and its outlying neighborhoods throughout the early 1950s.[14] In 1956, however, a study

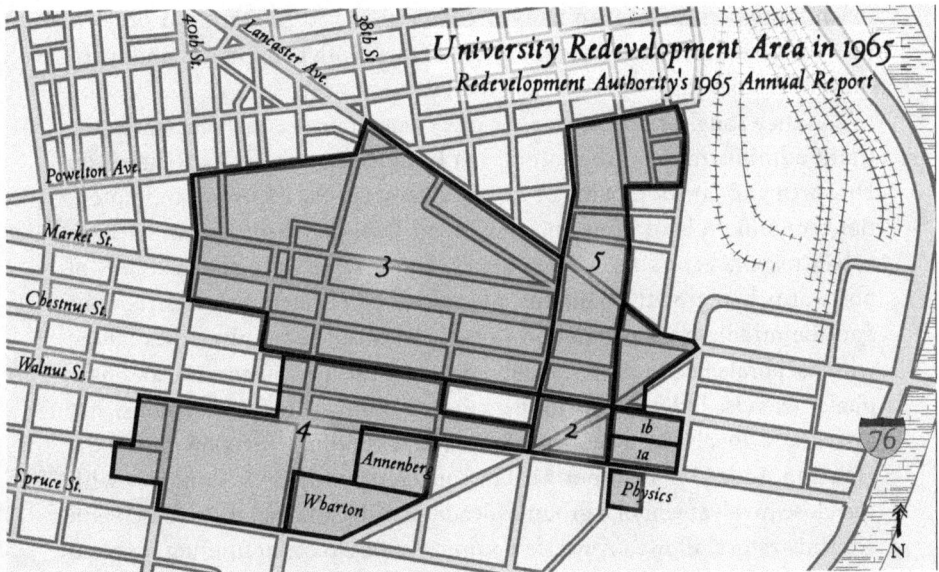

Figure 3. Map of the University City Urban Renewal Area, 1965. Courtesy of the Philadelphia Redevelopment Authority.

conducted by influential figures in the city's civic and planning establishments concluded that while downtown projects had succeeded, comprehensive redevelopment in deteriorating residential neighborhoods had not. Private investment had not followed clearance as expected, and, as in most cities, renewal had dislocated residents at a rate that far outpaced the construction of new housing.[15] The response to the Central Urban Renewal Area (CURA) study, as it was called, was twofold. First, there was a shift away from project initiation in the most distressed parts of the city. Funding and attention would now go toward "conservable" areas, where leaders resolved to focus on housing rehabilitation and code enforcement as opposed to demolition and clearance. Second, the post-CURA approach reflected growing alarm about the city's unemployment situation. Economists had identified a dismaying dispersion of jobs—particularly manufacturing jobs—to the Philadelphia suburbs as well as to southern states, and the region's economic base was adjudged to be weak as well.[16] In their urgency to shore up the city's employment base, Philadelphia officials and policy makers welcomed the 1954 revision of the federal government's Housing Act, which was much more permissive than its 1949 counterpart had been toward projects that replaced deteriorated neighborhood fabric with commercial and institutional (rather than strictly residential) development.

As they sought remedies for the city's economic decline, officials in the Clark administration and those of his Democratic successors Richardson Dilworth and James Tate took a strong interest in the expertise and potential economic role of local universities. In this, they behaved similarly to urban mayors across the United States. Universities were key members of postwar urban growth coalitions. Moored to city centers as industrial jobs and the middle-class population rapidly decentralized, universities (along with corporate headquarters, major corporate services businesses, and hospitals) exercised significant influence over municipal-level decisions, not least those involving federal urban renewal funding.[17] Section 112 of the Housing Act's 1959 reauthorization, conceived in the U.S. Congress with the close involvement of a group of academic advisors that included UPenn administrators, allowed America's municipalities to count funding supplied by universities and hospitals toward the "local match" required to unleash federal dollars. Section 112 proved extraordinarily valuable to cash-poor city administrators, and beneficial to their academic partners. Together with the power to use redevelopment funding under the Housing Act to undertake nonresidential projects, the provision would be a key factor in the creation of university-compatible neighborhood districts in Philadelphia during the 1960s, as it had been or would be in Chicago, Columbus, Buffalo, and New York City.[18] In West Philadelphia, university interests would soon overwhelm the city's stated commitment to prioritizing rehabilitation over demolition in urban renewal projects.

The West Philadelphia Corporation and
the University City Science Center

As changes to the city's urban renewal program and the federal regulations governing it were getting underway, a consortium of academic institutions led by UPenn founded the West Philadelphia Corporation (WPC) in 1959. A multi-institutional collaboration dedicated to transforming the neighborhoods bounding West Philadelphia's academic and medical campuses, the WPC comprised representatives from all of West Philadelphia's academic institutions and hospitals and some of its neighborhood associations. Its goals aligned strongly with city leaders' endeavors to shore up Philadelphia's economic position in the Delaware Valley region and in the nation. In the Corporation's 1962 annual report, a message from UPenn President Harnwell underscored the institution's deep connections to municipal government and its dedication to promoting University City as a new identity (today, we would say "brand") for the collection of neighborhoods adjacent to local university and medical campuses: "Philadelphia today is making an heroic effort to stem urban decline. But its bold, imaginative redevelopment program cannot accomplish this alone . . . five leading educational and medical institutions have formed the West Philadelphia Corporation to mobilize all the available resources, public and private, in developing University City—a residential and business community oriented toward education in its broadest sense and extending its welcome as well to applied research in medicine, engineering, and industry."[19]

From the start, the WPC seized on urban redevelopment as a means to shape University City as a special precinct for the pursuit of scientific knowledge. In 1961, the Corporation announced the intention to construct "a unique tower for scientific research and development" that would be located, along with ten smaller buildings, "between 34th and 36th Streets, Market Street to Lancaster Avenue."[20] The WPC board later amended the plan for a tall tower in favor of a bulkier, more campus-like atmosphere that could go head-to-head with suburban industrial competition.[21] The 1961 report's image of a multifacility complex in a modernist architectural style persisted, however, and this vision informed designs for the University City Science Center, which gained an identity as a nonprofit corporation on October 28, 1963.[22] At the formal announcement of the Science Center's formation, Mayor James Tate gave an interview to the University of Pennsylvania student newspaper in which he expressed the hope that the Science Center would help establish Philadelphia as "a brains capital of the world."[23] Historian Margaret Pugh O'Mara has argued that the Science Center initiative represented a path by which Philadelphia would become a generator of jobs in "advanced industry" that connected directly to basic research taking place at partner universities. University City was not just a location for research facilities but the expression of a more abstract idea: an aspirational "city of knowledge" where men of science, drawing on government-sponsored academic research, would revive and transform Philadelphia's faltering economy.[24] A 1962 West Philadelphia Corporation brochure conjured a future in which business activity in University City would mirror "the clustering of research firms around Harvard University and Massachusetts Institute of Technology." It noted, "Such laboratories can be physically attractive and economically salutary, and they bring to a community a responsible type of citizen."[25] From the perspective of the West Philadelphia Corporation's leadership, the advent of University City as a magnet for responsible citizens meant the dispersal of households and businesses in the Black Bottom, which lay a few blocks to the north of Penn's campus and immediately west of Drexel's.

"A Responsible Type of Citizen"

The catalytic event for the WPC's formation had been a violent murder. On April 25, 1958, twenty-six-year-old University of Pennsylvania graduate student In-Ho Oh left his home on 36th and Hamilton Streets in the Powelton neighborhood to mail a letter on a nearby corner. On the way back from the mailbox, he was viciously beaten to death by eleven young men in what was believed to be a robbery attempt. The ferocity of the attack "sent shock waves through the city";[26] exacerbated tensions between Powelton residents and those of the predominantly Black and economically distressed Mantua neighborhood to its north, where the youths lived; and heightened the anxiety of university administrators, who already were concerned that poverty and crime at their borders represented a threat to institutional stability.[27] University of Pennsylvania planning professor Martin Meyerson,[28] drawing on his knowledge of university-led efforts in predominantly Black areas of Chicago and New York City, had suggested in 1956 that West Philadelphia universities form an entity charged with upgrading the neighborhoods that bounded their campuses by dispersing their "residential slums."[29] By several accounts, the murder of Oh spurred the institutions to act on Meyerson's idea almost immediately.[30]

As the WPC's future members[31] coalesced, their interest in removing the households and businesses of the Black Bottom would drive the WPC's ambitious redevelopment program as strongly as would the desire to seed a new community for scientific research. A document drafted for a June 10, 1958, meeting expressed firm resolve to use urban renewal to remediate a perceived "infection":

In the rushing pell-mell growth of Philadelphia, this neighborhood was engulfed . . . Many of the once fine homes of this neighborhood were converted to apartment houses or rooming houses whose owners lived elsewhere. In turn, many of these houses deteriorated until only the desperate tenant would live in them. The blight of delapidation [sic] began its infectious spread through our area. . . . The best of our neighborhood is worth preserving; the worst should go. . . . The opportunities now before us to join together to preserve and improve our neighborhood are great and demanding.[32]

A 1961 letter from WPC Executive Vice President Leo Molinaro to Philadelphia Planning Commission Chair (and Penn Professor) G. Holmes Perkins laying out University City development priorities provides evidence of which neighborhood the institutions considered "the worst," and what they intended to do about it. "As far as possible," says the letter, "the first project area should be aimed at wiping out the worst slums in University City which lie just north of Market Street between 34th and 38th Streets. The impact of this not only on the economic base of University City but upon morale is immeasurable."[33]

Conditions in the area Molinaro described exemplified a racial and spatial transformation that was taking place throughout the urban industrial North. The neighborhood had undergone both absolute and proportional growth in Black population in the 1940s and 1950s, caused by a dual migration: the in-migration of Black households from the rural south and from elsewhere in Philadelphia, and the out-migration of white households to newly constructed (and racially exclusionary) working-class housing in the suburbs.[34] As in other neighborhoods of the so-called "2nd Ghetto," its poor environmental conditions emanated from the persistence of a real estate color line that crowded Black households into restricted areas, forced them to pay above-market rent for substandard housing, and excluded them from the mortgage market.[35] Widespread discriminatory and predatory housing practices, endorsed by realtors, appraisers and government agencies, were informally enforced through violence.[36] Thus, the dominance of "infiltration theory" in government and the real estate sector had helped to produce the dilapidated buildings and "desperate tenants" cited in the WPC document. Similarly, racism in the public education system, the job market, and the workplace had contributed to Black poverty and unemployment.[37]

But Molinaro and the institutions that employed him did not consider the ways in which racism fed the physical blight they were striving to eradicate, nor did they appreciate how the daily humiliations of labor market discrimination and the uneven enforcement of the law underlay high crime rates among African Americans.[38] Rather than identifying the economic distress observable in the Black Bottom as a symptom of injustice in the social order, university and city officials accepted and perpetuated a narrative that conflated substandard conditions with the residents themselves and set out to expunge both "decay" and decay-associated people from the area.

Planning and Protest in Unit 3

Upon its incorporation in July 1959, the West Philadelphia Corporation quickly moved to have a roughly hexagonal 82.3-acre tract of land stretching north from Market Street to Lancaster and Powelton Avenues and east to west from 36th to 38th Streets designated as University City Redevelopment Area Unit 3 and to obtain a consulting agreement with the Redevelopment Authority to assist in its planning.[39] WPC's leadership identified Unit 3 as "including some of the most blighted structures and conditions in University City" and pledged to "work closely with the Redevelopment Authority during the Survey and Planning period."[40] The aim of the Corporation was that the city clear the eastern section of the area in anticipation of a scientific and medical research complex, with much of the western part of the area to be taken up with an expansion of Presbyterian Hospital.[41] The Redevelopment Authority's 1961 annual report announced simply that "a great educational and research center, with institutional and private research facilities . . . and with living and shopping facilities available" would be "the first major project in the concept of University City." It noted that the WPC was acting as an unpaid consultant.[42]

Unit 3 was home, according to the 1960 Census, to an estimated 1,203 dwelling units and 3,423 residents.[43] The housing stock consisted primarily of single-family row houses, many of which had been divided into apartments. Commercial and industrial uses were interspersed among the housing, as was common in Philadelphia's working-class neighborhoods; a study cited by the WPC in a 1963 memo had counted twelve small manufacturing operations, five auto repair shops, five laundries, five service stations, five printers, and thirty-five other service and retail businesses.[44]

According to the website "The Black Bottom," which is maintained by civil rights leader Walter Palmer, the neighborhood extended south beyond

Market Street, which was Unit 3's southern boundary, but was otherwise coterminous with the Unit 3 redevelopment area.[45] Originally known as Greenville, it had experienced two significant bursts of African American population growth in the twentieth century, first during and after the First World War and then in the early 1950s. Many who had migrated to Philadelphia in search of work settled there, having been uprooted by changes in the agricultural economy in the southern states or by the intolerability of life under Jim Crow.[46] Compared with people who lived at the "Top," west of 52nd Street, people living in the Bottom were less likely to have steady jobs or high-quality housing, and they were more likely to be from the South. "To come north," according to one informant, "That was the promised land. It felt more free. Harassment was not absent but it was less. Lower on the meter." Yet this informant also emphasized the precarity and instability that characterized the lives of people who had come to Philadelphia expecting a better life but who faced frequent displacements and evictions: "Constant movement, it never stopped. People felt like they were pretty safe in the north. But the same thing happened all over again. They had to move out. They had no power to do anything about it. It's a wonder that people could actually be as normal as they were, given this constant movement."[47]

The viability and legitimacy of the Black Bottom as a neighborhood entity in the early 1960s was disputed at the time, and it remains a point of disagreement between historians and former residents.[48] But whatever their level of cohesion in the eyes of others, residents were well versed in the *modus operandi* of urban renewal planning. When, in December 1961, the *Philadelphia Tribune* reported that the federal Urban Renewal Administration had approved the Redevelopment Authority's request for initial planning and survey funds for Unit 3,[49] residents acted immediately. Perhaps fortuitously, the Redevelopment Authority was at that moment piloting a new program designed to engage households who would be subject to urban renewal relocation. As outlined in two 1962 working papers, the aim of the RDA program was to establish rapport with families, assist them in organizing themselves into committees and block groups, communicate information about urban renewal ("Why it is necessary—its opportunities—its problems" according to the first of the working papers), and learn about future relocatees' needs, which they would then attempt to alleviate through social work interventions.[50] Unit 3 residents volunteered to participate, and on February 15, 1962, an informational meeting at the Drew Elementary School about the renewal planning process attracted 350 people.

Figure 4. 30th North 36th Street in 1947. Photo courtesy of PhillyHistory.org, a project of the Philadelphia Department of Records.

This meeting did not go well for official representatives of the Redevelopment Authority and the West Philadelphia Corporation,[51] as Black Bottom residents loudly expressed their dismay at the prospect of being relocated to make way for the Science Center. There is no evidence that staff or board members of the WPC ever again met with Unit 3 residents after this 1962 meeting. But the RDA was a city agency with a modicum of public accountability. RDA outreach worker Troy L. Chapman, following the protocols of the agency's citizen engagement policy, scheduled a follow-up session at a local church, Tabernacle Presbyterian, and proceeded with the organization of the Citizens Committee of University City Redevelopment Area Unit 3.[52] Throughout 1962, he and members of the committee called on hundreds of households "in order to inform them of pending urban renewal and the

Citizens Committee." On April 12, Chapman wrote in a memo to his supervisor that "the Citizens Committee of University City Unit 3 and the Steering committee as of this date have made . . . great strides toward becoming a well-knit working organization."[53]

Based on available documentation, it seems that the most active members of the committee were homeowners at the eastern end of Unit 3, between 34th and 38th Streets north of Filbert Street. The group began to focus on this area, several acres of which had gone unclaimed by firms or institutions in official redevelopment plans, as a site where homes might be rehabilitated in line with the RDA's relatively new policy of avoiding clearance where necessary. While it is unclear how open the members of the Citizens Committee were with Chapman, he referred in his memo to the drafting of a "policy statement" that articulated a rationale for an alternative to demolition and relocation:

> In certain sections of the city where absentee ownership predominates . . . properties have been allowed to disintegrate, where over crowding [sic] and rent gouging are common practice. In such areas rehabilitation poses severe problems and total clearance may be necessary. In Area III of University City this is not the case. Here most of the houses are two or three story houses. Many still in single family occupancy; according to the 1961 edition of the real estate directory about half the units in the area bounded by 36th Street, Filbert, Saunders Ave., and rear property lines along Powelton and Lancaster Avenues are owner-occupied. . . . Redevelopment would force these people to sell at "fair market value." However, this area has been certified for redevelopment since 1950, and this has artificially depressed the price of housing. Thus, the present owners would probably not get enough money from the Redevelopment Authority to buy comparable housing elsewhere . . . Should Area III be designated for total clearance extraordinary pressure would be placed upon the adjacent areas to house the families which would be displaced. This would re-open the threat of overcrowding and rent gouging . . . Negroes caught up in the relocation process currently are forced by a limited open housing market into ghettoes and slums.[54]

Regardless of what its frontline staff knew when, if Redevelopment Authority leaders had hoped that Unit 3 residents would accept a community

participation program oriented exclusively toward education and social up-
lift, they were disappointed. On May 16, 1963, a few days after being informed that the Authority's plan for Unit 3 made no provision to conserve
any homes in the area, forty members of the Citizens Committee occupied
Mayor James Tate's City Hall office, demanding an audience. The sit-in was
in many respects a brilliant move. Tate, to whom the mayoralty had passed
a year earlier when reform leader Richardson Dilworth had left office to run
for governor, was now running for mayor in his own right. He belonged to
the "regular" (or machine) faction of Philadelphia's Democratic Party and
would prove to be much less committed to liberal reform in his governing
strategy than either of his two Reform Democratic predecessors. Now, however, he faced a Reform candidate, Walter M. Phillips, in a Democratic mayoral primary that was just days away, on May 21.

Tate declined to meet with the Unit 3 delegation, but he ordered the
city's redevelopment executives to see them that day.[55] After an hour of negotiations, Citizens Committee representatives obtained the signatures of
RDA Chair Gustave Amsterdam, City Council President Paul D'Ortona,
City Planning Commission Chair G. Holmes Perkins, and Mayoral Development Advisor William Rafsky on a document that committed the RDA to
spare as many homes as possible in Unit 3, to strive for representation by the
Citizens' Committee on the West Philadelphia Corporation's board, and to
afford the committee an advisory role with the Redevelopment Authority
going forward.[56] After Tate left his office "accompanied by nine policemen
and detectives," the protestors received a memorandum he had dictated. It
asserted, "the policy of the city administration is to avoid tearing down any
property where it is possible to save the structure."[57] Tate won the May 21
primary and was narrowly reelected the following November on the strength
of the Black vote.[58]

A Commitment Unravels

With a public agreement between the Citizens Committee and the Redevelopment Authority, the stage now appeared to be set for a renewal plan that
included some housing rehabilitation and new construction for current residents. In November 1963, the RDA's planning consultant presented its executive board with a comprehensive plan for Unit 3 that was consistent with this
goal.[59] Its major features were the expansion of the Presbyterian Hospital on a

newly created superblock at the western boundary of the site and an eighteen-acre Science Center complex on either side of a widened Market Street, at the site's southeastern corner.[60] The acreage north of the main Science Center site on the eastern side was divided into smaller parcels, designated for the Science Center, Drexel research facilities, public schools, and rehabilitated housing. But the West Philadelphia Corporation's board and staff (who were present at the executive board briefing) were unhappy that the RDA had conserved a seven-acre parcel between Filbert Street and Lancaster Avenue between 36th and 38th Streets (marked "5" in Figure 5) for continuing occupancy by incumbent residents.[61]

In the contentious period from 1964 to 1966, Molinaro relied on a dual strategy with respect to what he called the "controversial 7-acre parcel."[62] First, he insisted that the University City High School, a science-specialized high school that the WPC had begun to conceptualize as part of its neighborhood educational improvement portfolio a few years before, had to be

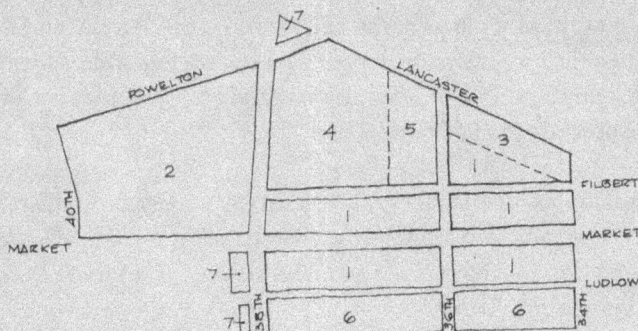

Figure 5. Unit 3 Diagram presented by the Redevelopment Authority to the West Philadelphia Corporation in 1963. RDA officials planned to facilitate the construction of housing for incumbent Black Bottom residents in the section marked "5." Special Collections Research Center, Temple University Libraries, Philadelphia, PA.

sited in the part of Unit 3 designated for replacement housing.[63] A high school is mentioned in a set of comments submitted in March 1963 to the Redevelopment Authority as "an extraordinary opportunity . . . to provide education at a secondary school level for Philadelphia youth" in proximity to the Science Center.[64] In December 1963, following the RDA's revision of the Unit 3 plan in the wake of the Citizens Committee agreement, Molinaro appealed directly to RDA Executive Director Francis Lammer, noting that "industrial leaders . . . see the need for this resource if Philadelphia is to prepare more young men and women for scientific careers in the industries of Greater Philadelphia."[65] WPC files also document outreach to educational experts and philanthropic leaders seeking advice and endorsement. After over a year of resistance to the school siting plan on the part of RDA officials who considered themselves obligated to their agreement with the Citizens Committee (as well as to an urban renewal plan that the federal government had already approved), the WPC executed a consulting agreement with the Philadelphia School District stating that Molinaro would assist in preparing the district's 1966 capital budget.[66] In March 1966, the Board of Education submitted a proposal to the Redevelopment Authority to acquire the controversial seven-acre parcel for the purpose of constructing a high school.

The second element of Molinaro's strategy was a sustained effort to denigrate the Citizens Committee, its leaders, and its allies. After the City Hall action in May 1963, he sent a memo to the WPC Board of Directors, with a pointed cc to the city officials who had brokered the agreement. His memo asserted that the demonstrators represented an area that had neither "'neighborhood' identification, nor organization" and accused Citizens Committee leaders of operating in bad faith:

The self-appointed leaders of the current citizen protest are Mr. Robert Coleman, employed by the Tabernacle Presbyterian Church at 37th and Chestnut Streets and Mr. John H. Clay, an attorney. Both are Negroes.

a. Mr. Coleman resides in Powelton Village, outside the Unit #3 project boundaries. He bases his interest upon the fact that his church, which is just across from the project, has parishioners in the project area. No evidence of this has been produced but it may well be the case.

b. Mr. Clay's interest is even more spurious. He resides at 56th and Catherine Streets, almost two miles from the project. Almost two years ago, Mr. Clay came to the Corporation and made it clear that he intended becoming active in a speculative way for profit in Unit #3. . . . From all evidence, it is clear that Mr. Clay's interest in University City #3 is that of a speculator holding property and not that of a resident protesting displacement.[67]

That John Clay had invested in Unit 3 property is clear; many entrepreneurs had done so in response to rumors of imminent acquisition there by the RDA. He also sought to benefit financially from the rehabilitation and new construction to which the Redevelopment Authority had committed itself, forming the University City Citizens Development Corporation (UCCDC) and becoming its executive director for this purpose. As a Black businessman, however, Clay had to overcome the perception that he was incompetent, dangerous, or both. This was a perception that West Philadelphia Corporation leaders were only too happy to exploit; they actively intervened with members of their social networks to derail Clay's applications for bank financing.[68] Clay ultimately submitted two proposals that the Redevelopment Authority deemed unworkable: one because the rehabilitated housing it proposed would be too expensive for existing residents, and the other because it involved all-new low-cost housing as opposed to rehabilitation of existing buildings.[69] A private background investigation of Clay's business dealings (commissioned by Molinaro) revealed that Clay had also been involved in a questionable real estate transaction in the Cobbs Creek neighborhood that may have disqualified him as a redeveloper in University City. It is also clear, however, that throughout 1964, 1965, and most of 1966, Redevelopment Authority officials were attempting to broker a viable residential project on the seven-acre site, with or without Clay's involvement. The project they envisioned entailed a private for-profit or not-for-profit developer who would undertake an economically feasible combination of rehabilitation and new construction. Several religious groups, including the Presbyterian Church and Philadelphia's powerful Episcopal Diocese, offered technical assistance and potential financial aid. But the officials of WPC and its associated institutions stymied these efforts. Rather than follow the RDA's lead, they diligently worked to undermine the legitimacy and reputability of Black Bottom residents and to portray them as dupes of Clay. Their narrative cast residential redevelopment as impracticable and reinforced the idea that replacing occupied homes with a new high school facility was the only reasonable path forward.[70]

As the possibility that the Redevelopment Authority would follow through on its commitment to the Citizens Committee faded, Black Bottom residents pulled every lever available to them to change the power dynamic. They enlisted the assistance of the NAACP, the Congress on Racial Equality (CORE), the Student Nonviolent Coordinating Committee (SNCC), the Episcopal Archdiocese, and other church groups. They made desperate written appeals to Mayor Tate, President Johnson, Housing and Homes Finance Agency administrator Robert Weaver,[71] and influential members of Congress. In November 1965, the University City Citizens Development Corporation filed suit against the RDA, WPC, and the Philadelphia City Planning Commission in U.S. District Court; their complaint, which argued that these entities were violating the plaintiffs' civil rights, was dismissed in July 1966.[72] When the Board of Education requested the controversial seven acres from the Redevelopment Authority later that month for the purpose of building a school, a delegation from SNCC, the NAACP, and CORE met with the regional administrator of the very young new federal agency, the Department of Housing and Urban Development (HUD), and succeeded in stalling the release of federal redevelopment funding for a few more months.[73]

But the clearance of a Black neighborhood in the view-shed of the Science Center was the West Philadelphia Corporation's express priority and constant preoccupation. In October, the Redevelopment Authority asked HUD to approve an amendment to the Unit 3 Urban Renewal Plan that granted all but 2.2 of the controversial seven acres to the School District.[74] HUD consented, and in November 1966 approved $12 million to clear Unit 3 and prepare it for "new structures and uses."[75] Clearance and relocation began in earnest in 1967, over continuing protest from residents and allied civil rights groups.[76] A Redevelopment Authority document from May of that year lists 156 Unit 3 owner-occupants and provides tabular data about their incomes to members of the West Philadelphia Realty Board, which was cooperating with the RDA to advise displaced homeowners about relocation options. Judging from the income data reported in the document and the "limited open housing market" cited in the Citizens Committee's policy statement, it is difficult to be optimistic that many were able to move to comparable housing. Given that over a thousand renter households were also displaced, the statement's prediction that total clearance would diminish housing quality and living conditions in adjacent areas also seems likely to have been validated.

Figure 6. Lot in Black Bottom cleared for University City redevelopment, May 5, 1968. Photo by Jack Tinney. Special Collections Research Center, Temple University Libraries, Philadelphia, PA.

Redevelopment Authority officials had continued through the summer of 1966 to insist that the controversial seven-acre site would be redeveloped for residential use as they had promised the Citizens Committee. But they ultimately bent to the WPC's will. Their capitulation was driven by the universities' power and by the irresistible economic and political bargain presented by urban renewal. Urban renewal meant millions of federal dollars for infrastructure. It meant new positions in the unionized construction trades at a time when the city was hemorrhaging working-class jobs. And it meant an opportunity, as Harnwell had put it, to "reverse the tide of urban decline" that, whether consciously or not, was associated in the dominant public imagination with materially poor Black people. "A responsible type of citizen" was considered necessary for the Science Center—and the advanced research-oriented economy it represented—to thrive in West Philadelphia. In the eyes of those with economic and political power, no one in the Black Bottom looked like that type of citizen. Further, university and city authorities were incapable of perceiving the ways in which generations of racialized inhumanity had contributed to this.

Liberalism, Pragmatism, Racism

By the time of the student sit-in in February 1969, the Redevelopment Authority had cleared over 500 structures from Unit 3 and other University City urban renewal areas, and new construction had begun on almost $50 million in new projects including University City Science Center Building Number Two and University City High School.[77] Leo Molinaro had left the West Philadelphia Corporation to join developer James Rouse in a new town-building venture in Maryland. A new nonprofit group, Renewal Housing Inc., had been selected by the Redevelopment Authority to develop the remaining 2.2 acres in Unit 3 that were still reserved for replacement housing. Few residents remained; a Tabernacle Presbyterian Church-affiliated group called the Volunteer Community Resources Council lamented in its May 1968 newsletter that "what was once a community has become a wasteland."[78] Even the 2.2 acre commitment would eventually be whittled down to rehabilitation on a single block, Warren Street between 36th and 37th Streets, where eight houses that were once part of a neighborhood of thousands of residents remain standing today.

Under these circumstances, the 1969 student sit-in's achievement had to do with something more abstract than housing. In her work on inclusive political communication, Iris Marion Young emphasizes the importance of acknowledgment and recognition in a functioning democracy. "It is not uncommon," she says, "to hear a complaint from individuals or groups who have tried to make claims and arguments in a political discussion that they have been ignored, or worse, spoken about by others as though they were not there, deprecated, stereotyped or otherwise insulted." As a result, she argues, public acknowledgment is "a specific communicative gesture with important and not sufficiently noticed functions for democratic practice."[79] Throughout the West Philadelphia Corporation's first decade, it lent assistance to residential rehabilitation and development projects in the

Figure 7. Survivors of the demolition of the Black Bottom: homes on Warren Street between 36th and 37th Street, 2020. Photo by author.

majority-white Powelton Village, Cedar Park, Spruce Hill, and Garden Court neighborhoods, proudly profiling them in annual reports and promotional brochures.[80] Its board and staff consulted regularly with neighborhood associations in those areas.[81] But after the uncomfortable public meeting at the Drew School in February 1962, WPC and University of Pennsylvania officials assiduously did not acknowledge the Black Bottom activists' existence in official publications or communication, and made contact with them the responsibility of Redevelopment Authority personnel. The universities' erasure of Citizens' Committee members' and allies' time and effort on behalf of themselves and their community was official and total as University City came into being.

Walter Palmer, who held a managerial position at Penn's Children's Hospital and had a citywide profile as a civil rights leader, was a point of contact before and during the College Hall sit-in between student activists and a group of Black leaders (Clay no longer among them) who had emerged as spokespeople for the interests of the now-scattered Unit 3 residents. They included Herman Wrice and Andrew Jenkins, whose work in the Mantua neighborhood is the subject of the next chapter. Wrice and Jenkins were both board members of Renewal Housing Inc., the nonprofit development corporation that the Redevelopment Authority had designated to rehabilitate and construct housing. The February 1969 sit-in was freighted with new-left sectarian disputes,[82] and it must have been galling to Wrice and Jenkins that in order to get basic acknowledgment from the president of the West Philadelphia Corporation, they had to append themselves to the activities of student radicals barely out of their teens. Nevertheless, over the six days in College Hall, representatives of Black civil society were full participants in a process that forced university administrators to recognize them as a consequential constituency with claims on West Philadelphia's future. While they would have to continue fighting in the decades that followed not to be "deprecated and stereotyped," they would no longer be ignored.[83]

For scholars of Philadelphia's political history, the transformation of the city by the simultaneous advent of an activist federal government and the election of liberal Democratic reformers to citywide office in the 1950s and 1960s has been a rich vein for exploration. Most have noted the progressive strides made by the groundbreaking 1949 City Charter, the pragmatic, good-government orientation of the Joseph Clark and Richardson Dilworth administrations, and the professionalism and efficiency of downtown redevelopment under famed City Planning Commission Executive Director Edmund Bacon.[84] As historian Guian McKee notes, however, "divisions of race bifurcated the economic policy initiatives that Philadelphia's post-War liberalism undertook and constrained the results that they achieved."[85] The deeply problematic nature of liberal pragmatism is on display in the archival documents that trace the fate of Black Bottom residents as they formed the Citizens Committee for Urban Renewal Area Unit 3, fought for their homes, and lost. It is also evident in the testimonies of liberal luminaries of the era, who minimize, in retrospect, the forced sacrifices of Philadelphians of color who had very little wealth or power (and whose sacrifices consistently hampered their efforts to accumulate any). In his political memoir, Kirk Petshek, an economist and a celebrated reformer in the Clark and Dilworth administrations, would again articulate the enabling fiction that there had been no choice but to clear the entire Black Bottom neighborhood: "Most urban

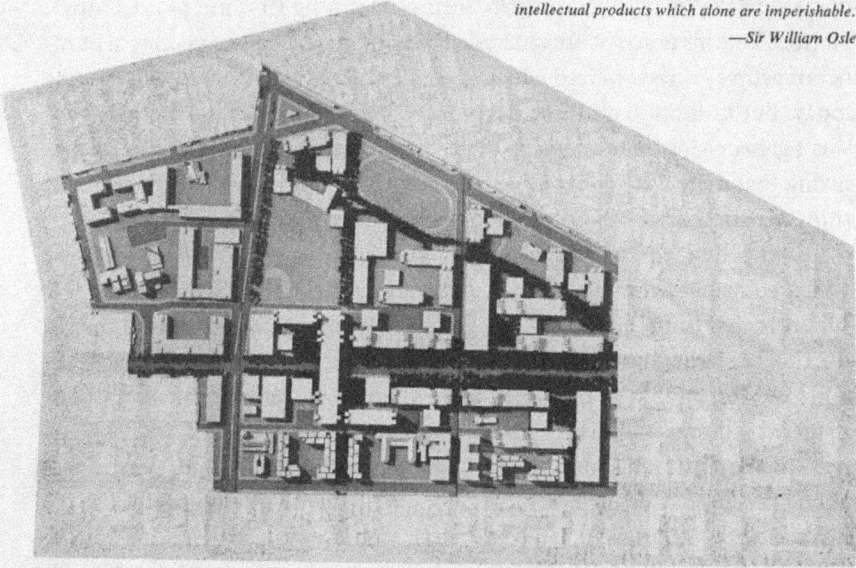

"We forget that the measure of the value of a nation to the world is neither the bushel nor the barrel, but mind; and that wheat and pork, though useful and necessary, are but dross in comparison with those intellectual products which alone are imperishable."

—Sir William Osler

Photograph of a model showing illustrative site plan for University City Science Center

Figure 8. Photo from the West Philadelphia Corporation's 1963 Annual Report, showing an architectural model of the proposed University City Science Center. The quotation at the top right is by Sir William Osler, a Canadian pathologist and cofounder of the Johns Hopkins University Hospital. The quotation reads: *"We forget that the value of a nation to the world is neither the bushel nor the barrel, but mind; and that wheat and pork, while useful and necessary, are but dross in comparison with those intellectual products which alone are imperishable."* Special Collections Research Center, Temple University Libraries, Philadelphia, PA.

renewal plans in University City had been for conservation areas emphasizing rehabilitation, with only occasional sore spots being cleared. But in the area proposed for the Science Center complex the story was different. If a center of the dimensions projected was to be built near the university, total clearance would be necessary."[86] Similarly, in an oral history interview conducted by Walter Phillips in 1976, former Planning Commission Chair G. Holmes Perkins noted of university-led redevelopment in general that "a number of people . . . were moved which is an idea that is anathema to most people today. But in those days these decisions were evaluated as to whether there was a gain or a loss in relationship to the total community. And although recognizing that there were going to be hardships for a few individuals those hardships were in general subordinated to the welfare of the total community."[87]

Black Philadelphians were acutely aware of the racialized patterns by which gains tended to be weighed against losses and the hardships of a few subordinated to the welfare of the whole.[88] And they had witnessed the reduction to official invisibility of their efforts to prevent imbalanced hardship and loss. This awareness prompted them to mistrust planning and redevelopment institutions and, when possible, to seek avenues for civic and political participation that relied minimally upon them. As Walter Palmer remembers about the period of civic reform and its effects on the communities he worked with, "Clark and Dilworth were seen as white knights in shining armor. However, Blacks got very little out of all this excitement that liberals generated. Those of us living it were trying to find a way to restructure the conversation."[89]

Efforts to "restructure the conversation," however, were rarely free from the discourses of value and progress articulated by the academic scions of University City, as we will see in the next chapter.

CHAPTER 2

West Philadelphia's Great Society

Student and community activists and Penn trustees had ended the February 1969 student occupation of College Hall with an agreement to create a Commission on University-Community Development, consisting of five student representatives, five faculty members, five trustees, and five community members.[1] This "Quadripartite Commission" had two stated purposes. First, it would oversee and direct the financial commitment the university had made to advance community development in the neighborhoods adjacent to Unit 3. In addition to obligating the university to provide, "initially," $75,000 per year for the commission's staffing and operations, the agreement stated that "the Board of Trustees individually and collectively agree to concert their efforts, through the corporations, businesses, institutions and agencies to which they have access, to develop the funds and funding sources needed for community renewal programs with the goal of establishing a community development fund with resources of $10,000,000."[2] Second, the commission was "empowered to review and approve all existing plans involving future land acquisition or development of currently owned land contiguous to existing residential neighborhoods."[3] Although the University City Science Center and University City High School were by that point under construction, not all the property in Unit 3 had been transferred to the Redevelopment Authority, and the area still contained some occupied housing. As chartered, the commission supposedly had authority both to provide a check on the university's future expansion and to participate in decision-making as development activity in Unit 3 progressed.

Although it would take more than a year for the commission to officially fall apart, fault lines were immediately evident. At the group's first meeting on March 10, 1969, community representatives expressed an eagerness to proceed with the rehabilitation work they believed the February agreement authorized their organization, Renewal Housing Inc., to undertake in Unit 3. Faculty representative Russell Ackoff proposed that the commission immediately incorporate as a community development corporation that would receive university funds, which might then be distributed to groups working on the ground.[4] Although commission members endorsed the incorporation proposal, however, there was no consensus about whether and how university funds would flow to local organizations. Community representatives imagined creating a core development staff with the baseline $75,000 and then drawing on the university's $10 million commitment to finance housing construction and rehabilitation, as well as other projects.[5] It gradually became clear, though, that the university did not intend to contribute its own funds; the agreement had stated, after all, only that the trustees would "concert their efforts . . . to develop funds and funding sources."

The Quadripartite Commission never incorporated. In December 1969, after months of tension, faculty representative John W. Eckman instructed the university's legal counsel to halt the process, citing the danger that "the incorporation . . . will only serve to focus undesirable and perhaps critical scrutiny on the interpretation of the Trustees [sic] much-debated $10 million promise of last February."[6] While the university and West Philadelphia Corporation contributed a few hundred thousand dollars to the Young Great Society and Mantua Community Planners organizations in the years afterward, the ambiguous and perhaps deceptive $10 million commitment in the February agreement was never fulfilled.

Conversation at the March 10 meeting about the agreement's "review and approve" clause also foreshadowed future dissension. As community representatives, student representatives, and some faculty representatives understood it, the sit-in agreement empowered the commission to revisit the question of how to save parts of the Black Bottom neighborhood from the bulldozer. At the commission's March 17, 1969, meeting, "Mr. Wrice noted that there are ten existing houses known as Shedwick Place whose occupants anticipate relocation in Society Hill. He suggested that the Commission should use its influence to prevent demolition of Shedwick Place and to have [Renewal Housing Inc.] designated as the redevelopers. Mr. Ackoff moved that the Chairman appoint a subcommittee to investigate the possibility of retaining Shedwick Place and the designation of RHI as the redeveloper."[7] This interpretation of the commission's remit, however, was not acceptable to the university. In late April, when the body passed a contested resolution requesting "a temporary setting aside of all present plans for institutions' expansion in Unit 3 on lands presently not irrevocably contracted" (so that some sites could be re-examined as potential locations for housing retention),[8] university adminis-trators equivocated. Their efforts to avoid even discussing the resolution with the full Quadripartite Commission—let alone implementing it—made the commission's powerlessness evident.[9] In late June of 1969, co-chair and Re-newal Housing Inc. President Lorenzo Graham and two other community representatives resigned. In the following year, lacking authority and dis-tracted by neighborhood-level disputes about the legitimacy of the commu-nity representatives who remained, the commission faltered. A few months after Martin Meyerson replaced Gaylord Harnwell as UPenn's president in September 1970, he formulated a new structure for university-community engagement that superseded the Quadripartite Commission.[10] The remain-ing members of the group voted to dissolve on February 9, 1971.

Herman Wrice and Andrew Jenkins, established leaders in the Mantua neighborhood, were the community representatives who remained on the Quadripartite Commission after it became clear that the university would not renegotiate the disposition of Unit 3 land. Mantua was north of Unit 3, a full mile distant from Penn, and separated from the Drexel campus by the Powelton Village neighborhood. Although predominantly populated by low-socioeconomic-status Black households, it was not considered part of the Black Bottom (see Chapter 1). The minutes of Quadripartite Commission meet-ings in late 1969 and 1970 make it clear that community groups that identified more closely with the Black Bottom itself favored renewed protest in response to the University of Pennsylvania's retreat from its February 1969 commit-ments. In the previous few years, however, community development organ-izations headed by Wrice and Jenkins in Mantua had attracted notice and tentative financial support from the university, and the Unit 3 struggle and stu-dent sit-in had given the institution further motivation to engage with their work. Pragmatism now dictated that they remain at the table.

Mantua and the Young Great Society

As a neighborhood concept, "Mantua" dated to 1809, when local landholder Richard Peters subdivided his estate, called Belmont, and sold a portion of the land for development. Over the course of the nineteenth century, the construction of moderately priced row homes and the extension of trolley lines turned the area into a populous, predominantly Irish, working-class neighborhood.[11] Mantua was easily accessible not only to Center City Philadelphia across the Schuylkill River but also to West Philadelphia factories; per one account, it was a "service community"—an area of modest dwellings for domestics employed in the statelier homes of Powelton Village.[12] In the early and mid-twentieth century, the factors precipitating changes in population and housing conditions in the Black Bottom operated in Mantua as well. Black households were a majority of its population by 1950, which was also the year the neighborhood's population peaked, at just over 19,000.[13] A decade later, the Philadelphia Housing Authority constructed the 18-story, 153-unit Mantua Hall in the 3500 block of Fairmount Avenue. Like the majority of Philadelphia public housing, it was located in a segregated neighborhood and tenanted by Black residents, many displaced from other areas by urban redevelopment projects.[14] The families of Andrew Jenkins and Herman Wrice were among the first to move into Mantua Hall when it opened in 1961.

Not long after, the two men (then in their twenties) founded a scout troop, Cub Scout Pack 422, as a way of keeping boys in the neighborhood from getting drawn into fighting among the neighborhood's six rival gangs. In mid-twentieth-century Philadelphia, participating in gangs enabled young men excluded from and alienated by mainstream institutions to find supportive social outlets and to express loyalty to peers and community.[15] Jenkins and Wrice had themselves been gang leaders; it was clear from interviews conducted for this study that the experience, while frightening, was also a source of pride and affirmation.[16] But gangs also threatened public safety. Groups identified with different "corners" fought frequently for them, endangering bystanders. Once out of their teens,[17] Wrice and Jenkins saw virtue in peacemaking. By Jenkins's account, the turning point occurred when the men's wives were nearly killed in crossfire while shopping in a local store.[18]

In addition to providing younger children with an alternative to the community of the "corners," Jenkins and Wrice worked with teenagers who were already involved in gangs. Their work drew on their familiarity with the gangs' structure and on their empathy for their members' exclusion from the primary economy. It soon evolved into a multipurpose organization, the Young Great Society (YGS). YGS sponsored athletics, tutoring programs, and summer camps in Mantua.[19] It also initiated several for-profit subsidiary businesses that employed dozens of young people at a time. News articles in the late 1960s referenced a housing rehabilitation enterprise, a community medical clinic, an infant care center, a football league, a pallet-repair business, and clubs and classes for teenage girls.[20] Media accounts, though often paternalistic in tone, emphasized the transformative impact on YGS members of an organization that combined personal affirmation and self-discipline with neighborhood revitalization. An early 1968 article in the *Philadelphia Evening Bulletin* described the group's intervention with a young man named Robert: "The Young Great Society is a self-help group which has

Figure 9. Members of Young Great Society removing junk from house, February 24, 1968. Photo by Meyer. Special Collections Research Center, Temple University Libraries, Philadelphia, PA.

literally blanketed the Mantua area with educational programs. It has received funds from public and private institutions and according to Wrice, has helped some 11,000 persons. Robert says, 'Wrice is the first adult who could speak my language and show me respect as a man. . . . If I went out and got into trouble, I'd feel as though I let them down.'"[21]

A key part of YGS's influence was its leaders' ability to draw on motivation and intelligence for which teens in Mantua otherwise had little outlet. Recalled one interviewee:

> We were used to guys that were gamblers, hanging out, running numbers . . . Herman and Andy were different. They were educated, and they were job-oriented, family-oriented and they wasn't afraid of us. And that really made a difference. . . . From the Young Great Society I learned how to be constructive instead of destructive in the community—I learned how to respect other people's feelings and properties. And I also knew that I could become a businessperson. Because if I had the skills to be a gang leader, I had the skills to be an organizer and a community person.[22]

This same interviewee attested to a more basic function that the Young Great Society fulfilled for those who joined it: "Andy and Herman were the fathers, Jean [Wrice] and Pat [Jenkins] were the mothers. So now we saw family."

Mantua Community Planners

The 1967 founding of the Mantua Community Planners (MCP) had several impetuses: the increasingly national profile of the charismatic Wrice, who was ambitious to expand YGS beyond Mantua;[23] Jenkins's desire to head an organization of his own; and the increasing salience of community-based planning both in the national discourse and in local struggles against the destructive outcomes of top-down redevelopment.[24] MCP was an umbrella group that confederated Mantua's YGS chapter with other organizations in the neighborhood: church groups, block associations, and even the Mantua-based outpost of the Philadelphia Anti-Poverty Action Committee, Philadelphia's version of President Lyndon Johnson's Community Action Program. While Jenkins was its director and public face, many of MCP's most effective leaders were women.

The portfolio of the Mantua Community Planners organization over-lapped with that of the Young Great Society—Jenkins touted its role in gang-violence prevention—but the group also focused on resident-led physical planning and environmental design for the neighborhood. A 1968 article in the *Philadelphia Evening Bulletin* highlighted MCP's chief organizer and treasurer, Doris Hamilton, who located the group's origin in her discovery that in the midst of Penn's and Drexel's politically contested expansions into adjacent neighborhoods, there seemed to be no clear plan for Mantua's future.[25] This was concerning: if there was no plan for Mantua, it might be swept up in a future University City land grab. The *Philadelphia Inquirer* reported on a February 1967 meeting that drew one hundred residents and a local Democratic politician: "Although no large scale renewal program is currently in the works for Mantua, more than 100 area residents turned out at a community meeting Monday night to have their say on what kind of redevelopment they would like to have when it does come . . . Arlin Gordon, who chaired the meeting, said the interest of residents will determine whether they become 'participants in redevelopment, or victims of it.'"[26]

Why planning? Certainly, having witnessed the erasure of the Black Bottom at the hands of the University City growth coalition, Wrice and Jenkins saw the importance of forming a countervailing apparatus in case Mantua should enter officials' sights. Mantua Community Planners, with its motto, "Plan or Be Planned For," articulated a commitment to redevelopment that incumbent residents would lead and in which they would have a strong voice. But leaders' ambition to formulate a plan for their neighborhood also connected with a determination to link Mantua residents to well-paid work. The logic was that having attracted public and private funding to implement a locally devised plan, MCP leaders would be able to enlist their own neighbors—and, crucially, to pay them—to build and maintain new physical and social infrastructure. Jenkins and Wrice envisioned Black-owned businesses, like those they had started through YGS, in a position to receive construction, building services, and other contracts from federal and local redevelopment agencies. Through community-controlled redevelopment, they would build and strengthen Black-led economic institutions from within the neighborhood, generating employment and wealth.

Mantua residents' embrace of planning was one of many neighborhood-based and citywide efforts to advance the social mobility of Philadelphia's Black population in the late 1960s. In the earlier part of the decade, Reverend Leon Sullivan of North Philadelphia's Zion Baptist Church had gained

Figure 10. Chuck Baker, David C. Porter, Charles Collins, and Carolyn L. Walker at the Mantua Community Planners workshop at 3625 Wallace Street, October 11, 1968. Photo by Anthony Bernato. Special Collections Research Center, Temple University Libraries, Philadelphia, PA.

national recognition, first with his work to place unemployed Black youth in jobs and then by successfully confronting employment discrimination through selective patronage campaigns, which encouraged the city's Black residents "don't buy where you can't work."[27] Sullivan went on to found a highly regarded training program, the Opportunities Industrialization Center, and to spearhead the Progress Movement, which dedicated itself to creating jobs by promoting and capitalizing Black-owned businesses.[28] Other organizations, such as local chapters of the National Association for the Advancement of Colored People (NAACP) and the Congress on Racial Equality (CORE) turned to protest to address economic marginalization.

CORE and NAACP fought a bitter six-year campaign to end Jim Crow practices in unionized construction; this struggle culminated in the 1969 Philadelphia Plan, which became the blueprint for federally mandated affirmative action in employment.[29] But efforts centered on facilitating assimilation into the existing economic order produced fierce resistance among whites and impatience among Blacks who continued to face formidable obstacles getting jobs and securing loans. By the late 1960s, CORE, the Student Nonviolent Coordinating Committee (SNCC), and other groups were engaging in what historian Matthew Countryman refers to as "community organizing with a Black nationalist agenda," advocating for independent institutions that controlled "the public resources necessary to fuel the economic development of poor black communities."[30] 1968 and 1969 saw the rise and decline of two groups, the Black Coalition and the Black Economic Development Conference, whose simultaneous advocacy for financial support and independence from the white power structure proved organizationally fatal.[31]

The Young Great Society and the Mantua Community Planners did not align themselves with race radicalism, or with the civil rebellions that had forced Philadelphia officials and business leaders to take at least nominal steps toward economic inclusion for more members of the Black community. Wrice in fact co-chaired the meliorist Philadelphia Urban Coalition, a public-private task force created by Mayor Tate to quell unrest in the aftermath of Martin Luther King Jr.'s assassination in 1968 (and which ultimately absorbed the Black Coalition). He was also on record as a "good friend" of Frank Rizzo, a police official notorious for authorizing brutality against Black protestors and for exploiting racial animus to consolidate personal power. Nevertheless, YGS and MCP were operating in a tradition of self-help that was informed by a strong desire for Black economic autonomy. Wrice and Jenkins advanced a vision of community-controlled economic institutions that would enable people to transcend, on their own steam, the color bars they faced in the mainstream labor and capital markets.

Paradoxes of Self-Help

The impulse to seek collective advancement by creating an autonomous economic base is a recurrent theme in Black social thought. Booker T. Washington, Marcus Garvey, and W. E. B. Du Bois had expounded versions of this philosophy, differentiated by their reliance on individualistic versus

cooperative behavior and by their orientation toward white-dominant institutions.[32] "Self-help" was the name that Leon Sullivan gave to his 1962 10-36-50
plan, which drew on the financial resources of middle-class church congrega-
tions to capitalize the Black-controlled business ventures affiliated with the
Progress Movement. But as Sullivan's example showed, self-help and "community capitalism" involved contradictions, in that their instigators were
trying to create niches for Black Americans within an economy deeply and
path-dependently infused with unacknowledged racism. Moreover, self-
help organizations often relied on government and philanthropic cooperation for their survival.[33]

YGS and MCP, while they strove for autonomy, also operated in this problematic milieu of civil rights liberalism. Money to support the organizations'
work—primarily their interventions with gang members—came initially
from the Lutheran Mission Society and the Episcopal Diocese of Philadelphia. Then, in 1968, they formed two critical partnerships with the University of Pennsylvania. First, Dr. Howard Mitchell, a psychologist and director
of the university's Human Resources Center, raised federal funds for a
program to train young leaders from Mantua in "organization for neighborhood development, the development of neighborhood communications,
problems in home improvement . . . recreation leadership, and the effect of the
city power structure on neighborhood needs."[34] That same year, the groups
entered into a relationship with the Wharton School's Management Science
Center, working with faculty and students and supported by funding from
the Anheuser-Busch Charitable Trust and later the Ford Foundation. Under
the arrangement, according to Wharton's Russell Ackoff:

> We offered to employ any three people from the community to work
> on the development of their community in any way that those so em-
> ployed saw fit. The three were selected within a day. They were ANDY
> JENKINS, President of the Mantua Community Planners and Vice-
> President and co-founder with Herman Wrice of the Young Great
> Society, RICHARD HART, and MRS. DORIS HAMILTON, Trea-
> surer of MCP. A fourth employee on the staff of YGS was added a
> short while later. Those employed were given office space (which they
> never used), secretarial aid (which they used occasionally), and a
> graduate student to serve as an assistant (whom they used exten-
> sively). It was made clear to the Mantua team members that the fac-
> ulty involved would volunteer nothing but were available to help

them as they saw fit. They were told that they would be completely self-controlling, even with respect to hours, location, and content of their work. They had no need to come to the University except to pick up their pay checks.[35]

This extract is from Ackoff's "A Black Ghetto's Research on a University," which appeared in the academic journal *Operations Research* in 1970. The paper, which he framed as a lesson for operations researchers about how to "learn from effective ghetto leaders" in confronting social problems, made bold claims about the projects YGS and MCP had initiated under the university's patronage:

YGS has set up nine manufacturing firms that grossed a little more than $1.5 million in 1969 and employed about 125 people from the community. . . . With University aid, MCP and YGS have been instrumental in obtaining loans from banks for the establishment and operation of a number of small businesses in Mantua and in providing these enterprises with needed technical and managerial assistance. Much of the latter has been provided by Wharton graduate students. Both MCP and YGS provide employment services and have placed several hundred Mantuans in the last two years. Furthermore, these two organizations themselves employ about 330 people in activities that they manage . . . YGS and MCP operate an Architectural and Planning Center and a Joint Workshop that are staffed by University faculty and students as well as by members of the community. The Center and Workshop have produced neighborhood development plans to which about $6 million has already been pledged. . . . Physical and mental health services have been initiated within the community. These include two medical centers, a mobile clinic that goes to the people, and a drug-addiction treatment center . . . MCP arranged for the City's Department of Recreation to convert two city-owned parking lots into recreational areas. MCP sponsors a basketball league that uses these facilities . . . MCP has held a number of outings for neighborhood children; the most recent was attended by more than 800 children. Use of the University's indoor swimming pool by neighborhood children was arranged for the summer. MCP sponsors dramatic, music, and dance classes in the community. Last year the students of the dance put on an evening

program in the University's auditorium that was exciting in concep-
tion and professional in execution. It also made a profit. I could go
on and mention the recently opened Day Care Center, the Nursery
School, the free legal, social, and welfare services, and many others,
but I think I have gone far enough to provide a picture of what has
been and is happening.[36]

Ackoff's breathless enumeration of YGS/MCP projects may have been fueled
by the hope of attracting additional financial support as well as by genuine
enthusiasm and personal vanity. It is clear from press accounts, however,
that the groups' ambitious array of projects was beset by almost constant financial and managerial instability.[37] The hope of receiving funds through
the federal Model Cities program evaporated when the Department of Housing and Urban Development ordered the City of Philadelphia to change its
application so that the program targeted a smaller population.[38] The Mantua-
Powelton Mini-School, a celebrated experiment funded by the School District
and the Rockefeller Foundation, encountered administrative difficulties and
financial problems; it closed in June 1970, a year before the departure from
the School District of its lead advocate, liberal superintendent Mark Shedd.[39]
Many of the initiatives cited in Ackoff's article were conceived as one-time
"demonstration" projects and were not sustained beyond a "seed grant" period. The University of Pennsylvania's Howard Mitchell himself lamented a
"bandwagon effect" that motivated faculty at his institution to win demonstration grants for publicity-generating projects which they were not then
prepared to sustain once their funding ran out.[40]

In spite of Ackoff's glib insistence that "ghetto" managers had no use for
budgets or "arbitrary fiscal blocks,"[41] funding difficulties at YGS and MCP
were surely compounded by the relative inexperience of their administrators at governing formal organizations. For-profit enterprises were particularly challenging. A 1971 *Business Week* article recounted the struggles of
the Mantua Industrial Development Corporation (MIDC), the umbrella for
the manufacturing firms mentioned in Ackoff's article.[42] MIDC quietly dis-
banded in 1973 after defaulting on a Small Business Association loan that
had been used to acquire a 90,000-square-foot building. Some of the businesses survived, but their connection to YGS and MCP did not. Wharton
operations researchers had imagined that with their help, YGS and MCP
could make Mantua a living testament to the power of self-help and community capitalism. The results they achieved were more ambiguous.

The planning ventures gained more traction. Mantua Community Planners produced a neighborhood-led urban renewal plan and succeeded in convincing local and federal officials to support it. A November 1969 article in the *Philadelphia Evening Bulletin* reported that MCP and YGS had "played a dominant role" in formulating an urban renewal plan for Mantua, and that the U.S. Department of Housing and Urban Development (HUD) had committed $1.4 million for the first year of implementation. The Philadelphia Redevelopment Authority, according to the article, planned to acquire ninety-nine properties in Mantua for housing rehabilitation and new construction by as-yet-unidentified nonprofit developers. The Authority also intended to prepare sites for a privately developed neighborhood health center and an "urban university" to be sponsored by the Young Great Society: "Community leaders emphasize that Mantua, from the beginning, took the 'initiative' with the Redevelopment Authority. Young Great Society and Mantua Community Planners are establishing a 'joint workshop' which will act as 'development coordinator' of the area, selecting contractors, assisting contractors with Federal Housing Administration financing, assisting black contractors, and implementing on-the-job training programs for neighborhood youths."[43] A few months later, however, HUD balked at authorizing the community control that MCP and YGS had expected to exert. Another article from the *Bulletin* quoted Jenkins as saying, "We won't put up with dictation. . . . It's equality or nothing. We can't rely on the city or the federal government for the security of Mantua. We can only rely on ourselves. We intend to be planning jointly side by side with the other authorities." The rejoinder of Philadelphia's HUD representative was clear: "The [Redevelopment Authority] cannot share its responsibility on an equal basis. This is something we will not permit. . . . It has always been HUD's policy that the role of the citizen groups is advisory."[44] A diminished governance role over the plan coincided with declines in funding in the ensuing years as the Nixon administration consolidated and cut national anti-poverty programs.[45] While the MCP's "Plan for Mantua" was later remembered as having "guided public investments in the neighborhood for several years,"[46] it did not become the engine of endogenous development and economic revitalization its authors envisioned.

Although both Young Great Society and Mantua Community Planners survived into the late 1970s, available evidence suggests that they ceased to reliably support full-time staff beyond 1972. The Quadripartite Commission collapsed in 1971, and the groups lost Ford Foundation support shortly thereafter, following a falling-out with faculty in the Management

Science Center at Wharton. There is no documentation of what caused the relationship between the "ghetto" leaders and their university partners to attenuate. It is mysterious that the break occurred so soon after the exuberance expressed by Ackoff in his *Operations Research* article.

YGS and MCP leaders also faced opposition within their own community. In addition to resenting their cooperation with Penn and Drexel, members of a group called East Powelton Concerned Neighbors protested Wrice and Jenkins's acquiescence in a grand city-led plan for a World's Fair to mark the nation's Bicentennial—a plan that entailed a billion-dollar megadevelopment at the edges of Powelton Village and Mantua.[47] The Mantua leaders initially opposed the city's proposal to create a four-mile-long structure above the 30th Street railyards between Mantua and the Schuylkill River but changed their position after being offered a $40,000 planning contract by the Philadelphia 1976 Bicentennial Corporation.[48] Other local groups accused them of "selling out" the neighborhoods, but the dispute subsided after the national Bicentennial Commission rejected the plan altogether.

In 1971, Andrew Jenkins took a job at the Philadelphia Anti-Poverty Action Committee (PAAC), the agency that Mayor James Tate had created to receive and distribute federal antipoverty funds.[49] This was the first in a series of increasingly senior positions that Jenkins would hold in city government over the next three decades. Herman Wrice remained with YGS but was more and more frequently called away from Philadelphia to speak and consult about gang-violence prevention.[50] In 1977, he and his family moved to Atlantic, Iowa, where he had accepted a job heading the Cass County Alcohol Assistance Agency.[51] An article about YGS in the *Bulletin* the following year depicted a troubled, rudderless organization.[52]

Mount Vernon Manor

The centerpiece of the plan that MCP had drafted in the late 1960s was a project of "intensive rehabilitation" in a sixteen-square-block area east of 34th Street between Spring Garden Street and Mantua Avenue. The plan called for a mixture of housing rehabilitation and new construction, along with an indoor recreation center at 34th Street and Haverford Avenue. It was this northeastern corner of the Mantua neighborhood, MCP members believed, that was "most vulnerable to speculation if a Bicentennial exhibition [were to be] constructed at 30th and Market Streets."[53] In short order in the early 1970s, however, the federal government's fiscal pullback scuttled the city's ambitious Bicentennial plans, and the national economy went into recession. President Richard Nixon's January 1973 declaration of a moratorium on direct federal funding for housing and community development imperiled projects across the country, including MCP's.[54] Still, Jenkins and Wrice continued struggling to assemble funds for Mantua-based urban regeneration—Jenkins now from within city government, where the political climate had shifted as well.

The heyday of YGS and MCP had taken place against a backdrop of increasingly militant activism on race and poverty issues across Philadelphia. This conflict had also changed Democratic politics in the city. The New Deal coalition that had bound working- and middle-class voters of both races to organized labor and liberal business interests in the 1950s and early 1960s fractured as the city continued to lose industry and population; as Black-led organizations from the NAACP to the Black Panther Party mobilized to protest persistent racism in public education, the workforce, and the housing market; and as figures like Frank Rizzo advanced the narrative that Blacks themselves were to blame for "crime in the streets and the problems in the school system and whatever else is bad about Philadelphia."[55] In order to consolidate the support of conservative Democratic voters—whom he needed to retain his grip on power as liberals abandoned him—Mayor Tate elevated Rizzo from the post of deputy police commissioner to the job of commissioner in May 1967. As Tate's police chief, Rizzo both fueled Black protest and visibly combated it, relishing the politics of polarization as he unleashed spectacular violence on militant and peaceful demonstrators alike. The election of Rizzo to the mayor's office—as a Democrat—in 1971 was in many ways emblematic of what historian Elizabeth Hinton characterizes as a shift from the War on Poverty to the War on Crime as an organizing principle for urban policy in the United States.[56] Rizzo continued to have access to substantial federal resources throughout the 1970s, but his administration dedicated many of these to policing and to punishment. The New Deal urban coalition that had fused organized labor with Black leaders and white liberals had irremediably fractured.[57]

Amid this turmoil, Wrice, Jenkins, and the organizations they led sidestepped controversy and hewed to violence prevention and self-help. Movement activists regarded the groups' unflagging support of Philadelphia's Democratic machine, and their cultivation of university patronage, as self-serving. However, Rizzo's election to the mayor's office charted a path to the realization of the Mantua Community Planners' neighborhood development plan that—ironically—would not have existed absent the Mantua leaders' loyalty to an increasingly racially regressive local regime.[58] Despite Nixon's 1973 moratorium on housing funding and an unfavorable national economic picture, significant federal funds continued to flow to cities in the 1970s, through the Community Development Block Grant Program and through federal "revenue-sharing." The new arrangements removed HUD from a direct grant-making role, but the effect of this was to endow local officials with additional discretion over the use of federal funds. In this context, the Mantua leaders' support of Rizzo allowed them to claim an outsized share of the city's federal cash.

The project that would become known as the Mount Vernon Manor Apartments took several more years to materialize. After the suspension of urban

Figure 11. Andrew Jenkins, John Sturgis, and construction workers at the site of the Mount Vernon Manor Apartments, July 8, 1979. Photo by William Owens. Special Collections Research Center, Temple University Libraries, Philadelphia, PA.

renewal funds in 1973, Wrice and Jenkins worked with Pennsylvania Senator Hugh Scott to resuscitate the project under HUD's Section 236 program, which offered private developers mortgage interest subsidies combined with federal loan guarantees that enabled them to raise debt financing. The Philadelphia City Planning Commission authorized the project in July 1974, with Young Great Society as the developer.[59] But then there were further delays, likely because the Mantua organizations still needed to raise equity. A January 1978 article announced the revival of the 122-unit development, citing support from the State of Pennsylvania's Department of Community Affairs, the Philadelphia Housing Development Corporation, and the Philadelphia Redevelopment Authority.[60] Jenkins's influence in local government (he was at that point the chairman of Rizzo's Citizens Advisory Committee on Community Development) likely helped to secure the supplemental city and state resources required to bring the project to completion.[61] News items about the Mount Vernon Manor Apartments emphasized the continuing link between neighborhood-based development and avenues to better-paying work for local residents. Construction on the project, MCP executive director John Sturgis told a reporter, had "helped reduce Mantua's high rate of unemployment."[62]

High School Politics

As self-help efforts in Mantua alternately foundered and recovered, the fraught, racialized politics of Philadelphia public education were playing out at University City High School (UCHS). UCHS had originally belonged to a portfolio of projects that the West Philadelphia Corporation pursued as part of a broad-based effort to improve public schools in university-adjacent neighborhoods, the Universities-Related Schools Program. University leaders conceived of the high school as a science "magnet" with an innovative curriculum—an educational complement to the University City Science Center's employment hub. Plans for the school incorporated contemporary ideas about progressive education: inquiry-based learning, an interdisciplinary curriculum, and an "open-plan" layout that defied traditional concepts of the classroom. But West Philadelphia Corporation officials' insistence that the School District locate UCHS at Filbert and 36th Streets, exactly where the Redevelopment Authority had proposed housing rehabilitation for residents of the Black Bottom, belied the notion that their aims were purely educational. Further, by the time the school opened in 1971, the School District

Figure 12. Student Government officers Helen Wilson and Jeff Marriott lay the cornerstone of the University City High School with Dr. Alec Washco of the Philadelphia Board of Education, May 2, 1973. Special Collections Research Center, Temple University Libraries, Philadelphia, PA.

was facing fiscal problems and was under constant attack by the city's newly elected mayor—that is, Frank Rizzo, the former police commissioner. The West Philadelphia Corporation and the University of Pennsylvania were by this point plagued by budget woes and were in the process of withdrawing financial support for the school improvement program.[63] These factors curtailed the school's ability to implement the progressive curriculum that District and WPC officials had initially envisioned.[64]

A related problem at UCHS went straight to the challenge of racism in West Philadelphia, both its origins and its legacies. The WPC's Universities-Related Schools Program had focused on making public education a palatable option for university-affiliated families who, then as now, were predominantly affluent and white. University City High School was part of this thrust. But many parents who participated in public discussions about the school's "feeder pattern" were concerned about overcrowding at the area's other high schools. They opposed an enrollment plan that catered to students "magnetized" from affluent households while leaving their own children in substandard, overburdened facilities and segregated classrooms. Officials split the difference: "The huge building was divided into pods for students assigned to different academic programs. There was to be one section for the science magnet program—originally, the vision for the entire school—and other sections that would presumably have accommodated rank-and-file West Philadelphia students. While a small number of students from university-affiliated families enrolled initially at UCHS, these numbers quickly dwindled."[65] In the ensuing years, the University City High School grew increasingly segregated by class and race. Gang conflicts erupted, giving the school a reputation for the violence and disorder that middle-class white Philadelphians had come to associate with low-socioeconomic-status Black neighborhoods and the people who lived in them. The school was heavily policed, and teachers' focus was on discipline and security.[66]

* * *

Documentation on Mantua in the decades following the opening of Mount Vernon Manor is sparse. *Building Drexel*, an institutional history of Drexel University published in 2017, notes the devastating effects of crack cocaine on the neighborhood.[67] Herman Wrice and his family returned in 1984, and Wrice started a new organization, Mantua Against Drugs (MAD), which became known for its direct confrontation of neighborhood drug dealers.[68] In a trademark white hardhat, Wrice led marches and oversaw the demolition of crack houses. Just as they had lauded his gang-violence prevention model, public figures embraced the "Wrice Process" for combating drugs; after being featured on the television program *60 Minutes* in 1990, Wrice consulted with local governments across the country and with the U.S. Justice Department and was made an honorary general in the U.S. National Guard. He passed away in 2000 while in Fort Lauderdale, Florida, to lead an anti-drug march.[69] Jenkins was continuously employed by the City of Philadelphia from 1971 to 2007, working under six mayors, including as deputy mayor for housing under Mayor Edward Rendell. He continues to live in

Figure 13. Mural honoring Herman Wrice at 33rd and Haverford Streets, August 22, 2020. Photo by Elizabeth Rose.

Mantua and now serves as the vice president of the Mantua Civic Association, which he regards as the successor organization to the Mantua Community Planners. He was president of the board of directors of the Mount Vernon Manor Apartments until 2010.

The work of the Young Great Society and Mantua Community Planners organizations in 1960s and 1970s Philadelphia was an experiment in Black self-determination. But the groups' attempt to build autonomous reserves of capital for Black-controlled businesses and good jobs for Black residents relied on the goodwill and sponsorship of mainstream, white-dominated organizations: church groups, philanthropies, the government, and universities. The institutions were not reliable sponsors, and their support came at a cost. In order to maintain their backing, the so-called "ghetto leaders" had to refrain from challenging institutional racism. They had to tacitly acquiesce to a hegemonic narrative that held that "ghetto" residents needed only to be peaceable and work harder in order to economically succeed. This narrative fed (and was fed by) the myth that in America, social mobility was linked solely to merit; it bypassed the fact that the nation's economic might had been built in part through the subjugation and enslavement of Black Africans, and it ignored the fact that this subjugation had been rationalized through a persistent story about Blacks' inherent inferiority.

In response to these constraints, Wrice cultivated an "outsider" persona, that of the former gang leader who had achieved a rough-hewn moral clarity and could show troubled youth a path to personal responsibility. Jenkins was more defiant, but this led him to break with university and philanthropic sponsors and ultimately to attach himself to a different system—that of Philadelphia's local Democratic political regime. Fifty years afterward, Walter Palmer chided both Jenkins and Wrice for being accommodationist. His remark about their relationship with the University of Pennsylvania expresses a general view that the era's radical activists held with respect to interactions between Black leaders and white-dominated society: "They thought they could make deals with [university administrators]," Palmer said. "I said, 'Your vital interest doesn't coincide with theirs.'"[70]

Jenkins's and Wrice's achievements were significant. They and their organizations constructed Mantua as a significant place. They cultivated young leaders, many of whom attribute their survival and professional success to their involvement with the Young Great Society and Mantua Community Planners organizations.[71] They provided jobs and income for many local residents in the 1960s and 1970s. Their work is still visible in the physical fabric of the neighborhood. Yet while YGS and MCP left a legacy that contemporary activists eagerly took up in the 2010s, the groups were not able to transform Mantua, or even halt its decline. The civil rebellions to which elected officials and urban universities were warily responding in the late 1960s and early 1970s emanated from many structural conditions and factors—material poverty, state violence, and political marginalization. Leaders of self-help movements were ultimately able only to treat the symptoms of these conditions. In the end, intensified policing and incarceration were the government's preferred responses not only to the politics of protest and rebellion but also to the politics of self-help.

In the ensuing decades, Mantua households continued to struggle. When university-sponsored redevelopment came around again, median income in the neighborhood was under $25,000, and educational attainment remained

Figure 14. A Mantua Community Planners sticker affixed to a door on Spring Garden Street, 2016. Photo by author.

low. Mantua was still a "bad neighborhood." University administrators and faculty—working under a new moniker, that of the anchor institution—were still trying to be responsive to the communities adjacent to their campuses, and they were still pursuing their own institutional imperatives while doing this. The next chapter describes the way that universities and community-based organizations alike used planning to consolidate political resources and advance political objectives in University City in the 2010s.

CHAPTER 3

Plans on the Ground

On October 25, 2013, in his keynote address at the annual Leadership Exchange event of the Economy League of Greater Philadelphia, Drexel University President John A. Fry announced the Drexel Innovation Neighborhood. In a speech highlighting the institution's 2012 Strategic Plan, "Transforming the Modern Urban University," he emphasized Drexel's signature co-op program, its expansion into new fields of academic study and instruction, and its aspiration to continued leadership in online education and entrepreneurship. He then moved to a discussion of Drexel's ambition to "transform our very surroundings in University City." Although he offered few concrete details, he alluded to "twelve acres of undeveloped or underdeveloped property" that the university had acquired, and to "a series of mixed-use projects built in partnership with private developers," which he believed to be "the future of major university development." Through such development, he argued, it would be possible to "build an innovation cluster as well-located as any in the world," blending research with commerce and leading economic transformation in the Philadelphia region.[1]

With this announcement, and with the land use and development planning that underpinned it, Fry was connecting his institution to an increasingly prevalent phenomenon in North American cities: universities and property developers collaborating, through a "higher education P3" structure, on mixed-use development conceived with economic innovation in mind. The idea that synergy between research universities and commercial enterprise could drive economic dynamism in a city was not new; the West Philadelphia Corporation had constructed the University City Science Center itself on this principle fifty years earlier. What was distinct about twenty-first-century Innovation Neighborhoods was twofold. First, the federal government was largely absent from the conceptualization and execution of these projects. Second, the program of this innovation-driven, university-adjacent development was to be mixed-use, with housing, retail stores, restaurants, open space, and other amenities in addition to offices and labs. The projects that Drexel would spearhead in University City in the coming years—uCity Square and Schuylkill Yards—reflected a pattern that was animating urban economic development policy across the country. And in University City, as in other places, innovation-centered mixed-use development was being promoted as a means of sparking desired transformation in neighborhoods that had also been sites of transformation—and contestation—during the urban renewal period.

This chapter analyzes Drexel's institutional progression toward innovation-centered campus expansion in the early 2010s, juxtaposing the university's Campus Master Plan, released with its Strategic Plan in 2012, with plans for two Drexel-adjacent neighborhoods that community organizations created during this same period. These were the Directions Plan, published in 2011 by the Powelton Village Civic Association, and the Mantua Transformation Plan, published in 2013 by the board of directors of the Mount Vernon Manor housing development in Mantua. Drexel's campus plan, while it committed the university to work collaboratively with neighbors, also embodied administrators' intention to establish distinct new neighborhoods in the area—neighborhoods they hoped students, workers, firms, and investors would come to identify with the university and its innovation agenda. The Powelton and Mantua plans, in contrast, expressed the interests and anxieties of residents in and near this newly Drexel-defined territory.

The chapter is structured around these three "plans on the ground" because the claims on community identity that each plan asserted would become important in the years that followed, as neighborhood groups negotiated with Drexel and its partners over the costs and benefits of the uCity Square and Schuylkill Yards developments. Before describing the plans, however, it is important to understand the larger context from which they emerged. Thus, the chapter begins by unpacking the origins of the innovation district in urban economic development theory and practice, and by explaining the concept's centrality to universities' ambitions, and to public policy discourse, beginning in the 2000s.

The Logic of the Contemporary Innovation District

The conceptual origin of today's innovation district can be located in foundational research in economics and economic geography. In a 2005 review of this literature,[2] James Simmie draws on a definition of innovation advanced by the European Commission: "the commercially successful exploitation of new technologies, ideas or methods through the introduction of new products or processes, or through the improvement of existing ones."[3] In 1939, Joseph Schumpeter named innovation as the prime source of capitalist economic dynamism.[4] Innovation has since preoccupied both academics and policy makers, who seek to create conditions for its successful emergence and diffusion. Researchers have noticed and investigated the spatial concentration of innovative activity, establishing that enterprises that succeed in commercializing new inventions agglomerate in geographies where auspicious combinations of factors are present—for example, human capital, dynamic supplier-purchaser relationships, and social environments in which entrepreneurs inform and inspire one another. Scholars have combined Schumpeter's work with that of the economist Alfred Marshall, who used the term "industrial district" to characterize places where ideas and know-how "spill over" to firms in related industries.[5] Jane Jacobs's work on urban industrial diversity also serves as a key reference point for scholars of place-based innovation.[6] Recent scholarship places research universities at the center of these dynamics. Henry Etzkowitz and Loet Leydesdorff propose the metaphor of a "triple helix" to characterize the intertwined roles of universities, firms, and government in promoting innovation-led growth in particular locales.[7]

The relationship between these insights and the public policy regime supporting the contemporary urban innovation district is attenuated. As noted above, the theory that deliberate spatial connection between academic science and private enterprise could yield economic growth animated the creators of university-proximate research complexes, including the University City Science Center, as early as the 1950s. This theory emerged both from the work of Schumpeter (whom the annual reports of the West Philadelphia Corporation quoted approvingly) and from the realities of Cold War science—the federal government's high-tech military research budget having replaced active wartime mobilization as a stimulus for production and employment.[8] But as a number of scholars have pointed out, science-led economic development in the post–World War II period happened overwhelmingly in suburbs and exurbs. Urban research complexes like the Science Center were exceptional, and only modestly successful. The most celebrated innovation clusters thrived along freeways, and in office parks designed to be self-contained and distant from the urban fray. Much of the academic research on spatially concentrated innovation in the United States has focused not on cities but on metropolitan regions.[9]

In contrast, proponents of the twenty-first-century innovation district embrace the urban core. Bruce Katz and Jennifer Wagner, in an influential Brookings Institution monograph, herald a "remarkable shift" by which "innovative firms and talented workers are choosing to congregate in compact, amenity-rich enclaves in the cores of central cities."[10] Moreover, instead of the self-contained single-use research complexes that characterized the mid-twentieth-century wave of university expansion, present-day innovation development includes housing, retail, hotels, and public spaces in addition to offices and labs. "To ensure the next crop of innovators doesn't live and work in an environment as sterile as one of the clean rooms in the Science Center," said a 2015 *Philadelphia Magazine* article about uCity Square, "development in the new neighborhood will be anchored by walkable streets, plenty of retail and a lively square."[11] Thus, while economic development policy makers extol innovation districts as spaces conducive to groundbreaking discoveries and the translation of science into commerce, residential and leisure environments are equally if not more central in their conceptualization. A case study of SkySong, a district associated with Arizona State University, highlights the Scottsdale-based institution's decision to "accommodate design-heavy retail development anticipated to appeal to both local restaurateurs and the targeted consumer groups patronizing their businesses." The goal, writes the author of the study, was "a live, work, play setting."[12]

The prevalence of the live/work/play concept in the innovation district conversation reflects the key role that real estate developers and property investors play in universities' efforts to gather innovators together in urban environments. Private interest in this particular version of the higher-education public/private partnership stems from the conviction that there are favorable returns to be gained from creating mixed-use development on university-owned or university-adjacent land. In a 2017 paper based on interviews with professionals involved in four innovation districts, Dustin Read and Drew Sanderford assert: "innovation districts were generally conceptualized in a manner very similar to other types of real estate development involving cross-sector collaboration. Public-private partnerships were perceived as a means of mobilizing parties capable of effectuating change, speculative investments in real estate development were seen as a legitimate use of government resources, and place branding strategies were identified as a useful tool to attract financial and human capital."[13] In this context, the "triple helix" has a different configuration. Innovation scholars originally conceived the metaphor to describe the process by which academic researchers collaborate with industry entrepreneurs to transform government-funded basic science (pharmaceutical compounds, computer technologies) into saleable inventions and, ultimately, profitable industrial companies. In innovation district projects, in contrast, university real estate departments collaborate with property entrepreneurs to develop new urban spaces, with the expectation that they will become destinations for technology-intensive firms and skilled labor. The logic is that because they are "collision points for innovative people,"[14] innovation districts stimulate economic development. But while thriving businesses are the end goal, property investment (rather than product development) is the turnkey. Rather than acting simply as a source of commercializable knowledge, the university acts as a development partner. In three of the four cases analyzed by Read and Sanderford, academic institutions "stepped forward to master lease space and/or guarantee debt financing in order to procure private sector investment."[15]

The government-side component of this arrangement is also significant. Certainly, federal agencies continue to fund a large share of university basic science,[16] and it makes sense to locate incubators and accelerators for startup companies close to university facilities and to support them with government funding. But the value proposition of the innovation district rests not just on the production of technology but on consumption, by would-be innovators, of housing, culture, street life, and other urban amenities.[17] These are neighborhoods, and as such they implicate local government in myriad ways. First, cities shape innovation districts' built and social form, through zoning and permitting.[18] Second, they maintain the quality and safety of their streets and sidewalks. Third, governments subsidize these projects through an array of economic development incentives and tax abatements. Case material on innovation districts outlines the multiple mechanisms—tax-exempt bonds, tax increment financing, historic preservation tax credits, and New Markets tax credits—that inject public capital into their financing structures.[19] Schuylkill Yards and uCity Square benefit from the City of Philadelphia's ten-year tax abatement on new development, from the State of Pennsylvania's Keystone Opportunity Zone program, from the federal Opportunity Zone program, and from state capital grants.

The establishment of the Drexel Innovation Neighborhood via the uCity Square and Schuylkill Yards projects is a far cry from the development of the University City Science Center. Philadelphia's City Planning Commission is not treating inhabited neighborhoods as blank slates. Its Redevelopment Authority is not condemning property or relocating residents. The federal government is no longer providing generous grants that enable the municipality to acquire occupied businesses and homes. But the innovation district rising in University City today calls on government authority and resources in more subtle ways, relying on city and state officials' capacity to forego revenue and to regulate development in particular actors' favor.

Drexel's Ambition to Innovate

The public/private partnerships to which Fry alluded in his 2013 Economy League address were increasingly common among universities in the early 2010s. Drexel's institutional path toward the innovation neighborhood, however, was not a foregone conclusion. The school, which financier Anthony Drexel had established in 1891 as the Drexel Institute of Art, Science and Industry, had lived much of its existence in the shadow of its close neighbor, the University of Pennsylvania. Penn, which was founded by Benjamin Franklin, became the first university in the continental United States in 1765. While it was originally a teaching college, its leaders had begun by the late nineteenth century to recruit eminent scholars, build an elite reputation, and "transition . . . to a Humboldtian-model research institution."[20] Drexel, in contrast, was a technical institute, founded at the peak of Philadelphia's prowess as a manufacturing city, with low tuition and an explicit brief to respond to the educational needs of the working class and the industrial firms that employed them.[21] Drexel soon began awarding bachelor's degrees and had become, by the 1930s, a "general purpose institution of higher education."[22] Nevertheless, in its orientation to applied subject matter and its well-known cooperative education program (through which students interspersed classroom work with employment), it identified primarily not as a research institution but as a place to acquire practical knowledge and prepare for the workplace.

Following a dip in enrollment during the Great Depression and World War II, Drexel's physical footprint and institutional scope grew during the postwar period. This occurred as a result of both Cold War research spending and soaring college participation rates nationwide (subsidized, as was suburban expansion, by federal largesse). Drexel grew in the two decades following the war, even as jobs and population left Philadelphia. In the 1980s, however, the institution entered a decline born of competition from other schools, a difficult transition to formal status as a research university, and the slipping fortunes of Philadelphia itself. Enrollment dropped by 38 percent, from over 12,000 to around 9,000, between 1986 and 1995.[23]

A turnaround occurred with the 1995 appointment of charismatic civil engineer Constantine Papadakis as Drexel's president. Papadakis, an adept financial manager and a master marketer, simultaneously overhauled enrollment management and undertook a massive rebranding strategy. Under his leadership, Drexel went through the final stages of evolution from an institute of technology to a comprehensive university, opening a law school and acquiring a school of medicine as well as making improvements to undergraduate arts and sciences programs.[24] Its enrollment grew to 16,300 by 2002 and would continue to increase over the following decade.[25] While some criticized Papadakis's corporate orientation (he uncritically referred to students as "customers"), his style was compatible with a growing trend on the part of university administrators to regard their institutions as competitors in a larger higher education industry. Professional consultants had expanded their role in higher education in this context, advising institutions on performance benchmarking, public relations, brand-building, and asset management.

John Fry's appointment as Drexel's president in 2010 after the unexpected death of Papadakis continued this business-oriented leadership, while also bringing Drexel's trajectory closer to that of Penn. After completing a master's degree in business in 1986, Fry had worked as a management consultant, often advising higher education clients. One of these was the University of Pennsylvania, and in 1995 Penn President Judith Rodin appointed Fry as an executive vice president of the university and put him on the team responsible for executing the institution's new strategic plan.[26] Here he became closely associated with the West Philadelphia Initiatives (WPI), Rodin's well-known effort, starting in 1996, to increase safety and prosperity in the troubled neighborhoods to the west of Penn's campus through a combination of physical and social interventions. WPI's programs encompassed public education, neighborhood security, commercial revitalization, economic inclusion (through changes to institutional purchasing practices and workforce development), and housing.[27]

While they are generally celebrated in the academic literature on university-community relations, Penn's West Philadelphia Initiatives have left a complicated legacy. Scholar Harley Etienne, who documents neighborhood perspectives on the initiatives in his book *Pushing Back the Gates*, demonstrates that the concept of making neighborhoods "clean and safe" contains assumptions both about the people and activities for whom revitalized areas are intended and about the sources of danger and deterioration *from* whom these people need protection. Even as they improved the public realm, increased purchasing from local vendors, and made jobs and career ladders more accessible to unemployed and underemployed West Philadelphians, administrators guided a set of actions that, in making Penn-adjacent neighborhoods more hospitable to the university-affiliated, culturally and physically excluded many people of lower socioeconomic status.

The WPI's signature public education initiative, the Sadie Tanner Mossell Alexander University of Pennsylvania Partnership School (in brief, the Penn Alexander School, or PAS), offers a stark example of this. The school is born of a public/private partnership between the University of Pennsylvania, the Philadelphia School District, and the Philadelphia Federation of Teachers. On a development site donated by the university, the school, which now enrolls children from preschool through the eighth grade, first opened in 2001.The university supports the school with resources from its Graduate School of Education and with an annual per-student subsidy that enables enrichment and reduced class sizes.[28] The school's reputation for quality has led to an increase in housing prices in the surrounding residential blocks from which it draws its student population (known as its "catchment area"). Many low-income families living in the in the Penn Alexander catchment area have lost their leases as market rents have outpaced the value of the federal housing vouchers that subsidized their rent. A 2016 study found that the catchment had undergone "drastic" changes in household wealth and racial composition since 2000, while socioeconomic indicators outside the catchment area remained low.[29] The fraught politics of PAS, and their bearing on discussions of a middle school planned for uCity Square during the 2010s, are discussed in the next chapter.

Etienne argues that while the West Philadelphia Initiatives typically are understood as a coherent, integrated set of programs, the multiple actors who implemented the initiatives frequently found themselves at odds philosophically. Some WPI leaders, he says, prioritized bringing students, faculty, and non-university-affiliated community members together on equal footing, whether in the classroom or in jointly managed cultural venues such as the Rotunda arts space. Other administrators employed "ambitious corporate-style

institutional management" to promote university-friendly real estate development and to manage streets and other public spaces as effective extensions of
campus territory.[30] Fry, Etienne implies, stood squarely on the corporate
side of this divide and squarely amid the WPI's internal contradictions.

As he became president of Drexel in 2010 after an eight-year stint as
president of Franklin and Marshall College in Lancaster, Pennsylvania, Fry
was positioned to carry forward Papadakis's unfinished agenda while making his own mark on University City's less renowned university. The project
of building an innovation district fit with Drexel's educational ambitions,
with its interest in drawing investment to Philadelphia, and with its aspiration to compete with higher education institutions across the region and
nation. The aim of making social inclusion a central aspect of the innovation district project also fit the institution's agenda. It reflected lessons that
Fry had absorbed thoroughly during his previous turn in West Philadelphia.

In building a narrative of Drexel's evolution toward innovation district
development, it is instructive to juxtapose *Building Drexel*, the 2017 institutional history on which parts of this chapter draw, with Puckett and Lloyd's
2015 *Becoming Penn*, the study whose account of the University of Pennsylvania's twentieth-century expansion is cited in Chapter 1. The two volumes
can be read in dialogue with one another. *Becoming Penn*, as Puckett and
Lloyd state in their conclusion, traces "a progression from alienation and drift
to reconciliation and revival":

> In the case of the Science Center in the mid-1960s, Penn was heavily
> implicated in the displacement of poor and working-class African
> Americans for the sake of an enterprise that fell short of being a true R
> & D hub. The shortfall of the Science Center added insult to the injury
> inflicted on displaced poor people by the unilateral decision making of
> Penn's surrogate, the West Philadelphia Corporation, and the RDA.
> Embracing the ethic of positive engagement in West Philadelphia that
> Sheldon Hackney introduced in the 1980s, Judith Rodin managed to
> achieve the 1960s WPC's goal of building a compatible neighborhood
> for Penn, without the insensitivity or lack of transparency that at-
> tended federally sponsored urban renewal in University City.[31]

Puckett and Lloyd portray the West Philadelphia Initiatives as having re-
dressed the injuries the university inflicted on its Black neighbors during the
urban renewal-era. Penn's efforts, in their view, served to reconcile the institution

with its neighbors and set the stage for a more harmonious future. But while they engage in some prospective reflection, Puckett and Lloyd's work is largely historical. *Building Drexel*, on the other hand, looks forward as well as backward. Its final chapter, "The Promise of a New Century," cites the West Philadelphia Initiatives as the inspiration for the university's outreach work in Mantua and Powelton Village. It also introduces Drexel's real estate ventures in the context of Fry's stated hope that they will create "a tidal wave of business and civic innovation, as well as social and economic equity."[32] As they describe the innovation neighborhood they are planning for the area around their campus, Drexel officials are stating two tacit objectives: to make good on the Science Center's only partially fulfilled economic development promises, and to emulate and improve upon Penn's neighborhood work.

The Urban Renewal Legacy in Powelton Village

Like Penn, Drexel fought bitterly with its residential neighbors during the urban renewal period. As described in Chapter 1, Philadelphia's City Planning Commission had created two redevelopment areas in the easternmost part of West Philadelphia in 1948 and consolidated parts of each into the "University City Redevelopment Area," with five numbered subunits, in 1957. As the West Philadelphia Corporation struggled to clear Unit 3 for the Science Center and as the University of Pennsylvania expanded into the area demarcated as Unit 4, Unit 5 (a vertical strip running east to west from 32nd to 34th Streets and north-south between Powelton Avenue and Chestnut Streets) fell into Drexel's ambit. In 1964, planning consultants recommended an enlarged campus to accommodate a projected 85 percent increase in enrollment (to 14,000 students) by 1970. They produced a development blueprint that extended Drexel's footprint into Unit 5, which contained a number of occupied homes.[33]

Even before being officially announced, however, Drexel's vision for a high-modernist remaking of the area ran afoul of residents of the adjacent low-density residential community of Powelton Village, known for its Victorian homes and impressive flower gardens as well as its climate of political activism. The protest and litigation ignited by this and subsequent expansion plans lasted for over two decades and involved politically active students as well as Powelton Village households.[34] While Drexel ultimately was able to build most of the structures it had planned in Unit 5, Powelton groups succeeded in forcing a negotiated process that saved some properties from the bulldozer and allowed residents a measure of influence over the architectural character of new development. Powelton Village residents also successfully pushed Drexel, starting in the 1970s, to penalize disruptive partying and other antisocial behaviors among students living off campus.

The dynamics between Drexel and Powelton Village residents were distinct from those that existed between the West Philadelphia Corporation and Black Bottom residents, for two reasons. First, Drexel, which did not officially become a university until 1970, was a less powerful player in Philadelphia than the University of Pennsylvania. As early as 1948, Drexel leaders had expressed dismay that the City Planning Commission and Redevelopment Authority responded more readily to requests from the more prestigious institution.[35] Second, as a group dominated by white homeowners (albeit politically progressive ones, in many cases), Drexel's adversaries in and around Urban Renewal Area Unit 5 had political access and financial resources. At key junctures, community groups hired architects to produce counter-plans for the neighborhood, as well as attorneys to contest the city's interpretation of redevelopment law.[36] While some homes in Powelton Village were condemned and demolished during the urban renewal period, successful advocacy and negotiation preserved the neighborhood's basic fabric. In 1985, the community and the university achieved a détente of sorts when Drexel President William S. Gaither negotiated an agreement with the Powelton Village Civic Association for the construction of a new dormitory at 34th and Arch Streets. Civic leaders and the university hailed the "Dormitory Agreement," which established a process for neighborhood consultation and review on university projects going forward, as the start of a new era of partnership.

The Powelton Village Civic Association's Directions Plan

But Powelton residents, from their own perspective, continued to lose ground in the succeeding decades. For while the university was no longer striving to develop property in Powelton Village, its operations were continuing to have an unwelcome impact. The Powelton Village Civic Association (PVCA)'s Directions Plan, released in 2011, characterizes existing conditions in Powelton Village in terms of a single central concern: the impact on the neighborhood of accelerating growth in student housing. According to the introduction, "Powelton Village is at a tipping point. On one side is the Powelton Village of spectacular homes, supported by strong market values and diligent home-owners. On the other side is the Powelton Village of deteriorated homes, carved up into rental units—often bereft of basic maintenance—typically owned by absentee landlords. . . . Amongst some homeowners, there is a sense that the delicate fabric of Powelton Village is tattering house by house."[37] Several pages later, the plan identifies the tattering's source di-rectly: "In 2010 the Drexel student population exceeded 22,000 students. . . . Only about 17% of students actually live on campus. This drives demand for rental units close to Drexel. As a result, much of Powelton's housing has been purchased and reconfigured as student rentals. In many cases, these units hold well over the limit of three unrelated individuals per household."[38] While the Powelton Village Civic Association serves several functions, such as sponsoring annual block parties, advocating for local schools, and main-taining a community playground known as the Tot Lot, seven of the nine objectives outlined in its bylaws document are cognate to the first stated objective: "To exert influence, whenever and wherever possible, for the pres-ervation and improvement of the residential character of Powelton Village."[39] Though the Directions Plan contains sections about school quality, retail development, and urban greening, the struggle to curb what one civic asso-ciation member termed "incompatible development," both in and adjacent to the neighborhood, is the binding agent. Interviews with association offi-cials and observations at meetings underscored active residents' attachment to a specific collective perception of the community—represented by the twin pillars of architectural distinctiveness and the presence of conscien-tious owner-occupants.[40]

The Directions Plan explains the decline in owner-occupied homes as a function of the laws of housing economics, which favor investor-ownership. The income value of a home that has been converted for room-by-room rental by students exceeds the price a single-family homeowner would pay for that same property. Investor-purchasers outbid prospective owner-occupants, and absentee-owned student rental properties become increas-ingly prevalent (the plan observes that owners of 34 percent of Powelton Village's housing stock have off-site mailing addresses). While it is techni-cally illegal under Philadelphia's housing code to rent a housing unit to more than three unrelated individuals, PVCA leaders argue that the city's Licenses and Inspections department does not reliably enforce the code, due to capacity constraints. The Association has considered seeking government interventions—such as historic designation—that could prevent so-called "boarding house" conversions. The Directions Plan, however, makes Drexel the target of its appeal for change.

PVCA is descended from the Powelton Civic Homeowners Association and Powelton Neighbors, groups formed to resist Drexel's expansion into the neighborhood five decades ago. The Directions Plan's four-page section on neighborhood history traces decades of conflict and cooperation between the university and homeowner representatives: protest and litigation in the 1960s and early 1970s; a thaw in the late 1970s; and the cooperative review process established with the "Dormitory Agreement" in 1985. It also details conflict over residence hall construction and open space in the early 2000s, as Drexel began concerted efforts to house more of its growing student body on campus. Noting a nationwide "warming trend" between academic institutions and their surrounding communities, the Directions Plan calls on the university to maintain contextually compatible design at the border of Powelton, to regulate illegal conversions, to help increase the population of owner-occupiers, and to attract more young families with children. It also pledges the Association's support for "the kind of urbane, mixed-use development that will make for a safer, more attractive and stable Powelton Village neighborhood."[41] This gesture of comity toward Drexel links subtly to a warning (tacit in the plan and mentioned explicitly during interviews) that homeowners are prepared to litigate against development plans they deem inconsistent with their goals. Interviewees spoke with pride of having successfully used legal action to achieve modifications to a plan for a university-sponsored student housing project in 2008, noting that the PVCA's relationship with the university had changed as a result. "We started having biweekly meetings with Drexel after that," said one interviewee. "We didn't have a veto, but we had a seat at the table."[42] As they anticipated the university's expansion in the early 2010s, Powelton Village leaders fully intended to occupy that seat.

Drexel in Mantua

Powelton community residents had consistently tangled with Drexel over development and quality of life issues from the 1960s onward. In contrast, the university's engagement with Mantua—directly to the north of Powelton across Spring Garden Street—was more ministerial. In the final chapter of the book *Building Drexel*, Drexel history professor Scott Gabriel Knowles and his coauthors Jason Ludwig and Nathaniel Stanton cite the institution's

Table 1. Goals and action steps of the Powelton Village Civic Association Directions Plan, 2011.

Goal	Action steps identified
Promote home ownership and better maintenance practices for neighborhood houses	• Work with agencies to increase code enforcement • Identify sites for housing and mixed-used development while supporting more student housing on campus • Establish "educational housing district" or "provisions for universities, students, landlords and property managers to abide by" • Integrate green technologies to preserve architecture while cutting utility costs • Consider establishing a neighborhood improvement district (NID) • Market Powelton Village assets to potential homeowners
Support Powelton Village schools	• Identify funding for materials • Green schoolyards • Repurpose some school sites for mixed-use development
Create livelier Main Street environment on Lancaster Avenue	• Recruit restaurants and other retail • Improve the appearance of retail frontage • Improve public realm at key intersections
Improve connections to key area destinations, such as Fairmount Park and Center City	• Improve traffic flow • Improve biking and walking infrastructure • Incentivize public transportation use • Strategic lighting installation, planting of street trees, repaving of sidewalks
Improve parks and streets to encourage commercial growth, greening, and recreation	• New programming on Lancaster Avenue and at Drexel Park • Public art and landscaping near institutional buildings • Maintain and enhance tree canopy • Stormwater management • New bikeway

SOURCE: Adapted by author from Powelton Village Civic Association Directions Plan.

efforts during the 1960s and 1970s to organize arts courses for community members and to open Drexel's athletic fields to neighborhood children. Drexel students, they note, volunteered at the Mantua-Powelton Mini-School. Moreover, in the wake of a 1970 student-community sit-in in the university's Main Building, Drexel's Community Affairs office expanded its programming in Mantua to include consumer education and direct investment in schools as well as small business assistance and a youth employment program.[43] Knowles et al. also write admiringly of the work of the Young Great Society and Mantua Community Planners.

By the 1980s and 1990s, however, connections between the university and neighborhood leaders had weakened as Drexel faced administrative turmoil and as Mantua experienced population loss, high crime rates, and the attrition of stable working-class households. During this period, many people of modest means who were able to move from Mantua to other Philadelphia neighborhoods—or out of the city—did so; this included many of the people with whom the Young Great Society and Mantua Community Planners had worked during their heyday. Another factor in the community's population decline was the Philadelphia Housing Authority's 2008 decision to replace the 153-unit high-rise development Mantua Hall, where Herman Wrice and Andrew Jenkins had first offered services to neighborhood youth, with 101 lower-scale units. The demolition of Mantua Hall rid the neighborhood of a badly deteriorated and dangerous building. It also displaced some families and further thinned the neighborhood's population.

Drexel's enrollment growth in the first decade of the 2000s affected Mantua significantly. Drawing on Mantua's large inventory of vacant lots, residential developers constructed new buildings with units designed and priced for student occupancy and (as they had been doing in Powelton Village for several decades) converted older single-family homes into student rentals. There was a 73 percent increase in residents in the twenty- to twenty-four-year-old age range in Mantua between 2000 and 2010. Yet despite growth in its student population, Mantua's total population was only 65 percent of what it had been in 1980 when John Fry became president of Drexel in 2010.[44]

Early in his tenure, Fry began speaking publicly about the university's obligation to neighboring low-wealth communities and their residents. He also hired Lucy Kerman, with whom he had worked on the West Philadelphia Initiatives at Penn, as Drexel's Senior Vice Provost for University and Community Partnerships. In the next eight years, Kerman's office would oversee the development of the university-funded Dornsife Center for

Figure 15. Population loss in Mantua and other Lower Lancaster corridor neighborhoods caused vacancy to rise along Lancaster Avenue in the 1990s and early 2000s. Photo by author.

Neighborhood Partnerships in the heart of Mantua and help the City of Philadelphia and neighborhood organizations secure several grants and designations—such as a 2014 Promise Zone designation—that would inject government resources into the neighborhood. The selection of Mantua to receive a U.S. Department of Housing and Urban Development Choice Neighborhoods Initiative planning grant in 2011 was a keystone for this work.

Mount Vernon Manor and the Mantua Transformation Plan

Student renter households had moved into Mantua in the early 2000s alongside an incumbent population struggling with substandard housing conditions and limited employment prospects. Over time, the Mantua Community Planners and other groups that had organized the neighborhood in the 1960s and 1970s had given way to a fractious collection of small, under-resourced groups defined largely by the extent to which they commanded the favor of local ward leaders and politicians.[45]

A poignant emblem of this decline in cohesion was the state of the Mount Vernon Manor Apartments, the HUD Section 236 project that Mantua Community Planners had completed in 1979. By 2010, the nine-building development, controlled by a board of directors that MCP's Andrew Jenkins still headed, was in dire condition. Nearly 30 percent of its 125 units were vacant; water infiltration and mold had made ground-floor units uninhabitable; roof leaks had damaged upper-floor apartments; and drug-dealing was flourishing in run-down common areas. More to the point, the development was losing money and had been for years.[46] According to one close observer, the board of directors "had run the project into the ground," and the regional office of the U.S. Department of Housing and Urban Development (HUD) was on the verge of condemning the property.

In an unlikely way, the Mantua Transformation Plan emerged from this troubled situation. Recognizing that saving the Mount Vernon Manor Apartments from condemnation would require a financial restructuring, Andrew Jenkins reached out to a longtime professional acquaintance, Roy Diamond. A former legal assistance attorney who had known the work of Mantua Community Planners as a University of Pennsylvania student in the late 1970s,[47] Diamond had later parlayed ground-level knowledge of affordable housing law and finance into a successful consulting business. He agreed to help, and in the spring of 2010 HUD authorized Diamond's firm, Diamond and Associates, to step in as the management agent at Mount Vernon Manor. In exchange for their approval of this new arrangement, Philadelphia city officials insisted that Mount Vernon Manor's entire board of directors, including Jenkins, be replaced.[48]

Jenkins's cession of control over his signature community project in some respects removed the last remaining vestige of the Mantua Community Planners' presence in the neighborhood. At the same time, it set off a chain of events that extended the group's legacy and created a platform for ongoing political engagement. Initially seeking to build clout to compete for the scarce government-subsidized financing that would be needed to rehabilitate the Mount Vernon Manor complex, Diamond's firm applied to HUD's Choice Neighborhoods Initiative for a $250,000 community planning grant on behalf of the new Mount Vernon Manor board. Staff members at Diamond were by their own admission completely unqualified to facilitate a legitimate community-engagement process in Mantua.[49] But when they unexpectedly received the grant, they opened the door for others who were able to do so. The planning exercise that followed gave rise to two organizations—the Mount Vernon Manor Community Development Corporation and the Mantua Civic Association—that established continuity between past and present-day activism in the neighborhood.

The planning process funded by the Choice Neighborhoods Initiative got underway in the early summer of 2011. It was an awkward start. The grant application had been written largely by a young staffer at Diamond and Associates. Drexel's office of community partnerships had helped. There had been no involvement from Mantua-based groups. "We didn't know about the Choice grant," a Mount Vernon Manor board member later recalled. "We were just trying to save the housing."[50] The abrupt appearance of $250,000 for a neighborhood plan represented an opportunity, but it was an opportunity of which Mantua's community organizations were wary, having learned to mistrust both outside institutions and one another. A diagram featured in an early document prepared by the planning consultant, Kitchen & Associates, highlighted "perceived neighborhood boundaries" separating distinct areas of the neighborhood where residents and local leaders operated in isolation from one another and in some cases harbored resentments rooted in intra-neighborhood class differences.[51] Several

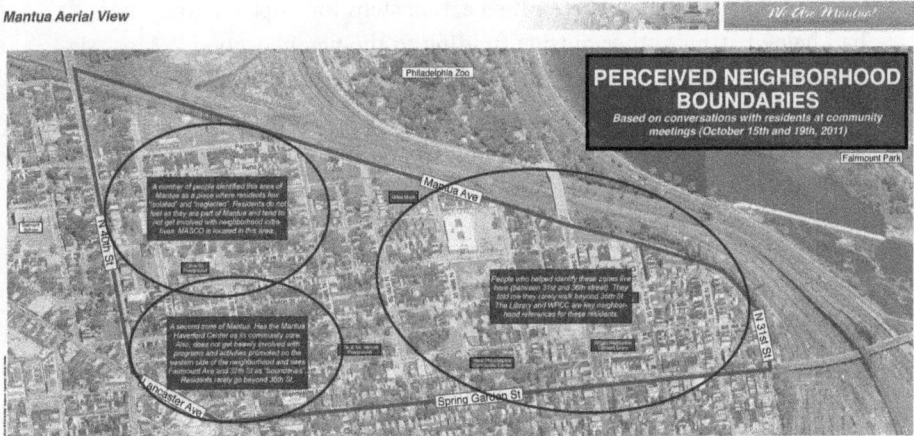

Figure 16. "Perceived Neighborhood Boundaries," from Kitchen & Associates' preliminary planning document for the Mantua Transformation Plan (Philadelphia, 2013). Reprinted with permission from Kitchen & Associates.

interviewees described the boundaries separating these territories as "invisible walls" left over from decades-old gang disputes, or "old east-west stuff," as one interviewee put it.[52]

The Philadelphia office of the Local Initiatives Support Corporation (LISC), a community development intermediary, contributed funding for a community liaison, Donna Griffin, who worked closely with the consulting planners and the new Mount Vernon Manor board.[53] With her help, a twenty-five-member steering committee coalesced; issue-based task forces began meeting; and input sessions and open houses were held across the neighborhood at a variety of venues. The Mount Vernon Manor board developed the tagline "We Are Mantua!" to encourage enthusiasm for an intentional process in which action steps that people suggested along the way would not wait for a complete plan. "It was planning and doing," says one interviewee. "The plan was informed by what was being done and simultaneously it was informing what was being done."[54] "Invisible walls" began to seem less impenetrable as individuals and organizations began coordinating more closely.

By the time the Mount Vernon Manor board submitted the Mantua Transformation Plan to HUD in June 2013, the "planning and doing" instigated by the grant had already accomplished much. It had paved the way for the board to finance the first phase of rehabilitation at the Mount Vernon Manor Apartments as a 100 percent affordable development.[55] It had articulated a range of goals and identified action steps for implementing them. It had helped attract other outside funding to the neighborhood.[56] Most significantly, it had established the Mantua Civic Association (MCA), whose members were positioning themselves to advance neighborhood priorities as a potential counterweight to those of Drexel and local politicians. As they evolved during the "We Are Mantua!"/Choice Neighborhoods process, MCA and the Mount Vernon Manor Community Development Corporation shook off, to an extent, the personal rivalries and managerial failures that had dogged past efforts to improve conditions in the neighborhood. At the same time, the new organizations also embodied the enduring effects of past community improvement efforts. Mount Vernon Manor's replacement board, which Jenkins had a strong hand in assembling, included several people who had been mentored by Jenkins and Wrice in the 1960s and 1970s. The general contractor for the Mount Vernon Manor redevelopment (and eventually the executive director of the Mount Vernon Manor Community Development Corporation) was Michael Thorpe, who had been an active member of the Young Great Society as a teenager. MCA, which in many ways supplanted a multiplicity of contentious smaller groups,[57] was seen by at least some leaders as an organizational descendant of Mantua Community Planners, ready to breathe new life into the neighborhood's tradition of advocacy. From the perspective of community members, the standing up of a civic association was far and away the most important accomplishment of the "We Are Mantua!" effort. And the civic association was important, according to a neighborhood leader interviewed in 2016, because "we were running behind the runaway train. . . . We had to come together to deal with the anchoring institutions."[58]

As the main anchor institution in question, Drexel cut a complicated figure. Kerman's office had helped put the Mount Vernon Manor rescue strategy in place and acted as a partner in the "We Are Mantua!" effort, with administrators and faculty participating on its steering committee and on several task forces. The university's Office of University-Community Partnerships provided financial support for aspects of the effort to begin

Figure 17. Mount Vernon Manor after Rehabilitation. Photo courtesy of Mt. Vernon Manor Community Development Corporation.

Table 2. Priorities and Strategies for Mantua as outlined in the Mantua Transformation Plan, 2013.

Priorities	Strategies
Improve capacity for civic engagement	• Establish Mantua Civic Association • Establish Community Home and School Association • Cultivate youth leadership • Expand Mount Vernon Manor Board capacity
Ensure quality education for Mantua's youth	• Pre-K and early literacy • Professional and curriculum development at McMichael School • Improved transition to high school • College opportunity paths • Parent involvement
Promote economic self-sufficiency	• Connect residents to adult education, career services, financial services • Pipeline to job opportunities • Construction trades skills development • Entrepreneurship support
Enhance community safety	• Boost enforcement at drug activity hotspots • Implement Neighborhood Watch • Encourage anonymous crime reporting at Mount Vernon Manor • Reinforce drug-free zone around community facilities • Improve lighting in strategic locations
Promote a healthier lifestyle	• Expand access to diverse and affordable food • Improve availability of basic healthcare • Expand opportunity for affordable exercising
Revitalize Mantua's physical environment	• Create neighborhood core that improves safety, activates vacant lots, reinforces pride in culture and history • Rebuild residential fabric west of the core by assembling public land for development, and by supporting home rehabilitation • Strengthen residential blocks east of the core by improving relationships among residents, students, and landlords • Targeted revitalization efforts on Haverford Avenue, Mantua Avenue, and the Olive Street Playground
Expand housing opportunities for all income levels	• Preserve existing homeownership • Expand affordable homeownership and affordable rental opportunities • Expand opportunities for mixed-income housing • Employ zoning to guide development

SOURCE: Adapted by author from Mantua Transformation Plan.

implementing neighborhood transformation during the planning process: it funded a youth advisory committee, established working partnerships with neighborhood schools, and announced the university's intention to build a community hub, the Dornsife Center, in Mantua. The office also helped to secure additional federal grants. At the same time, the unity that emerged during the "We Are Mantua!" process, and that propelled the Mantua Civic Association into an increasingly influential role, sprung from neighborhood leaders' desire to build greater power and voice for neighborhood representatives as Drexel expanded its footprint in University City.

The Mantua Transformation Plan's section on housing noted: "The threat of displacement is an ongoing concern among local residents and stakeholders and has been intensively discussed during the planning process. Development pressure will continue to increase due to Mantua's proximity to Center City and the expansion of its institutional neighbors. A set of targeted strategies protecting homeowners preserving and expanding affordable housing options will ensure that Mantua residents are able to remain and benefit from the neighborhood's transformation."[59] One key to this was to get resources to low-income homeowners in Mantua—both to prevent them from falling into arrears as their property tax assessments rose, and to help them make crucial repairs to their housing. The plan also stressed the importance of connecting Mantua homeowners to City of Philadelphia services aimed at resolving "tangled titles," tax liens, and other barriers to the transfer of homes between generations. Another critical opportunity was the substantial inventory of publicly owned vacant land in the neighborhood. In the plan, and at greater length in interviews, neighborhood representatives and citywide advocacy organizations identified the development and long-term stewardship of housing or commercial space on these parcels as a key to maintaining income diversity in Mantua as property values rose. Some interviewees proposed adopting transformative ownership strategies like community land trusts as a way of ensuring that community members, rather than market forces, would govern land use going forward. The Mantua Transformation Plan relied, however, on a standard market study that identified clusters of publicly owned parcels and proposed collaboration among for-profit and nonprofit developers and city agencies to assemble the funds required to develop them.

Figure 18. Publicly and privately owned vacant land in Mantua, as shown in the 2013 Mantua Transformation Plan, p. 28. Reprinted courtesy of Mt. Vernon Manor Community Development Corporation.

A Vibrant Urban University District

Drexel released its Campus Master Plan together with a Strategic Plan, "Transforming the Modern Urban University," in the fall of 2012. Anchored in four principles, the plan was introduced by President Fry as the product of an effort "to imagine a campus that strengthens Philadelphia and the region."[60] It highlighted the campus's location at a transportation hub on the Eastern Seaboard and underscored the power of urban design to promote economic development and bring people together. The document also brought forward the innovation district concept that Fry would feature in his speech to the Economy League the following year, asserting that the university's West Philadelphia setting presented "a special opportunity to integrate the activities of the campus, community, and workplace into a coherent, dynamic,

Table 3. Drexel Campus Master Plan Principles and Interventions, 2012.

Principle	Interventions
Distinguish Drexel's campus as a vibrant modern urban university district	• Preserve, intensify, and overlap college precincts • Emphasize close relationships and short travel times between related programs • Connect people to destinations through public transit • Concentrate undergraduate teaching in the heart of campus • Encourage private development and investment • Build a larger, more active university city neighborhood
Bring the campus to the street	• Improve the convenience and safety of walking • Implement "terrace" infill-development strategy • Improve transportation choices • Make streets into great public spaces
Draw the community together around shared places	• Better utilize the historic main building • Promote dialogue among diverse groups of people • Provide multiple forms and places of gathering to invite these conversations • Expand dining, retail, entertainment, and recreation amenities that bring people together • Turn the Armory into a hub for student activity
Expand the innovation community	• Intensify the overlap and magnitude of campus, workplace, residential, and amenity activities to foster creative innovation • Connect students with employers and the community beyond campus • Demonstrate sustainability innovations

SOURCE: Adapted by author from Drexel Campus Master Plan.

and fully accessible district that both facilitates innovation, and demonstrates its rewards."[61]

The Campus Master Plan also included projects, both anticipated and underway, that strengthened and defined the core of the campus and improved existing academic buildings. *Philadelphia Inquirer* architecture critic Inga Saffron praised the university's crowd sourcing of ideas from students, faculty, and neighbors, and noted the consolidation of student housing and classrooms into a tighter core "in an effort to end its destructive sprawl into the Powelton Village and University City neighborhoods."[62] Nevertheless, the plan was clear about the intention to enlarge the area of University City that students, employees, and visitors would identify with Drexel. This was most evident in the statement that Drexel officials planned to create "a twenty-first-century district marked by livability, amenity, and accessibility" that extended from 30th to 36th Streets and from Chestnut Street to Powelton Avenue. This area, the plan implied, would feature offices

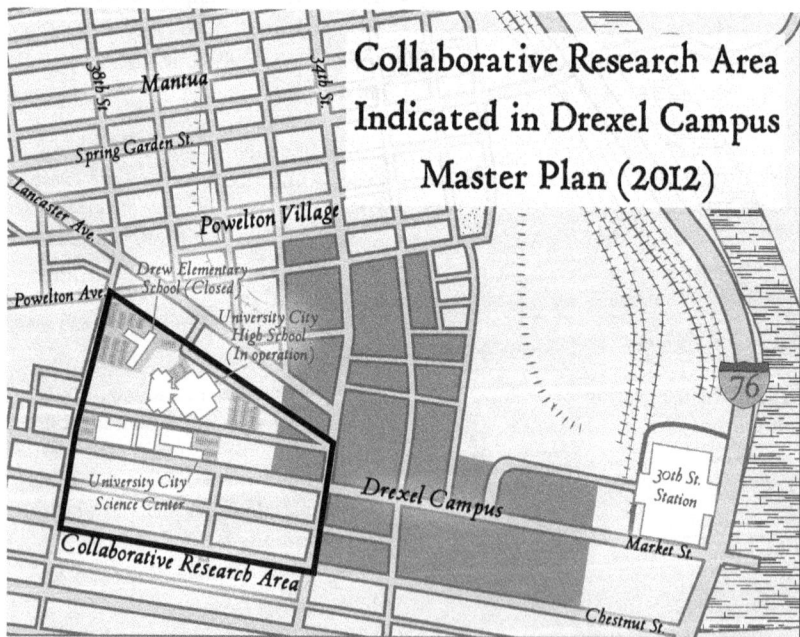

Figure 19. Urban University District boundaries proposed in the Drexel Campus Master Plan, 2012. Adapted by Elizabeth Rose from Drexel Campus Master Plan.

and labs, retail properties, a hotel, and market-rate housing to be developed in concert with private sector partners.

The blocks identified for the new urban university district encompassed the area occupied by the University City Science Center. They also encompassed the still-operational University City High School, the shuttered Drew Elementary School, and ten additional acres north of the Science Center and west of 36th Street that the School District had acquired in 1966 but never developed.[63] At this point, the empty acreage still belonged to the Philadelphia School District, as it had since 1967.

In Drexel's Campus Master Plan as well as in Fry's public statements, the expansion of the university's innovation footprint read as fully compatible with the goal of helping and collaborating with residents of neighborhoods near the campus. The extension work that was emerging from the Office of University and Community Partnerships—consonant with the institution's bid to become "the most civically engaged university in the nation"[64]—was presented as continuous with the remaking of the neighborhoods around the university. In fact, the development partnerships that Drexel was contemplating—and their anticipated instantiation in a mixed-use urban university district oriented toward the live/work/play preferences of innovators and knowledge workers—posed challenges for Powelton Village and Mantua households. For Powelton Village residents, the challenges had mainly to do with the scale of new development, and with the possibility that student housing demand would continue to accelerate undesirable trends. For Mantua residents, the threat was potentially more existential.

Acquisition of the University City High School Campus

As Drexel and neighboring community organizations were engaging in planning in the early 2010s, so too was the Philadelphia School District. Long-standing distress and dysfunction in the city's underfunded public schools had taken a new turn in 2002, when the State of Pennsylvania had taken the system over amid a dispute between city and state officials over low test scores and chronic budget deficits. After this, according to planning scholar Ryan Good, "public education in Philadelphia transitioned increasingly toward a 'diverse provider' model, in which a variety of private entities manage publicly funded schools, resulting in a dramatic expansion of charter schools in the city. . . . By 2012, 27 percent of all publicly funded students attended charter schools."[65] The growth of charter school attendance (which contributed to an enrollment decline of 49,000 between 2002 and 2012) and further cuts by the state led to more financial problems. District officials began to see closing schools as a fiscal necessity. In December 2012, Superintendent William Hite recommended that 37 school buildings—almost one-sixth of 240 in the city's portfolio—be closed. One of these was University City High School.

As discussed in Chapter 2, University City High School had never become the innovative, science- and math-specialized high school that the West Philadelphia Corporation and progressive school superintendent Mark Shedd had envisioned. From the start, it had been ensnared in conflict: conflict over the decision to displace people and businesses from the Black Bottom; conflict over whether UCHS would be an integrated school that treated white and Black students equally; and a citywide conflict over segregation and equal educational opportunity that persists today.[66] Since opening in 1971, UCHS had been an undesirable school known for disciplinary problems and violence.[67] In 2010, in a turnaround initiative for struggling schools, Superintendent Arlene Ackerman named the school a "Promise Academy," and with an influx of committed new teachers, counselors, and support staff, students showed progress.[68] Nevertheless, for the School District officials identifying schools for closure in 2012, University City High School more than met the criteria of underperformance and resource underutilization. In a school designed for 2,500 students, only 500 were enrolled.[69]

Efforts to prevent the school's closure were immediate and fierce. Students, teachers, and alumni organized and gave testimony at public meetings. One teacher, A. J. Schiera, put the history and future of the school at the center of his AP Government course in 2013. Preserved on the University City High School Digital Time Capsule website (which Schiera and his students compiled) are videos of students and alumni calling decision-makers to account: "If the state is responsible for our well-being," says one student, "how could they have let the School District come to such deficit?"[70] But on March 13, 2013, the School Reform Commission rendered a final decision to close UCHS and distribute its 500 students among two other district schools.

In this context, the School District's announcement in February 2014 that it had agreed to sell the University City High School site to Drexel and a development partner, Wexford Science + Technology, elicited further consternation. While Penn and not Drexel had engineered the original taking of the land, many saw the purchase as part of a long-term plan on the part of cooperating institutions: Drexel, Penn, and the School District. In the words

Figure 20. Images of a mosaic commemorating the Black Bottom, formerly located at the entrance to University City High School. Photos by Elaine Simon, PhD, Co-Director, Urban Studies Program, University of Pennsylvania.

of one interviewee: "The neighborhood narrative on UCHS has always been 'they wanted that site to do what they wanted to do.' . . . The simplest answer is to think that it was very valuable land that they wanted to take and develop sixty years ago. And it just probably always remained on the books as an option if the high school wasn't as successful as they wanted it to be. And it wasn't successful, so they went back and they pulled it back out as an option. Which is very sad."[71]

Ryan Good points out that parents, students, and community members invoked the spatial race- and class-patterning of officials' choices about which schools to close at this time. The decision to shutter University City High School and other predominantly Black schools, closure opponents asserted, would exacerbate historical inequalities and further destabilize Black communities' claims to space.[72] Because only about 20 percent of the students at UCHS in 2013 came from within walking distance, their claim to the school was not expressly about their attachment to it as a neighborhood institution. The school was important to the neighborhood nevertheless, in part because of its connection to racialized displacement two generations earlier.[73]

New Neighborhoods

Regardless of the site's meaning in the community, it would soon be caught up in the churn of redevelopment. Philadelphia's City Council passed an ordinance that rezoned the site for dense mixed-use development in June 2014, after a hastily organized community engagement process sponsored by city council member Jannie Blackwell. Drexel acquired it for $25.1 million shortly afterward. Deconstruction of the fortress-like University City High School building began in early 2015, producing images that echoed those of cleared land in the Black Bottom nearly five decades earlier. Former teacher Schiera remembered experiencing "something like a death" as demolition contractors pulled down the building. Because they had intended it to be a magnet school with a model curriculum, School District officials had built University City High School to a higher standard than other school buildings of the period: it contained indoor swimming facilities, technology labs, and a darkroom. Said Schiera, "I thought of the building as a graveyard for assets that our school could have had if it had been kept up."[74]

Figure 21. University City High School in the midst of demolition, 2015. Photo by Elaine Simon, PhD, Co-Director, Urban Studies Program, University of Pennsylvania.

In June 2015, Philadelphia's business press reported the formation of a new development partnership[75] between the University City Science Center and Wexford Science + Technology, a Baltimore-based company specialized in "vibrant, mixed use, amenity-rich Knowledge Communities."[76] On September 15 of that year, the entities held a press event. On the roof of a parking structure at 37th and Market Streets, overlooking the twice-cleared University City High School site, they announced uCity Square, which would come to fruition on ten of the fourteen acres Drexel had purchased the previous year.[77] Drexel would retain title to the land and issue a ninety-nine-year ground lease to Wexford. Wexford would expand the University City Science Center campus and add offices, labs, apartments, a hotel, and retail spaces. As an article in *Philadelphia Magazine* put it, "The massive development project will see the Science Center swell from over 1 million square-feet to 6 million square-feet by the time the 10-year, $1 billion (plus) plan is completed. The addition of the University City High School site directly north of Market Street makes it all possible to create this new live/work/play environment, with what developers Wexford Science + Technology call 'a community of ingenuity' full of a mix [sic] cutting edge lab, office and retail space."[78]

The second Drexel-affiliated innovation venture announced in the 2010s relied on a similar development partnership. Here, the complex rebranding work that accompanied the transformation of the University City High School site was not required. The ten acres the university assembled for the Schuylkill Yards project lay on the other side of Drexel's campus, between 30th and 33rd Streets abutting the 30th Street train station. It included parking lots, vacant land, and a few underutilized commercial buildings, including one that had housed the *Evening Bulletin* newspaper from 1954 until it ceased publication in 1982. Drexel's Fry and Gerard H. Sweeney of Brandywine Realty Trust introduced the project on March 2, 2016, unveiling a dramatic before-and-after rendering that juxtaposed a dull scene of highways, surface parking, and railroad tracks with an image of eight towers of varying heights sprouting up from a verdant, garden-like base. The Schuylkill Yards Innovation Development would be built in at least two phases, eventually encompassing fourteen acres and offering "entrepreneurial spaces, educational facilities and research laboratories, corporate offices, residential and retail spaces, hospitality and cultural venues and public open spaces."[79] Brandywine already owned the Cira Centre, a massive curtain-wall skyscraper just north of 30th Street Station on the Schuylkill River, and was in the midst of building two other towers on the Schuylkill. Press coverage of the announcement focused on the new project's "network of open and green spaces" and on the potential of the development to be a magnet for high-tech companies and an economic engine for the Greater Philadelphia region.[80]

uCity Square and Schuylkill Yards resemble other innovation district projects pursued by universities around the country in the 2010s.[81] They use ground lease mechanisms, with a developer leasing land from an academic institution with a nonprofit status. Their mixed-use character—the inclusion of retail, hospitality, and residential spaces—is a central component of their value proposition for investors. They propose new neighborhoods, and their branding relies on images of brilliant new arrivals working, living, and playing among amenities that are conferred by urban density and supported by city infrastructure. Finally, they draw on tax abatement and direct government subsidy. Projects in uCity Square have received a total of $7.5 million in direct grants through the State of Pennsylvania's Redevelopment Assistance Capital Program.[82] As noted above, uCity Square and Schuylkill Yards are located in a State of Pennsylvania-designated Keystone Opportunity Zone, which exempts resident companies from many city and state taxes.[83] The land they sit on is also part of the federal Opportunity Zones program established by the Tax Cuts and Jobs Act of 2017, which discounts or eliminates capital gains taxes associated with the sale of property or businesses in designated areas. Further, ground lease payments (unlike the principal portion of debt service payments) are exempted from the federal corporate income tax. University City's innovation districts are not as fiscally enmeshed with their host city as some of the examples mentioned earlier in this chapter, but they are intimately tied in with the fiscal politics of Philadelphia and the United States—both as potential generators of revenue and as potential venues for investors whose returns are boosted when they are able to shield cash flows from tax liability. The university lies at the center of this dynamic.

The question city officials rarely ask as urban universities propose new neighborhoods in partnership with developers is how their benefits—the wealth they generate—will be distributed among residents, the public sector, and property investors. The distribution of potential costs as nearby "old" neighborhoods change also goes unexamined. Policymakers assume a path from innovation-centered real estate development to the attraction and growth of innovative firms, and from there to broad-based economic prosperity and well-being. Their confidence in this path is such that they unquestioningly incur the opportunity costs associated with subsidizing such development.

At midcentury, in Philadelphia and across the United States, people of color in the path of urban renewal projects made outsized sacrifices as they confronted the destruction, at the hands of the state, of residential and commercial districts to which they possessed social and cultural attachments.[84] The selling point of the developments that destroyed their neighborhoods was that generalized economic growth would benefit all urban stakeholders: by revitalizing deteriorated built environments, by stemming the loss of firms and middle-class households, and by providing the tax revenue needed to serve incumbent residents, including the poor. But concentrated exposure to urban renewal relocation was part of a decades-long pattern of dislocation, exploitation, and dispossession, which, along with inequitable treatment in the criminal-legal system and exclusion from mainstream housing, labor, and credit markets, kept low-wealth households—particularly Black households—from thriving or building wealth in twentieth-century urban economies.[85] Urban economic development did not develop their communities, and it often harmed them.

The intergenerational impacts of past economic development practice, and the persistence of racism, are evident in the current racial wealth gap as well as in high poverty and unemployment rates in predominantly Black urban communities. Today, new neighborhoods created in the innovation district mold rarely directly dispossess or displace these households. Yet the capacity of innovation districts to deliver benefits to them remains constrained, because the developers of these new urban spaces are designing them—physically, economically, and institutionally—around the capital, credentials, and purchasing power of people who already possess high socioeconomic status. To the extent that they succeed, these spaces will overwhelmingly confer wealth on the already advantaged. This is the challenge facing those who would aspire to integrate social and economic equity as goals of innovation district development: the pull of the existing economic structure is working against them.

Conclusion: Plans on the Ground

The next chapter discusses efforts to disrupt this dynamic—to make innovation-centered development a force for social and economic inclusion. But it is useful at the conclusion of a chapter structured around plans to make some general observations about how the Directions Plan, the Mantua

Transformation Plan, and the Drexel Campus Master Plan function as discursive documents. John Pløger (2001) argues that in the past three decades, planners have increasingly and consciously used narrative and images to "produce an imagined community."[86] Plans draw on claims of shared history; they invoke common beliefs and values; and they argue that the measures they propose are rooted in those beliefs and values. As they document existing conditions in places and put forward expert determinations about how to achieve preservation or change, plans are making assertions about space and to whom it belongs.[87]

Each of the plans created for the Lower Lancaster section of University City in the 2010s produced an imagined community. The imagined community of the Directions Plan affirmed a virtuous tradition of single-family home ownership and architectural distinction. To civic leaders, these were the essential qualities of Powelton Village, and the primary goal was to preserve them in the face of change. The imagined community of the Mantua Transformation Plan was one in which current activists would draw on the incomplete work of past leaders to improve an economically distressed neighborhood. The lives of community members would change for the better, as the neighborhood remained recognizable as an actual and symbolic space belonging to current Mantuans. The imagined community of Drexel's Campus Master Plan was one that did not yet exist; the innovation district would bring it into being. The shared history it invoked was the history of the urban university as an economic engine. The common faith it affirmed was twofold: a faith in the capacity of innovation to generate economic prosperity, and a faith that real estate development would create the conditions for innovation. In successive years, each of these visions would be in conversation with the others, as Drexel and its partners negotiated the public approvals necessary to the initiation of the uCity Square and Schuylkill Yards developments. The bid to achieve inclusion along with growth formed the backdrop for these discussions.

CHAPTER 4

The Contradictions of Inclusion

After announcing Schuylkill Yards, Drexel and its partner Brandywine Realty Trust hoped to break ground quickly. The project required zoning modifications, however, which had to be vetted by both the Philadelphia City Planning Commission and the city council. On January 17, 2017, the Planning Commission expressed its support for the zoning amendments that facilitated Phase I of the project.[1] But despite the planning commission's endorsement, questions from commissioners and testimony from community groups at the hearing made it clear that before the city council signed off on the changes, further negotiations were in store. "Unfortunately a[t] present, we have not seen a willingness from Drexel or Brandywine to provide mitigation for this project in a way that we believe is appropriate," Powelton Village Civic Association President John Phillips told a reporter, "but we are looking forward to working with all parties to resolve this in the future."[2]

This discussion of mitigation had to do partly with how to manage the impact a new mega-development would exert on the built environment. Advocates, particularly in Powelton Village, were concerned about how developers would design and place new buildings to be compatible with the built fabric of nearby areas, and with how they would minimize the effects of increased density on traffic and parking. But the conversation also had to do with the social environment—namely, how to prevent displacement and exclusion in Mantua and the Lower Lancaster corridor's other low-wealth neighborhoods. At the planning commission hearing, a commissioner repeatedly inquired as to whether Brandywine intended to include affordable housing units in the residential portions of the new Schuylkill Yards district (the answer was no). In his testimony, Michael Thorpe, the executive director of the Mount Vernon Manor Community Development Corporation, expressed concern that without preventive measures in place, real estate speculation would accelerate land price appreciation in Mantua and preclude affordable development by mission-driven organizations. Mantua Civic Association representatives also asked for commitments that jobs associated with the project would reach unemployed and underemployed residents of their neighborhood. They were particularly worried that—given the long-standing racial exclusivity of building trades unions—residents of their neighborhood would have difficulty accessing the construction jobs the project would bring.

There was already a forum in which neighborhood residents were seeking to exert influence over such questions, but it was not formally connected to city planning processes, or to Drexel. As she had done at the University City High School site, 3rd District Councilwoman Jannie Blackwell had conditioned her support for the desired zoning package on the successful completion of a community benefits agreement (CBA)—a package of developer commitments that responded to resident concerns about how the impacts of the project, both positive and negative, would be experienced in nearby neighborhoods.[3] A coalition of local civic and community organizations was negotiating a CBA with the private partner in the Schuylkill Yards project, Brandywine Realty Trust. At the January 17 hearing, Jerry Sweeney of Brandywine emphasized multiple efforts on his firm's part to create pathways to building trades employment for nearby residents, and to work with Drexel to support locally owned businesses in their bids to be selected as contractors and suppliers. But he also cautioned against the implication that the concerns being raised by community groups were the responsibility of his firm. "We need to make sure that we understand," he told the reporter, "that a development, as grand as Schuylkill Yards is, can't solve every single problem in every single neighborhood in the City of Philadelphia."[4]

While perhaps hyperbolic, Sweeney's response was understandable: Brandywine Realty Trust was a public company, listed on the New York Stock Exchange. Surely city officials and community groups did not hold a for-profit corporation responsible for social stressors in neighborhoods on the fringes of its investment. The CBA process was an important source of public sector leverage over Schuylkill Yards, and a lever that Councilwoman Blackwell unmistakably intended to use. But the community-based organizations were negotiating with an organization whose primary obligation was to its shareholders.

At the same time, Brandywine was poised to develop on property it was leasing from the country's self-avowed most civically engaged university. In the previous five years, Drexel representatives repeatedly had expressed confidence that Schuylkill Yards and uCity Square (University City's other Drexel-sponsored innovation neighborhood) would benefit the economically marginalized. As John Fry had put it in his March 2, 2016, announcement of the Schuylkill Yards partnership, "Inclusion is at the heart of this project. It's not a side benefit. This 20-year, $3.5 billion project will benefit thousands of low-income families without disrupting the fabric of their neighborhoods. Schuylkill Yards will *connect long-term economic development with sustainable social progress* on a level that's never been done before"[5] (emphasis mine). In light of the expectations this raised, and because the council member was insisting on a CBA, Brandywine, a real estate investment trust, had become part of a public conversation about how to enable low-socioeconomic-status residents to benefit from urban economic development. Executives at Wexford Science + Technology had been drawn into a similar conversation in 2014, as members of the council had debated the land use changes that would facilitate the uCity Square redevelopment. Both Wexford and Brandywine had entered into partnership with Drexel, forging relationships that gave them access to university-owned land, to public subsidy, and to desirable consumer populations. In doing so, they found themselves at the center of a struggle to define and achieve sustainable social progress at the intersection of private real estate development, municipal economic development policy, and university institutional strategy.

This chapter is about that struggle. It begins with a summary of the significant outreach and service efforts Drexel orchestrated in the neighborhoods to its immediate north starting in the early 2010s, including a new K-8 public school near the former University City High School site in the emerging uCity Square. It then examines how groups in Powelton Village and Mantua mobilized to advance and defend the communities imagined in the Directions and Mantua Transformation Plans earlier in the decade. The groups worked both separately and in coalition, engaging Drexel, elected officials, and Drexel's private sector partners Wexford and Brandywine. Mantua and Powelton groups joined forces, first to negotiate a CBA with the developer of the uCity Square project and then to forge a second CBA with the developer of Schuylkill Yards. A new group, the Mantua-Powelton Alliance, emerged to determine how to deploy funding supplied by Brandywine Realty Trust as part of the Schuylkill Yards CBA. The chapter focuses particularly on Mantua, where the Mantua Civic Association and Mount Vernon Manor Community Development Corporation—

organizations that had coalesced during the "We Are Mantua!" planning process—were making a place for themselves in conversations about redevelopment.

Civic mobilization undoubtedly shaped the conditions under which Drexel and its partners began constructing University City's twenty-first-century innovation district. Through astonishing investments of mostly volunteer time and with limited (though crucial) cooperation from elected officials and philanthropic sources, residents of Mantua and Powelton Village brought about measures designed to ensure that what they valued in their communities would survive and thrive alongside two massive investments aimed at a much wealthier population. By November 2017, when Drexel and Brandywine broke ground on the Schuylkill Yards project, mobilized citizens had achieved two pieces of new land use legislation aimed at decelerating speculative property trading affecting their neighborhoods. They had also obtained binding commitments from private developers that ranged from height limits on new construction to the commitment of millions of dollars to a Mantua-Powelton Community Fund administered by local organizations. In conjunction with investment by Drexel, these political victories generated optimism, a sense of forward momentum, and confidence in residents' ability to benefit from the wealth creation occurring in the innovation neighborhoods nearby. Civic mobilization had limits, however, as did a social reclamation model founded on the goodwill of a university and the real estate companies with which it had joined forces.

Drexel in the Neighborhoods

Through its Office of University and Community Partnerships (OUCP), Drexel University devoted extraordinary resources to outreach and service in the neighborhoods to the north of its campus in the 2010s. For example, Drexel was instrumental in bringing governmental and philanthropic resources to programs aimed at people of low socioeconomic status living in the neighborhoods around its campus. In addition to helping win the 2011 HUD Choice Neighborhoods grant that initiated the rehabilitation of the Mount Vernon Manor Apartments, the institution was a partner in a 2012 Mantua-targeted U.S. Department of Justice Byrne Criminal Justice Innovation grant. In 2016, Drexel became the sponsor of a five-year U.S. Department of Education Promise Neighborhoods grant aimed at supporting "cradle-to-career" interventions for children and families in poverty in a two-square-mile area encompassing Powelton Village, Mantua, Belmont, Saunders Park, and West Powelton. The neighborhood boundaries for the Department of Education grant (which was matched by contributions from two local foundations) mirrored those of a federal Promise Zone announced by President Barack Obama in 2014 on the fiftieth anniversary of Lyndon Johnson's 1964 declaration of an unconditional War on Poverty in the United States.

Drexel anchored and symbolized its commitment to its neighbors by creating a physical place, the Dornsife Center for Neighborhood Partnerships, at 35th and Spring Garden Streets. To establish the Dornsife Center,

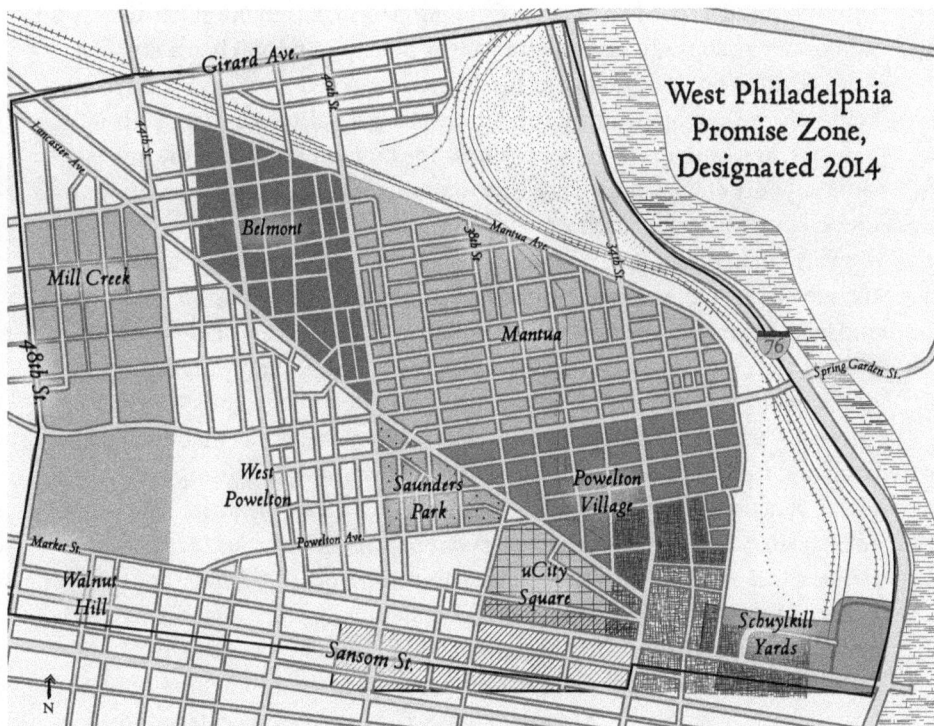

Figure 22. Boundaries of the West Philadelphia Promise Zone. Some saw the Promise Zone as a kind of complement to the innovation district, suggesting that the spaces would operate symbiotically to bring about inclusive prosperity. Image by Elizabeth Rose.

Drexel relied on two major gifts—one from Philip B. Lindy[6] to acquire a 1.3-acre parcel on the border of Mantua and Powelton Village, and a second from alumni David and Dana Dornsife to renovate a vacant mid-nineteenth-century mansion and two historic school buildings on the site. The center, which opened in mid-2014, houses meeting and gathering spaces, a computer learning lab, a health center (which offers primary healthcare to the uninsured), and kitchen and dining facilities. It hosts adult classes, after-school activities, discussion forums, and arts programs that are free and open to neighborhood residents and that engage Drexel faculty and students in addition to many local nonprofits. Administrators liken it to university-sponsored agricultural extension services that date back to the nineteenth century—but in an urban setting.[7] On a summer afternoon in 2020, at the height of the COVID pandemic, the "upcoming events" section of the center's website advertised an outdoor Qi Gong class and a remote panel discussion about recent advocacy to transform policing and public safety.[8] An April 8, 2020 bulletin linked to the homepage noted a variety of services being offered remotely, including *pro bono* legal assistance, help with job searches, and online writing workshops. The bulletin also noted the university's support of a Mantua Civic Association effort to distribute meals and groceries to Mantua households in quarantine.[9]

Particularly important to Drexel's economic inclusion efforts are initiatives to connect unemployed and underemployed adults with skills training and jobs. Before the Dornsife Center opened, OUCP staff assisted West Philadelphia job seekers with resumes and interview skills and worked to persuade managers in academic departments and operations units within the university to hire them. The "business case" they made was that managers could reduce attrition and increase worker commitment by hiring local residents vetted and prepared by OUCP employees.[10] Staff members have now consolidated GED preparation, career counseling, and referrals to training at the Beachell Family Learning Center within the Dornsife Center. Entrepreneurs and small business owners can access assistance with business planning and financing at the Beachell Center; they can also connect with Drexel's efforts (as well as those of its development partners) to direct procurement dollars to local businesses. Through another Dornsife-based center affiliated with Drexel's law school, employment-related legal assistance is available.

Drexel's work on pathways to jobs for adults has been increasingly integrated with that of the nationally recognized West Philadelphia Skills Initiative (WPSI), a project of the nonprofit University City District (UCD).[11]

Figure 23. Drexel's Dornsife Center for Neighborhood Partnerships, 36th and Spring Garden Streets. Photo by Elizabeth Rose.

Founded in 2009 in a broadening of UCD's mission, WPSI has been highly effective in placing unemployed and underemployed West Philadelphia residents in jobs in University City—in many cases, jobs with family-supporting wages and health and retirement benefits. WPSI staff design programs around the "bespoke" hiring needs of UCD's members, inquiring into employers' soft skill and technical skill needs and organizational cultures and shaping both participant recruitment and training content accordingly. Training combines foundational skills with technical instruction as needed, and candidates are compensated for their time during training in addition to having access to counseling and support services. Graduates have gotten jobs as bus operators, lab technicians, dental assistants, security officers, and certified medical assistants. A $5 million grant from the Lenfest Foundation in 2018 is enabling the development of additional credentialing programs

Table 4. Programs at the Drexel University Dornsife Center for Neighborhood Partnerships, April 2020.

Program Area	Offerings	Academic units involved
Adult education and workforce access	<ul><li>GED preparation (with dual enrollment at the Community College of Philadelphia)</li><li>B Smart (9-week business planning and coaching program for business owners)</li><li>Software classes (Microsoft Office, Google Suite, QuickBooks)</li><li>Big Idea Group (meeting group for entrepreneurs)</li><li>Career counseling</li><li>Resume review</li><li>Credentialing programs (Community Health Worker, Child Development Associate, Emergency Medical Technician, Building Performance Analyst)</li></ul>	<ul><li>Bennett S. LeBow College of Business</li><li>Center for Non-violence and Social Justice (Dornsife School of Public Health)</li></ul>
Arts and culture	<ul><li>Writers Room (writing workshops)</li><li>Dance and movement classes</li><li>Music classes for children</li><li>Computer-based music production workshops for teens and adults</li><li>Fashion design and merchandising program for middle school students</li></ul>	<ul><li>Department of English and Philosophy</li><li>Department of Performing Arts</li><li>Music Industry Program</li><li>Department of Design and Merchandising</li></ul>
Health and wellness	<ul><li>Community Wellness Hub</li><li>Cooking workshops and culinary arts courses</li><li>Community dinner (monthly)</li><li>Pet care clinics</li><li>Creative movement and martial arts courses</li></ul>	<ul><li>College of Nursing and Health Professions</li><li>Department of Culinary Arts and Food Science</li><li>Department of Performing Arts</li></ul>
Creating knowledge together	<ul><li>"Side-by-side" courses (in which community members participate in Drexel courses at no charge)</li><li>Public astronomy program</li><li>Neighborhood placemaking projects</li><li>Civic dialogues</li></ul>	<ul><li>Department of English and Philosophy</li><li>Department of Criminology and Justice Studies</li><li>Department of Physics</li><li>Department of Biology</li><li>Antoinette Westphal College of Media Arts and Design</li></ul>

Table 4. (*Continued*)

Program Area	Offerings	Academic units involved
Kids and families	• Family read-alongs • Museum Mondays • Science, technology, and art programs • Holiday programs	• Department of Performing Arts
Building educational opportunities	• Early learning supports (West Philadelphia Action for Early Learning initiative) • Mentorship and enrichment for middle school students • Career exploration • Free-access computer lab/digital literacy training • GED preparation (with dual enrollment at the Community College of Philadelphia)	• Lindy Center for Civic Engagement • Music Industry Program • Department of Materials Sciences and Engineering • College of Computing and Informatics
Individual and family supports	• Pro bono legal advice: criminal record expungement and estate planning • Community lawyering clinic • Free clothing pop-up shop • Wellness Hub health promotion programs	• Thomas R. Kline School of Law • College of Nursing and Health Professions

SOURCE: Compiled by author from https://drexel.edu/dornsifecenter/.

that will train and place newly minted child development associates, community health workers, and building performance analysts. The Lenfest grant also funds a partnership with the University City Science Center to expose youth and adults to workforce skills and acculturation to STEM (Science, Technology, Engineering, and Math) employment.[12] Perhaps the most important factor in the success of the WPSI intermediation model is an orientation toward participants as imminent professionals, combined with a respectful, trauma-informed approach to their experiences.[13]

Drexel has also made significant investments in primary education. Recognizing that even the most successful workforce pipeline programs cannot position adults without college degrees for the celebrated "knowledge worker" jobs expected at uCity Square and Schuylkill Yards, the university is dedicating resources to local K-4 and K-8 schools, on the theory that with a stronger start, children growing up in poverty near the university campus today will have a shot at the innovation jobs of the future. Faculty and students from Drexel's School of Education provide advice, tutoring, and classroom support at the Morton McMichael School in Mantua and the Samuel Powel School in Powelton, and the university also funds programs that expose middle school and high school students to STEM.[14] The U.S. Department of Education's Promise Neighborhoods grant (amounting to $30 million over five years) adds additional resources to a concerted effort to create a bridge between the low educational attainment and high unemployment conditions of the Promise Zone and the energy and opportunity of University City's new economic development projects.

Drexel's largest primary education initiative is a new K-8 public school in the uCity Square development. In 2016, the Science Leadership Academy Middle School (SLAMS)—a public school serving students in the fifth through eighth grades—opened in a building on the Dornsife Center campus at 35th and Spring Garden Streets. The opening of SLAMS was part of a staged project to unite the K-4 Samuel Powel Elementary School with a middle school in order to create a viable K-8 option for parents in the area. As a local news outlet reported, "Dornsife . . . is just a temporary location for the new school while plans are underway to build the school's permanent home on the site of the now demolished former University City High School and Drew Elementary School near 38th and Filbert."[15] In the following three years, Drexel officials worked tirelessly to assemble financing for a new school building, and in June 2019 the Board of Education approved a plan to co-locate Powel and SLAMS close to the site where School District management had elected to close the high school six years before.

The financing and ownership structure for the $40 million project is unorthodox: $7 million from the School District, $3 million from Pennsylvania's Redevelopment Assistance Capital Program, and the rest from a variety of philanthropic sources. Drexel will own the building, entering into a thirty-five-year lease agreement with the School District under which the District will pay a nominal $12.00 annual rent.[16] Yet despite the public/private financing and ownership arrangement, the new school will be public. Officials have expressed confidence that as a District school with a commitment to serving students from the immediate area, the new entity will dovetail with the "cradle-to-career" interventions that Drexel is coordinating in the Promise Zone. At the December 9, 2019, groundbreaking, one prominent

Figure 24. Powel/SLAMS K-8 school under construction at 36th and Filbert Streets, August 22, 2020. Photo by Elizabeth Rose.

city leader lauded Drexel's commitment to creating "a neighborhood school where anyone from the community could come."[17]

What Kind of Neighborhood?

Behind praise for the new K-8 school, however, anxieties swirled. From the perspective of the Powelton Village Civic Association and its members, the school was an unambiguous win. The PVCA's Directions Plan had noted that "besides educating community children, schools are a critical tool in recruiting new homeowners to the neighborhood and in creating a sense of community."[18] But Mantua's elementary- and middle-school-aged children

were assigned to schools in a different catchment area (zone of service coverage) from children in Powelton Village, and most would not be assigned to
the new K-8 school at uCity Square.[19] Moreover, policy experts and neighborhood leaders alike foresaw challenges in ensuring that a desirable school
at the heart of an innovation district would provide opportunities in the
medium and long term for the children that Drexel's cradle-to-career interventions targeted.[20] How could a neighborhood rich in affordable housing
be stabilized only blocks away from the innovation neighborhoods at uCity
Square and Schuylkill Yards?

The Penn Alexander School at 42nd and Spruce Streets loomed large in
these discussions. As noted in Chapter 3, the Penn Alexander School is high-
performing and has been a major factor in increased income and housing stability in the previously struggling community surrounding it. Accordingly,
the university-assisted school model is a well-established best practice in the
literature on university-community partnerships. Both scholarly analysis and
more anecdotal media accounts, however, have suggested that the school's educational innovations reach fewer of University City's low-wealth households
every year.[21] Questions posed to Drexel's Lucy Kerman at a June 19, 2019,
School Board finance committee meeting reflected members' awareness that
spots in the Penn Alexander School had become decreasingly available to
low-income students:

> McGiver asked whether there were studies about student growth in
> neighborhood areas that would identify how the demographic needs
> could change 10-15 years down the line, as Penn-Alexander is now
> experiencing . . . Wilkerson voiced the same concerns as McGiver
> and stated that Penn-Alexander "didn't play out the way we thought
> it would" in that although it initially included more African-American
> students and economic diversity, it has now "flipped completely." . . .
> She said no one had anticipated that the investments in new and ren-
> ovated housing prompted by the new school would actually push out
> long-term neighborhood residents who could not afford the higher
> property tax rates assigned to the area. Those factors led to the cre-
> ation of "a more privileged student body" at the school.[22]

Kerman responded that circumstances in the Powel/SLAMS catchment were
qualitatively distinct from those surrounding the Penn Alexander School,
owing in part to the active presence of the People's Emergency Center

CHANGES IN MARKET VALUE 2000-2018

GROSS MEDIAN RENT

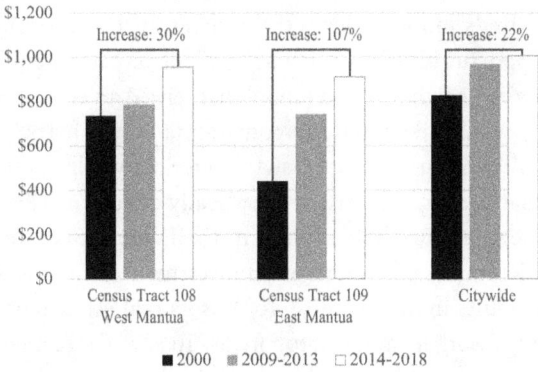

Increase: 30% Increase: 107% Increase: 22%

Census Tract 108
West Mantua

Census Tract 109
East Mantua

Citywide

■ 2000 ■ 2009-2013 ☐ 2014-2018

MEDIAN HOME VALUE

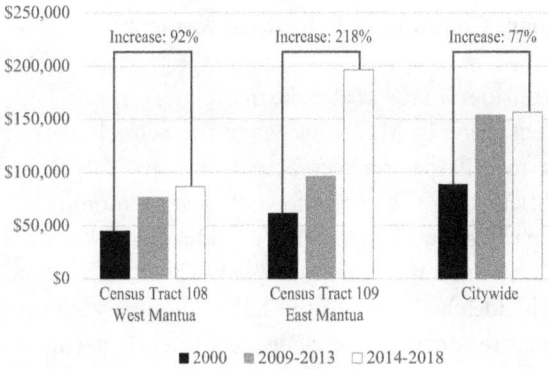

Increase: 92% Increase: 218% Increase: 77%

Census Tract 108
West Mantua

Census Tract 109
East Mantua

Citywide

■ 2000 ■ 2009-2013 ☐ 2014-2018

MEDIAN REAL ESTATE TAX

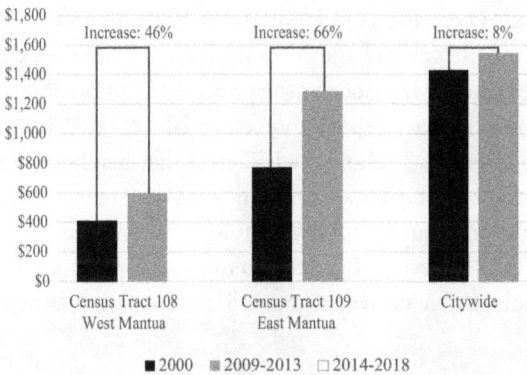

Increase: 46% Increase: 66% Increase: 8%

Census Tract 108
West Mantua

Census Tract 109
East Mantua

Citywide

■ 2000 ■ 2009-2013 ☐ 2014-2018

Figure 25. Changes in market value, 2000–2018, Philadelphia Census Tracts 108 and 109. Graph compiled from U.S. Census data by Elizabeth Rose.

(PEC), a nonprofit organization that manages shelters and transitional housing for formerly unhoused families. PEC's development arm was also building affordable homes in the area, she said. Moreover, because Powel/SLAMS
would accommodate hundreds more students than currently, there would
be additional and ample opportunities for students from "out-of-catchment."

Nevertheless, to maintain a neighborhood school that served an economically mixed student body would likely require constraints on the market-
driven appreciation of real estate near uCity Square and Schuylkill Yards.
With evidence in hand that such appreciation was already occurring (Figure 25), economically insecure households living in the Lower Lancaster
corridor faced a classic dilemma of neighborhood reinvestment: Drexel was
investing in children and adults in the Promise Zone as its real estate partnerships targeted knowledge workers and startup firms. To some, it seemed
doubtful that these investments could function symbiotically.

The uCity Square Community Benefits Agreement

An early opportunity to consider what was at stake in the latest wave of University City redevelopment came in May 2014, when the School District
announced its intention to sell the fourteen-acre University City High
School site to Drexel. Anticipating this turn of events several months before ("We knew something was going to happen but we didn't know when"),[23]
the People's Emergency Center and the Powelton Village Civic Association,
with funding from the Philadelphia office of the Local Initiatives Support
Corporation, had convened residents and civic leaders to elicit neighborhood priorities. A March 5, 2014, community input session and charrette
drew over one hundred participants representing multiple civic organizations;
a workshop followed on March 12 at which eight leaders representing Mantua,
Powelton Village, and West Powelton/Saunders Park collaborated with volunteer architects to "express the goals of the community . . . in site plan dia-
grams indicating proposed uses for the site and the preferred location of those
uses."[24] The professionally produced report that emerged—created by the
planning and design firm Interface Studio—made it clear that neighborhood
groups were paying attention to the site's imminent redevelopment. When
Drexel and Wexford sought city council approval for an up-zoning just a few
weeks later, Councilwoman Blackwell pledged not to move the legislation forward until the development partners had negotiated a community benefits

agreement with the organizations: "When it came down to [Drexel and Wex-ford] seeking the spot zoning for the site through the councilwoman, the councilwoman already had a heads up that the community's 'on it' and they are interested, so you gotta talk to them. . . . Civic groups were armed with that document."[25] Negotiations were tense and frenzied, driven by a mid-June deadline for the closing on Drexel's purchase of the site. Lawyers sat on both sides of the table. When the city council announced the agreement on June 14 (it was "Exhibit B" appended to the legislation authorizing the desired zoning changes), its terms were geared toward the priorities articulated in Interface Studio's *University City High School/Drew School Site Reuse: Community Input and Design Workshop* report. Among these were restrictions on building heights at the northern part of the site; an assurance that any housing on the site would not be constructed for or marketed to students; the inclusion of parking podiums on the site to "avoid the use of neighborhood parking re-sources by users of the Site"; and the statement of a joint goal to create a public school there.[26] The agreement also set forth some terms on which Drexel would provide financial assistance to other public schools in the area.[27] And it provided for the formation of a community advisory group to "provide mean-ingful advisory input" into future site planning.[28] Finally, as an additional ex-hibit (not part of the community benefits agreement), there was an Economic Opportunity Plan, signed by Drexel, Wexford, and city representatives, set-ting targets for female, minority, and local resident participation in construc-tion employment and contracting on the project. As described later in this chapter, the plan was a legal requirement and constituted a standard feature of major projects requiring city approvals or subsidy.

When the deal was done and the School District had conveyed the shut-tered University City High School and its surrounding acreage to Drexel, community signatories to the agreement had a chance to reflect on the rushed negotiation. The strengths of the agreement, one Powelton Village Civic Association member recalled, were twofold: first, the commitment to engage a community advisory group in site planning going forward, and second, limits on the height and character of development on the part of the site adjacent to Powelton Village. The conclusion from the March charette and design workshop that neighbors desired to see development "that har-monizes with neighborhood context . . . and creates a continuation of neigh-borhood fabric" had clearly been at the forefront. Another Powelton Villager emphasized the importance of getting in writing the development partners' goal of building a school. This interviewee noted that the negotiation process represented unprecedented cooperation between local civic groups and the "overcoming of economic and racial tension" between Powelton Village and Mantua. But interviewees also acknowledged that due to long experience engaging with Drexel and better organizational resources overall ("our neighborhood came up with a list of priorities quicker, more outlined"), the Powelton Village contingent had led the negotiation. The CBA reflected this: "Affordable housing never made the top-eight list."[29] A Mantua leader protested that the built-environment-centered focus of the discussions had eclipsed social concerns: "All they wanted to talk about was parking and trees."[30] Ultimately, Mantua representatives had been at the table for discussions that were largely about site design. Their concerns about displacement and exclusion had not gotten a hearing.

The Mantua Civic Association

If the 2014 community benefits negotiation left Mantua leaders feeling they had participated in a dance choreographed by others, they were determined to exert more influence going forward. One vehicle for this was the Mantua Civic Association (MCA), one of several concrete achievements of the "We Are Mantua!" Choice Neighborhoods planning process. The Philadelphia office of the Local Initiatives Support Corporation had provided technical assistance to the startup organization, and in December 2012 MCA had begun holding regular public meetings on the third Thursday evening of each month, alternating between locations in the eastern and western sections of the neighborhood.[31] Anyone was welcome at the meetings, but attendees were encouraged to pay a five-dollar fee and join the association as members. Members elect an executive board to govern the association and can also participate in working committees focused on seniors; education and youth; zoning and development; and "enrichment" or neighborhood beautification.

I attended a total of six civic association meetings between October 2015 and September 2017, and research assistants attended two additional meetings. Despite weather extremes that frequently made meeting spaces uncomfortably cold or warm, each of the eight meetings had between forty and sixty people in attendance. The typical configuration was rows of folding chairs in a gym or community room, with members of the organization's executive board seated behind a long table at the front. To the side, there was an information table containing an agenda, a sign-in sheet, membership application forms, and literature from local service providers such as the Dornsife Center and People's Emergency Center. There were refreshments (often Philadelphia soft pretzels with their distinctive figure-eight shape) at another side table. The median age of attendees was approximately sixty years old, although the association's president, De'Wayne Drummond, was considerably younger, in his mid-thirties. Drummond's two young daughters sometimes sat doing their homework or playing on electronic devices in the front row.

A lifelong Mantua resident who had been socialized into community politics by his grandfather and whose regular job was as a parent outreach coordinator for the Office of Head Start at the Philadelphia School District (all civic association leaders' work was done on a volunteer basis), Drummond called meetings to order and facilitated them tightly. His first order of business at the start of a meeting was often to hand out three-by-five note cards on which attendees could write suggested agenda topics for the following month's meeting. Drummond also consistently reminded people of ground rules: "No personal attacks: challenge ideas, not people. Phones off. Stick to the agenda." On some occasions, the meetings began and ended with a prayer, which was often led by Andrew Jenkins, the former president of Mantua Community Planners and now the vice president of the civic association.[32] Lasting between two and two and a half hours, the meetings featured reports by the group's subcommittees; presentations by city officials or development organizations; announcements and program recruitment by service provider organizations; and discussion of pertinent city legislation and policy. The group was close-knit and intergenerational (though older generations were more amply represented), and people seemed to relish the opportunity meetings provided for sociability and connection. At one point, yielding the floor to education committee member James Allen, who was about to announce a youth initiative, Drummond noted, smiling, "That's my fourth-grade teacher right there."

The wide-ranging agenda topics at MCA meetings during the period I attended reflected several fronts on which the civic association was working. First, the association was engaged in improvement projects in the neighborhood in partnership with city agencies and institutions, and representatives of those entities often attended meetings to solicit feedback or to report on progress. At several meetings, there were presentations by the Philadelphia Art Museum and Philadelphia Mural Arts project about ongoing plans for a

Figure 26. Bust and mural of Reverend Dr. Martin Luther King Jr. at 40th Street and Lancaster Avenues, August 22, 2020. King spoke to a crowd of ten thousand at the intersection on August 3, 1965, during a visit to Philadelphia in support of the movement to integrate Girard College. Photo by Elizabeth Rose.

new mural on the Spring Garden Street Bridge. The city's Parks Department and the Trust for Public Land were collaborating on a new playground at 37th and Mount Vernon Streets.

Second, ambassadors from the Dornsife Center, the Mount Vernon Manor CDC, the People's Emergency Center, and elected officials' offices informed attendees about new programs and resources. In May 2016, for example, a Mantua resident who worked as a liaison to the Dornsife Center announced the Center's monthly community meal as well as a pet food giveaway and workshops in quilting, cooking, and writing. At the same meeting, a representative from the People's Emergency Center announced a senior health fair at the 40th Street library, an early June event celebrating businesses on the Lancaster Avenue commercial corridor, and an upcoming meeting to discuss a proposed new historic district, the West Philadelphia Freedom District ("We want to be sure that our history gets recorded and remembered, so that as we build, we don't overgrow what was there before").[33] The proposed Freedom District, spearheaded by a Muslim-American cultural organization that runs a museum at 42nd Street and Lancaster Avenue, includes a mosque where Malcolm X and Wallace Muhammad once served as ministers as well as the site of Martin Luther King Jr.'s "Freedom Now" rally at 40th Street and Lancaster Avenue in 1965.[34] In maintaining a connection with the Freedom District as well as with commemorations-by-mural of Herman Wrice and artist Tim Spencer,[35] the civic association identified itself as an engine of cultural preservation as well as a source of social support for economically fragile households.

"Plan or Be Planned For"

The Mantua Civic Association's monthly meeting was also a space in which to counter and defy dominant narratives about the Mantua neighborhood—narratives that cast it as "poor," "disinvested," or "unsafe." Attendees focused on and affirmed the neighborhood's assets even as they worried about its persistent challenges and feared for its future cultural integrity. Often referring to the tradition of self-determination symbolized in the work of the Young Great Society and Mantua Community Planners, they hewed to a narrative that with solidarity and unity they could confront and overcome the problems facing the neighborhood. The barriers facing Mantua households did not get papered over, but neither were they a source of despair or panic.

For example, more than once, people discussing the importance of stemming violence among young teenagers in the neighborhood referred hopefully to part-time jobs, sports, and urban agriculture programs as ways of responding to adolescents' "knuckleheaded" behavior. The image of a knucklehead defied popular characterizations of teens in contact with the criminal-legal system—characterizations that portrayed them as dangerous and antisocial. The term was affectionate and implied that the confidence and guidance of respected elders, combined with viable employment and recreation options, could create environments in which young people were held and loved, not feared.

In addition to its commitment to self-help and mutual aid, the Mantua Civic Association became active in city politics, launching a campaign to preserve the neighborhood's character as the real estate market changed. In 2014, following the release of the Mantua Transformation Plan, the City Planning Commission designated the association as a Registered Community Organization (RCO)—an entity with the right to formally review applications for individual zoning variances within its territory. At the same time, residents were becoming increasingly alarmed about the acquisition of vacant land and homes in the neighborhood by housing developers. As a local news article put it: "Mantua has become a focal point for developers looking to cash in on the relatively cheap stock of rowhomes and vacant lots. Most of the building is aimed at students pushing north from pricier Powelton Village."[36]

Because the zoning in Mantua permitted multi-family housing development "by right," a few developers were already building twelve- and fifteen-unit structures there. The existing zoning rules had been in place since the 1950s, when planners had expected the city to grow by two million people in the ensuing decades. In mid-2015, leaders and members of MCA and Mount Vernon Manor CDC identified a neighborhood-wide downzoning as a tool that would arrest or at least slow student-oriented development. They proposed changing the zoning from multi-family to RSA-5, a category limiting new construction to attached or semi-detached single-family homes. Under this regime, developers would need to seek variances in order to build multi-unit apartment buildings, and this would involve a trip to the Zoning Board of Adjustment, where local RCOs had an advisory voice. "When developers get the property by right, they don't have to tell the community nothing," Drummond told a reporter in 2016. "That is why things are popping up and we don't have a clue about it. . . . This doesn't mean we want development to stop, it just means we want to sit at the table with our future neighbors."[37] In

WHAT DOES RE-ZONING MEAN FOR MY BLOCK?

The Mantua community has organized to change most of the zoning in the neighborhood from multi-family to single-family. Zoning determines the use and size of new construction. **Zoning is a way for the community to have a voice in future development!**

BECAUSE MY BLOCK IS ZONED "MULTI-FAMILY"...

- A developer can construct a new apartment building without alerting the community or seeking input from surrounding neighbors.
- Current homeowners and developers can convert rowhomes to multi-unit apartments without needing feedback from the community.
- The high cost and value of multi-family development will continue to dramatically drive up neighboring homeowners' property taxes.

IF MY BLOCK IS RE-ZONED "SINGLE-FAMILY"...

- Developers and property owners interested in building multi-family apartments need to seek approval from the Philadelphia Zoning Board and also hold a community meeting for residents affected by the construction to share their concerns or support.
- Single-family homes can help keep property taxes stable.
- Our community sends the message that we aim to preserve single-family homes in Mantua!

If you have any questions or concerns about re-zoning, please feel free to contact **Mt. Vernon Manor CDC** by calling **215-475-9492** or drop by our office at **631 N. 39ᵗʰ Street**, Monday-Friday, 9AM-5:30PM.

Figure 27. 2016 flier explaining a proposed zoning change in Mantua. Image courtesy of Mt. Vernon Manor CDC.

addition to being accorded the respect that came with a consultative role, advocates also wanted to discourage a glut of housing designed for student occupancy as they assembled the organizational and financial resources to sponsor housing interventions for a non-transitional population. As one MCA board member remarked at the May 2016 meeting, downzoning would "keep our community a neighborhood—not a transitional place where people stay twenty minutes and leave."

Sticking Points: Land

Achieving the downzoning of Mantua required advocates to vigorously push Jannie Blackwell, their reluctant city council representative.[38] Blackwell ultimately introduced the Mantua legislation (along with a "conservation overlay district" advocated by the Powelton Village Civic Association) only in the final stages of negotiation over the terms of the Schuylkill Yards development in June 2017. Policy experts who promoted dense development as a vehicle for greater affordability criticized the legislation.[39] Nevertheless, the achievement of a zoning classification that matched the existing housing typology (and that made it more onerous to build student housing) was a victory for Mantua and its newly mobilized civic association.[40] But while symbolically significant, the downzoning was an insufficient response to the twofold challenge of Mantua's preservation. Many barriers existed that were preventing homeowners and local non-profits from rehabilitating housing that had fallen into disrepair and financial delinquency.

Moreover, new resources and political approvals were needed if the civic association and its partners were to be able to leverage the neighborhood's vacant property as a resource for the kind of new development that they desired. Much like their counterparts in Powelton Village, Mantua leaders conceived of their community as resting on a foundation of homeownership. According to the Mantua Transformation Plan, just one in three housing units in the neighborhood was owner-occupied,[41] but perhaps ironically, even 33 percent ownership far exceeded the corresponding rate in Powelton Village. The problem was the precariousness of this housing. Homeowners were largely elderly people on fixed incomes who had purchased their century-old brick rowhomes decades earlier. Material constraints (both theirs and those of generations of owners and renters before them) had produced an epidemic of deferred maintenance. Plumbing and heating systems needed replacement, porches sagged, and roofs leaked, even as appreciation in surrounding areas triggered significant increases in assessed property values and corresponding taxes owed.

Mantua Civic Association leaders briefly explored a campaign to advocate for a moratorium on property tax increases in the neighborhood. But city housing officials were already instigating property tax relief for people with low or fixed incomes, particularly seniors; the larger issue was that many of the same homeowners with rising tax assessments were also behind on mortgage payments and utility bills. Loss of ownership through foreclosure was common,[42] and to avoid this fate many people were selling their homes for cash to real estate companies whose interest was in the land. The value of many of these properties from the standpoint of a real estate transaction was independent of the value of the houses that stood on them. The time and care that residents or former residents had invested in their houses and yards and the symbolic attachments they had to them were, in the domain of real estate economics, worthless. The 2014 "Funeral for a Home" project, in

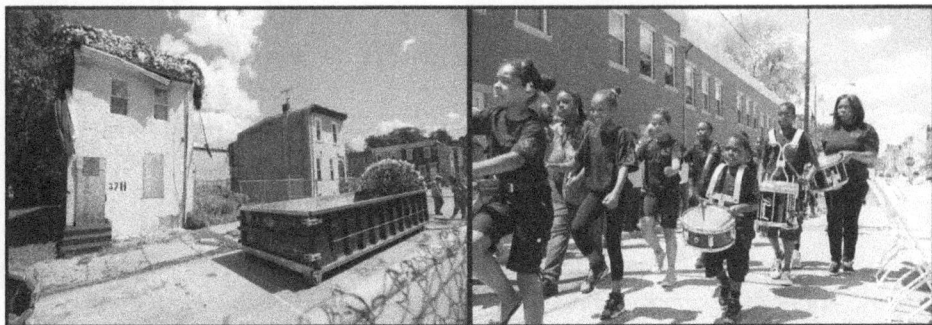

Figure 28. Funeral for a Home at 3711 Melon Street in Mantua, May 31, 2014. Photos by Jeffrey Stockbridge.

which the Mantua Civic Association was a key collaborator, poignantly highlighted this dilemma by staging an elaborate ceremony (complete with a choral performance and a procession to the junkyard to deposit "remains") around the planned demolition of one such house, at 3711 Melon Street.[43]

In addition to thinking about how to preserve existing housing, civic association members were also cognizant of the opportunities and risks posed by vacant property. The Mantua Transformation Plan noted, "vacant land represents 1/3 of the area of all parcels combined. For every five housing units, one is vacant."[44] Some of this vacant property was in private hands, but as of 2013 about half of it was publicly owned. To the extent that both property and subsidy could be obtained, this presented the opportunity for mission-driven organizations to initiate new development that existing residents saw as compatible with the character of their neighborhood: namely, renter- and owner-occupied units affordable to people with stable but relatively low incomes. But transforming publicly owned vacant land into affordable housing involved byzantine politics. At the city level in the early 2000s, elected officials and agency personnel had put a great deal of effort into creating the Philadelphia Land Bank, intended as a central repository for property owned by city agencies or strategically acquired by the public sector at auction.[45] The land bank's mission was to obtain clear title to these properties and convey them to firms and organizations who would then put them to use as sites for housing, green infrastructure, and urban agriculture. The land bank's work was complicated, though, by interagency politics and by the reluctance of city council members to cede their historical authority over public property disposition in their districts. At the May 2016 Mantua Civic Association meeting, a discussion about the downzoning proposal with a representative from the Philadelphia City Planning Commission turned to the question of how to exert community influence over the disposition of vacant land in the neighborhood. My gestural notes from the meeting read:

> Concern about how to find out what property the [Redevelopment Authority] owns in Mantua—"Is there information available that the community can look at? Do we keep up with the information on this? Is it possible for the community to keep up with proposals to do something in the neighborhood?" Mention of land bank, the fact that RDA can place properties in land bank, and the fact that the "councilmanic person" has some discretion over the properties in the land bank. Board president: "The councilmanic person can give that property to a developer." Relatedly, concern about records of private ownership and building permits issued. Board member: "Lots and lots of properties are owned by people who are not part of the community. They are holding them out for speculation."[46]

Even if developers such as the Mount Vernon Manor CDC and the People's Emergency Center succeeded in acquiring property through the Philadelphia Land Bank, the affordable housing finance landscape was bleak. Construction was expensive, and operating housing that offered feasible rent or mortgage terms to low-income people required significant subsidy. Federal and state subsidies, particularly for deeply affordable units, were scarce, and the City of Philadelphia was chronically in fiscal straits. Relatedly, one aim of the Philadelphia Land Bank was to use the public property disposition process to earn revenue for the city's general fund. This perceived imperative also cut against the civic association's hope that the land bank would be a source of inexpensive land for housing construction by nonprofit organizations.

Sticking Points: Work

Civic association members' anxiety about the effects of new development on the survival of the neighborhood's low-cost housing stock was matched by their urgency to tap into new employment opportunities. "We do support all these wonderful projects in our neighborhood," a member said to a

Philadelphia Parks and Recreation Department representative addressing the group in January 2016 about a playground project on 37th and Mount Vernon Streets. "But we have a concern with economic inclusion." The questioning of an Amtrak representative addressing the group in October 2015 had been blunter: "Do you have any plan to provide employment for this neighborhood?" These people were not asking for themselves (as noted above, civic association members tended to be at or near retirement age), but for their children and grandchildren, or for the children and grandchildren of relatives and friends. Civic association members understood that Drexel was investing in skill-building and labor market intermediation programs that were reaching increasing numbers of adults and youth in Mantua. They also understood the isolation of much of the community from the social, educational, and occupational networks through which hiring occurred. They wanted more people in their neighborhood to become a part of those networks, and their preoccupation was with jobs in the construction industry.

There was nothing new about this desire. The public sector's role as a sponsor or subsidizer of development had made the organized construction industry a target of anti-discrimination advocacy in Philadelphia since the early 1960s.[47] Activists from the NAACP and the Congress on Racial Equality had made some headway at that time. But while federal administrative orders had boosted non-whites' participation in union construction work in the 1970s, this had not been sustained, due to a decline in direct federal funding for urban development and to practices initiated by unions to maintain traditional prerogatives.[48] A worrying backdrop to statements proclaiming construction jobs estimates for uCity Square and Schuylkill Yards (4,300 and 10,000, respectively) was a 2013 study published by the news site AxisPhilly which found that the demographic composition of building trades workers in Philadelphia had changed very little since the 1970s. In an analysis of a sample of 5,400 (largely union) construction workers who were paid the prevailing wage between 2008 and 2012, the AxisPhilly analysis determined that 76 percent were white, and that 67 percent lived in suburbs rather than in the city itself.[49] The few Black workers who belonged to majority-white unions often faced ugly treatment in the workplace.[50]

That so little progress had occurred was particularly galling to Mantua leaders who recalled earlier struggles.[51] Civil rights activists in Philadelphia in the 1960s had, in the words of historian Thomas Sugrue, "demanded policies that broke open the closed circle of nepotism, friendship, and race that kept blacks out of one key sector of the urban economy."[52] Sugrue continues:

"The threat to that closed world sparked a powerful reaction from building trades unionists and their supporters, who belatedly adopted the rhetoric and strategies of postwar racial gradualism to defend their position. Although they lost their battle to thwart the Philadelphia Plan, their arguments—particularly their insistence on their racial innocence, their critique of affirmative action's 'discrimination' against whites, and their resentment of government—continue to shape the affirmative action debate."[53]

Forty years later, the leaders of Philadelphia's construction unions were continuing to frame their closed circle as a set of legitimate, merit-based arrangements threatened with violation by government overreach. The city's gradualism persisted as well. In an example of what historian Michael Katz refers to as a "mimetic reform,"[54] mayors had, over the years, sponsored multiple commissions and studies examining contracting and hiring disparities in construction and other sectors affected by public procurement.[55] One provision of the Philadelphia Code required the city and developers to establish Economic Opportunity Plans for major projects requiring city council authorization or receiving public funds or tax abatements. These plans set forth goals for minority contracting and labor force participation and stipulated that developers make good faith attempts to meet them.[56] But projects governed by Economic Opportunity Plans generally underperformed relative to stated targets, with few or no repercussions.[57]

As noted above, the city had appended a project-specific Economic Opportunity Plan to the 2014 zoning legislation that had allowed the uCity Square development to move forward. The Mantua Civic Association was one of several groups whose leaders received regular updates on Drexel and Wexford's adherence to its targets.[58] Another bright spot for Mantuans was a concerted effort by Drexel to encourage contractors doing campus construction to provide opportunities to local workers. At its June 2016 meeting, the Mantua Civic Association bestowed a community service award on Emily Bittenbender, managing director of Bittenbender Construction, and praised her for adhering to a commitment to local hiring that she had made several months prior (Bittenbender served as general contractor on many Drexel projects). Overall, however, union construction jobs were overwhelmingly occupied by white suburbanites. Some members of the progressive coalition that had elected James Kenney as Philadelphia's ninety-ninth mayor in 2015 had been optimistic that he could leverage his close relationships with leaders in the building trades to hasten cultural change and union compliance with affirmative action policies. But on this issue, Mayor Kenney was proving disappointing.[59] Said one interviewee:

> I don't understand all the dynamics, but it's hard to get people into the union, and this is a union job. There are a lot of excuses as to why this doesn't happen. Sometimes they talk about "Well, most of the people from the neighborhood have drug problems, so they can't pass the drug test . . ." or "They can't pass the math test," or "They don't understand the culture of the union so they get there on the job and they're late or they don't get along with their fellow employees . . ." and it's a bunch of BS, you know? I mean, what kind of math test is it that it's that hard to get people to pass? I mean, are you serious?[60]

The puzzle of job access (whether in the construction trades or not) was of course connected not just to the absence of pathways to employment but also to the barriers facing many who might seek to put themselves on those pathways. These barriers included low formal educational attainment, substance abuse, and what was by the late 2010s being referred to as "justice involvement." As noted above, a program at the Dornsife Center was dedicated to helping people earn their GEDs; another program, co-sponsored with Drexel's law school, helped people convicted of low-level offenses expunge their records. But for many youth and young adults, interactions with the criminal-legal system (whether in the form of direct penal supervision or exposure to its impact on their families and social networks) had impaired their capacity to succeed in the regular labor market. These interactions had exposed them to trauma, worsened learning and behavioral health issues, and rendered them ineligible for many jobs. Services offered by Drexel were inadequate to counteract system-level failure, as were the efforts of the Mantua Civic Association itself. One association leader, a professional educator, spoke at length about a multiagency program she had developed to help young people transition back to school after spending time in juvenile detention facilities. The process had been painful and difficult:

> Probation supervision was inadequate. There wasn't a comprehensive re-entry process. . . . To see how the systems are just so dysfunctional— well, it makes you sort of disappointed when you think about city services. . . . You see kids who are disengaged. And I said to the

whole group, "We've all failed these kids. The School District failed to teach these kids how to read and write and do math. You [Department of Human Services] failed to protect, to make sure that kid is safe. Probation, you failed to adequately supervise.... We need to collectively take responsibility for these kids that are out here and in trouble.... How do you send those kids back to the homes they came out of when you've done nothing with those families? How can you possibly send that kid back when you know it was the conditions at home that sent that kid out on the street? How do you send them away for nine to eighteen months and not work with their families?[61]

This interviewee's exasperating experience with state systems led her to be active in the Mantua Civic Association's youth programming, as well as in Drexel's work with the McMichael School, to which she dedicated hours each week. But she was grimly pragmatic about the limitations of civil society organizations to affect structural problems. She knew that systemic change lay beyond the capacity of a volunteer organization to effect: "We have no staff.... It's very overwhelming sometimes. We've done a lot with very few resources over the last several years as a group in its infancy. [Yet] there are some major issues that we struggle with as a community."[62] Between this person's work with the civic organization and her involvement with Drexel-sponsored educational programming, to get involved in a struggle over the terms of oncoming redevelopment seemed to her to be a bridge too far: "The Schuylkill Yards thing just makes my head hurt because the lower end of Mantua will be a whole new city. I don't even go to the meetings anymore 'cause I can't even get my head wrapped around what they're even talking about."[63] Perhaps ironically, the year following this interview would consume the Mantua Civic Association and several of its neighborhood-based counterparts in development negotiations.

The Schuylkill Yards CBA and the Mantua-Powelton Alliance

Schuylkill Yards—involving eight million square feet of live/work/play development projected to emerge on fourteen acres over the course of two decades—was part of a larger vision. Brandywine Realty Trust owned substantial acreage north and south of the 30th Street train station on the west bank of the Schuylkill River, some of which it had already developed; its holdings included the striking Cira Centre building which it had built on land owned by Amtrak. Also underway was a multistakeholder "Philly District 30" Plan for the entire 30th Street Station area—a plan that envisioned capping the Amtrak railyards to create 175 acres of new mixed-use real estate.[64] The idea that Philadelphia's downtown business district was moving west to encompass new Class A office properties in University City was a recurrent theme in the city's business press.[65] Schuylkill Yards, which was "really a subset area of Philly District 30," was a critical move in clinching that westward shift, and a critical move in putting Drexel at the center of it.[66] To initiate Schuylkill Yards required the blessing of 3rd District Councilwoman Jannie Blackwell, and to obtain that blessing required a community benefits agreement. Despite its social inclusion agenda and despite its role as a development partner for Schuylkill Yards, Drexel handed this task to Brandywine.

Community benefits agreements (CBAs) came about in the late 1990s as a mechanism to facilitate compromise between private developers and residents who stand to be affected by their projects. In a context in which subsidies and foregone revenue remain the dominant tools of urban economic development policy, CBAs "enlarge negotiations" over economic development to include a range of local interests.[67] In exchange for the support of groups negotiating on behalf of a local community, a developer who enters into a CBA makes a set of commitments—for example, to include affordable housing, hire union labor, or contribute cash to neighborhood improvement projects. While public opinion about individual CBAs is tied to numerous factors, one of the most important is the perceived advisability of the underlying development proposal. Much of the conflict over a 2008 CBA signed by two community groups with the developer of the SugarHouse Casino in Philadelphia's Fishtown neighborhood, for example, centered on whether the casino itself represented a worthwhile economic development initiative.[68] Efforts to distinguish "true" CBAs from illegitimate ones have long occupied practitioners and scholars. Julian Gross, a legal expert on CBAs, argues that the term *CBA* should be reserved for agreements that concern a single development project, that are legally enforceable, that address a range of community interests, and that emanate from a broadly inclusive process. Gross also draws a distinction between "private CBAs," or stand-alone agreements between community groups and developers, and "public CBAs," or agreements between governmental entities and developers that proceed from a CBA campaign conducted by local groups.

The Schuylkill Yards CBA fits neatly into neither of these categories. In this case, a local elected official with gatekeeping power over a land use approval conditioned that approval on a private developer's willingness to bargain with local organizations. Additionally, unlike in the 2008 casino case, there was no significant debate about the project itself. While there may have been dissent in some quarters about the advisability of Brandywine's $3.5 billion investment in University City, this dissent did not reach the mainstream, and city council approvals for Schuylkill Yards were clearly forthcoming once a CBA had been signed. Instead, two other issues were paramount: what the benefits would be and which organizations would represent the community for the purpose of negotiating them.

Thus, a major question hovering over the Schuylkill Yards CBA was one of representation. This made it typical. While Gross argues that only agreements resulting from "broadly inclusive processes" should be termed CBAs, it is often unclear whose interpretation of inclusivity should hold in any specific local context. In Philadelphia's Council District 3, the arbiter of this question had historically been Councilwoman Blackwell. In the past, said one interviewee, "Developers that wanted something from her—Jannie made that developer talk to a community contact. She is the one who deems the community representatives . . . [Moreover], in the past it turned into benefits for those particular people."[69]

For the uCity Square negotiation in 2014, Blackwell had called numerous groups to the table—the civic associations for Powelton Village, Mantua, and West Powelton; the People's Emergency Center CDC; the Lancaster Avenue Business Association; the 24th Democratic Ward Committee; and the Mantua Community Improvement Committee, an organization whose director had been a longtime close ally of Blackwell.[70] Conflict had emerged as some groups had advocated particularistic interests or attempted backdoor negotiations with Wexford outside of the official discussion forum. In the Schuylkill Yards case, perhaps having learned from this prior experience, Blackwell, in the words of one interviewee, "set the table" but left it to Brandywine to decide who would sit there.[71] For a time after the March 2016 announcement of Schuylkill Yards, Brandywine conducted one-on-one meetings with a variety of organizations whose members claimed standing to bargain for benefits in conjunction with the development. By the fall of that year, however, Brandywine had apparently determined that its negotiating partner would be a coalition of four organizations that called itself the Mantua-Powelton Alliance: the Mantua Civic Association, the Mount Vernon Manor CDC, the Powelton Village Civic Association, and the People's Emergency Center CDC. Strategic cohesion among these groups had begun with the University City High School negotiations and continued as the federal Promise Zone and Promise Neighborhoods designations, along with Drexel's community engagement efforts, had turned a spotlight on the Lower Lancaster corridor neighborhoods. The four groups had built enough mutual trust by 2016 to present themselves to Brandywine *en bloc* as an authentic representative of the community's interests, although they expected that the company would continue bargaining with multiple parties. In late summer of that year, the Mantua-Powelton Alliance learned that it was the sole counterparty in the Schuylkill Yards CBA negotiation.

The disparities in interests and political capital that had arisen during the uCity Square negotiation remained. While the relationship had often been fractious, Powelton Village leaders enjoyed a rapport with Drexel that carried over even into a negotiation from which the institution was nominally absent; their insistence on being taken seriously was taken seriously. Powelton Village Civic Association members also had the advantage of apparent reasonableness, in that their "asks" again primarily concerned the physical impacts of redevelopment: massing, traffic corridors, street trees. Some Powelton Village negotiators came to the process with thinly veiled distaste for a strategy that turned to a real estate development project as a vehicle for redistributing financial resources and social opportunities. But the collective strength of the Mantua-Powelton Alliance rested on its diverse membership, and there was also genuine support for an outcome that satisfied Mantua representatives, even if it was occasionally remarked privately that they were "going too far."[72]

For their part, the Mantua-based organizations and the People's Emergency Center enlisted the Philadelphia office of the Local Initiatives Support Corporation (LISC) to help coordinate strategy and to research nationwide best practices in community benefits advocacy. The research found that successful groups in other places had achieved benefits that amounted to around two percent of the total development costs of large mega-projects. Thus, the Mantua-Powelton Alliance, in addition to demanding an advisory role in the design and physical planning of the Schuylkill Yards complex, decided to ask Brandywine for $72 million in cash.[73] A direct financial investment from Brandywine, in this vision, would go toward housing programs, workforce development and education, small business development, and capacity-building for local organizations. If strategically used, went the logic, the money would create housing and social infrastructure that could ensure, in the words of the Mantua Transformation Plan, that "Mantua residents are able to remain and benefit from the neighborhood's transformation."[74]

Brandywine had other ideas about what was appropriate for the groups to request. As they met with representatives of the Mantua-Powelton Alliance in the summer and fall of 2016, Jerry Sweeney and his team were also arranging to fund several interventions targeted at local businesses and workers. One of these was the Grow Philadelphia Capital Fund, a partnership with a prominent West Philadelphia business development organization, the Enterprise Center, to expand the participation of local entrepreneurs in Brandywine's procurement "spend." The Enterprise Center would prepare local vendors and contractors to submit correctly packaged financial statements, and with Brandywine as a member of the loan committee, the fund would then extend very-low-interest loans to qualified businesses.[75]

Brandywine was also formalizing its financial support for a construction workforce effort, the Construction Apprenticeship Preparatory Program (CAPP). Run by a retired Black electrician named Walter McGill, CAPP had, in a previous, less formal incarnation, a successful track record of preparing minority candidates for union apprenticeship entrance exams. Brandywine's support of CAPP was tied to a goal, later inscribed in the city's Economic Opportunity Plan for the project, that 50 percent of the apprentice hours on the Schuylkill Yards project would be worked by members of minority groups and 50 percent by residents of the City of Philadelphia. This was an atypical goal for an Economic Opportunity Plan to include, and Brandywine later announced its intention to impose fines on contractors who did not meet the goals. For many, these commitments signaled Brandywine's intention to use its leverage to change embedded racial dynamics in access to large-firm procurement and building trades employment.

Having invested in economic inclusion programs on its own, Brandywine apparently anticipated that its conversation with the Mantua-Powelton Alliance would center on issues such as site design, traffic measures, and the public realm. Thus, Sweeney and his team were reportedly taken aback, even offended, when the groups requested cash. Nevertheless, Brandywine remained at the bargaining table. They did so because Councilwoman Blackwell did not withdraw her insistence that the developer and the community groups reach agreement before she introduced the desired zoning ordinance.

Behind the scenes, she was conducting her own negotiation of sorts with the neighborhood representatives: "The Councilperson set the table and then we had to fight. [We demanded $72 million]—and [the Councilperson's staff] told us, 'That's crazy,' and so we demanded a smaller amount and then the word came down: 'That's crazy—but you can go ahead and fight,' and she kept pushing them, making them come to the table."[76]

On June 13, 2017, although Brandywine and the Mantua-Powelton Alliance were still negotiating, Blackwell introduced the Schuylkill Yards zoning legislation. This move signaled that time was up; she expected them to reach an agreement in the days that followed.[77] Lawyers for Brandywine and the Mantua-Powelton Alliance executed the Schuylkill Yards Community Benefits Agreement a week later, on June 20.

The agreement set guidelines for community input into the development plan for the project. It established that Brandywine would confer with community groups on traffic mitigation and provide 6.5 acres of public space as part of the total project. It also committed $3.1 million—$620,000 per year for five years—to a fund that would be governed by a Community Fund Management Group (the CBA lay out highly detailed terms under which the group would select a fiscal agent, create operating procedures, make decisions, and ultimately disburse funding). The management group, per the document, would consist of representatives from the four members of the Mantua-Powelton Alliance plus an additional representative from the office of the 3rd District councilperson. When they approved the legislation enabling Schuylkill Yards to move forward, the council also passed remapping legislation prohibiting "by-right" construction of multi-family housing in Mantua and an ordinance creating a "Neighborhood Conservation Overlay District" in Powelton Village. Both measures were targeted at slowing speculation and preventing the development of housing aimed at students. Mantua Civic Association and Powelton Village Civic Association had been lobbying the councilperson on both for several years.

What did this mean? It depended upon one's perspective. Both during the negotiations and in the months that followed, officials at Brandywine and Drexel made it known that, in their opinion, the Mantua-Powelton Alliance and the councilperson had subjected the developer to extortion. In this view, a publicly beneficial project was held hostage for months by parochial interests making unreasonable, even unconscionable financial demands. Civic groups and CDCs had forced a development firm to attend to issues that lay beyond its control and outside its sphere of responsibility, and the result was an injustice and a bad precedent for the future. There was additional criticism of the civic groups' effort to limit high-density construction, since such development was viewed as the only way to bring housing costs down and create the opportunity for income-diverse development.

Others believed that mobilization around the CBA was a poor substitute for activism that questioned the basic mechanisms underlying University City's redevelopment. The Schuylkill Yards Innovation was only financially viable because of layers of foregone government revenue: the exemption of payments on Brandywine's ninety-nine-year ground lease with Drexel from federal income tax; the Opportunity Zone's exemption of investors from capital gains tax; the Keystone Opportunity Zone's exemption of tenants in the developments from a host of state taxes; the developer's exemption from municipal real estate taxes under the city's ten-year tax abatement; and Drexel's own tax-exempt status. The developers and Drexel advanced a

Figure 29. Some observers disparaged the community benefits negotiation as an insidious distraction. Cartoon by Meg Lemieur, 2018.

narrative that positioned subsidized property investment by the private sector as self-evidently and universally desirable—good for the city and the region. But this narrative conflated real estate investment and economic development and failed to account for the collateral impact the project would have on low-socioeconomic-status households absent an effort to de-commodify land and housing in their neighborhoods. To some critics, to be sure, the main problem with the CBA was that funding allotted to neighbor-hood preservation was paltry and would not go far, particularly given the cost of creating and maintaining below-market housing; an observer from inside city government called it "chump change."[78] But to others, the CBA process distracted community organizations from a deeper critique that would have countered conventional definitions of economic development and re-turn on investment altogether.

The Contradictions of Inclusion

In the era of the innovation district, both the economics and the politics of university-led redevelopment are new. Whereas in the past, direct public subsidy was the order of the day, today's university development entrepre-neurs structure deals that tap into liquid global capital markets and leverage tax-privileged investment. In the past, city governments backed university real estate projects to stem the suburbanization of firms and middle-class households. Today, the back-to-the-city trend among college-educated mil-lennials represents growth—growth that might eventually translate to reve-nue that helps public officials finance school systems, repair infrastructure, or provide homes to unhoused residents. The scene has also changed politi-cally. Mainstream policy makers and planners now disavow infiltration theory, a racist pillar of liberal redevelopment discourse fifty years ago. Un-like the West Philadelphia Corporation and its municipal partners, the sponsors of innovation-centered development in twenty-first-century Uni-versity City do not talk overtly about eliminating infectious blight or attract-ing responsible citizens, and they are not condemning occupied residential and commercial property. Drexel, the university partner in the emergent innovation districts, is investing actively in education, workforce prepara-tion, and other services directed at low-socioeconomic-status neighbor-hoods nearby. Further, representatives of majority-Black neighborhoods have claimed and wielded political influence that city and university officials bluntly denied to members of the Citizens Committee for University City Urban Renewal Area Unit 3.

In this environment, members of the Mantua-Powelton Alliance succeeded in asserting claims on place that their respective organizational ancestors (the Mantua Community Planners and Powelton Neighbors) would not likely have imagined possible. In addition to enabling a voice for residents in discussions about the environmental implications of new development, and in addition to cementing commitments to prevent the production of student housing in vulnerable neighborhoods, the Schuylkill Yards Community Benefits Agreement pushed Mantua leaders' concerns about displacement and cultural preservation into the public conversation. It validated those concerns by winning resources for a community-controlled fund dedicated to ensuring that economically insecure families could keep a foothold in their changing neighborhoods. But to achieve these gains, the organizations had to assimilate into a pared-down approach to social advocacy: one that attended to current neighborhood distress but that did not question how that distress had come about. For aside from the issue of legitimate community representation, another dilemma the advocates faced in their negotiations with Brandywine turned on the contrast between "mitigative" and "reparative" approaches to community benefits claims.

A mitigative approach anticipates the direct negative effects of new development and seeks measures that reduce or compensate for those effects. The inclusion of parking within a new development compensates for the anticipated shortage of parking in a nearby neighborhood. Height limits, parks, and street trees reduce the impact of new, dense development on the built environment and the public realm. In contrast, a reparative approach responds to cumulative social harm, addressing the legacy effects of dispossession and asset stripping in the areas now being "revitalized." The idea behind a reparative approach is that new development presents an opportunity to atone for the contemporary repercussions of past wrongs (i.e., persistent poverty and precarity) through measures that approximate redistributive justice.[79] If the city and university had casually demolished the homes of Black residents in the name of the total community's welfare in 1968,[80] maybe it was appropriate to take extra-large measures to address housing insecurity in Mantua in 2017. If the Philadelphia Plan, won after bitter struggle, had failed to promote greater representation of Black tradespeople in construction jobs, perhaps overrepresentation at the Schuylkill Yards worksite could achieve—or aspire to—retroactive justice.

As the logic of reparation finds its way into academic and policy discourse,[81] the arena of the community benefits negotiation presents an understandably attractive venue in which to argue for repair.[82] An impulse to relate current displacement risk to the traumatic history of redevelopment in University City underlay the Mantua Civic Association's demand (unmet) for affordable housing guarantees in the context of the uCity Square negotiation. It underlay the $72 million request the Mantua-Powelton Alliance brought to its discussions with Brandywine. A discussion of repair fit awkwardly, however, within the Schuylkill Yards bargaining process. Mitigation—the purer the better—was more consistent than repair with development norms, law and practice, and read in the dominant public discourse as the only reasonable frame of reference for a CBA negotiation.[83] As Jerry Sweeney had implied with his remark that a single development project could not be expected to solve all of Philadelphia's problems, a reparative approach—one aimed at addressing the structural roots of poverty, joblessness, and justice-involvement—conflicted with Brandywine's fiduciary identity. The Mantua-Powelton Alliance had to agree to confine community benefits advocacy within the narrow bounds of impact mitigation to keep their seat at the bargaining table.

A second (and related) contradiction lay in the fact that Brandywine was negotiating the Schuylkill Yards CBA as a lone actor. While municipal government, the university, and the real estate investment trust were all implicated in the political and financial machinery that underlay Schuylkill Yards, Brandywine became the project's community-facing protagonist. Civic representatives were puzzled by the absence of Drexel, and moreso the city. One interviewee said, "The politicians are happy to let us fight it out, let the volunteers go up against the developers. There is nothing inherently wrong with developers—they're not terrible people. But there needs to be somebody other than schoolteachers and artists to line up against these people."[84]

Indeed, the community benefits process emblematizes—for many—the shrunken role that the government has come to play in the provision of collective goods in contemporary cities. At the time of the controversy over the University City Science Center, the federal government was in the midst of an era of unprecedented intervention in—and unprecedented funding for—urban programs, including housing construction and rehabilitation, water and sewer infrastructure, early childhood education, and legal services. Soon afterward, however, a conservative political turn and the imperatives of the conflict in Vietnam shifted presidential and congressional priorities, and a gradual but steady withdrawal of federal resources from urban programs—aside from those associated with policing and criminal justice— began. By the 2010s, Philadelphia and other high-poverty cities had long since been subsisting without much in the way of federal transfers for housing, education, or jobs. During Barack Obama's presidency, the White House Domestic Policy Council launched the Promise Zone initiative and, partly on the strength of the Mantua Transformation Plan, chose Mantua and several adjacent University City neighborhoods to be in the first round of grantees. The designation of two square miles of West Philadelphia as a federal Promise Zone led two years later to a $30 million U.S. Department of Education Promise Neighborhoods grant award. But the Promise Zone designation itself came with *de minimis* funding. According to one interviewee, it "kicked out little peon resources."[85] Another interviewee quipped, "The problem with the Promise Zone is there's no money. I can promise to take you to dinner, but at dinnertime you're still hungry."[86] During the Obama era, argues sociologist Hilary Silver, "federal urban policy consisted of small-scale reformed versions of the few programs that had survived years of attrition" since the Great Society's heyday.[87] For all the attention the West Philadelphia Promise Zone received as an organizing principle for community-led revitalization, the financial resources associated with the Promise Zone paled in comparison with those commanded by University City's other zones and districts—those that marked territory where financial returns on real estate investment received tax-exempt status (Figure 30).

State and local government resources for Lower Lancaster's economically struggling communities were hardly more plentiful. The leaders of Pennsylvania's Republican-controlled state legislature saw no reason to support urban systems or programs that they viewed as benefiting undeserving populations. The legislature's denial of resources to the School District, and its support for charter schools, had helped to set off the crisis that led to the closing of University City High School and other public schools in 2013. Lack of intergovernmental revenue left the City of Philadelphia with little choice (at least as officials saw it) but to offer unequivocal support to property development as an economic development tool. Mayor James Kenney and a majority of city council members rejected calls for inclusionary housing regulation and taxes on new construction, fearing that such measures would have a chilling effect on capital investment and, by extension, municipal revenue capacity.[88] City officials saw publicly owned land that might

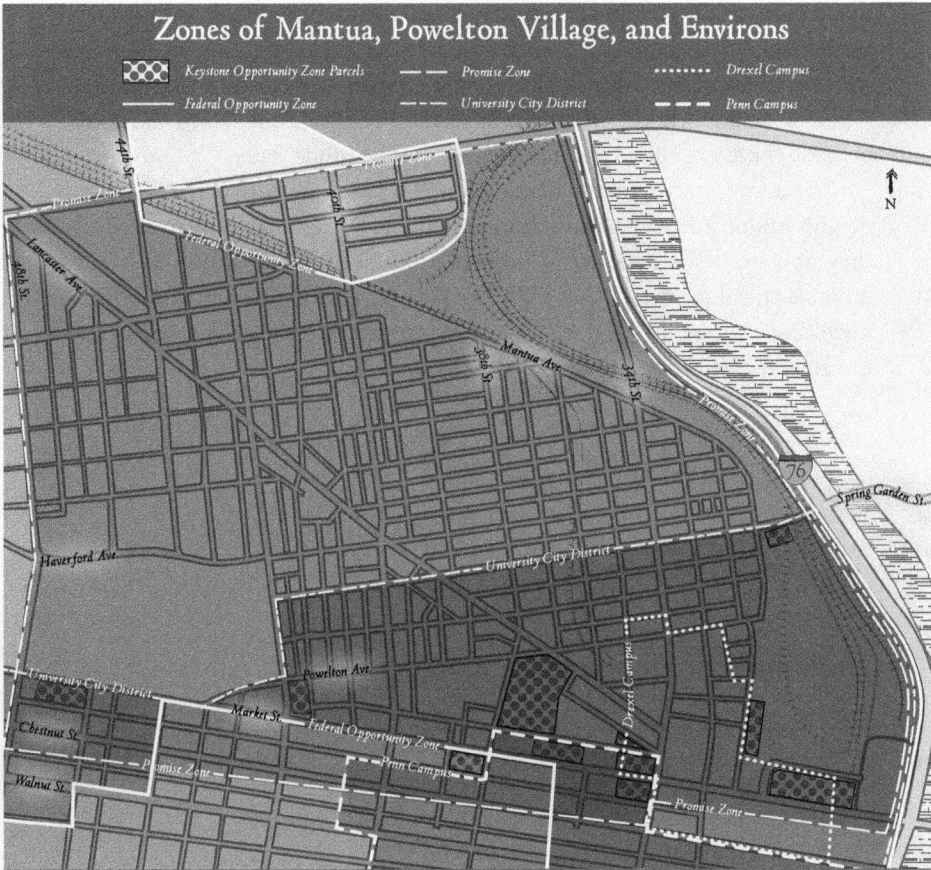

Figure 30. Zone boundaries in University City north of Market Street. Image by Elizabeth Rose.

have become a collective resource primarily in terms of its immediate fiscal value.

There was nothing atypical about the tax privileges the Schuylkill Yards and uCity Square projects enjoyed. As noted above, there was less public sector subsidy claimed by investors in these ventures than by investors in comparable innovation district development projects elsewhere in the United States. From the city's perspective, the logic of juicing university-led real estate development seemed inescapable; how else could Philadelphia build on its "eds and meds" specialization (which was based on the economic dynamism of tax-exempt academic institutions) to promote the private sector growth that would put the city in a better fiscal situation in the long term? If community organizations could squeeze something from Brandywine for neighborhood preservation in the Promise Zone, all to the good, because there was little capacity to direct public funds there.

The community benefits negotiation laid bare the reality that although neighborhood advocates had achieved political power, the polity over which they now exerted a measure of influence had been hollowed out. The "sustainable social progress" that John Fry had extolled at the Schuylkill Yards unveiling was possible (if it was possible) only because the private sector and the anchor institution were paving the way.

CONCLUSION

On November 8, 2017, less than five months after the community benefits agreement broke the regulatory logjam created by Councilwoman Blackwell, Drexel and Brandywine broke ground on Schuylkill Yards. Officials and executives celebrated with a press conference at 30th and Market Streets, at a surface parking lot that they would soon transform into an elliptical park called Drexel Square. The park opened to the public in June 2019; alongside it, the development partners were renovating the Bulletin Building (a mid-century structure that had once housed the now-defunct *Philadelphia Evening Bulletin* newspaper) for the gene therapy company Spark Therapeutics. August 2019 saw the unveiling of eye-catching preliminary designs for two new multistory buildings—one an office, lab and retail building, the other an office-residential condo—planned for John F. Kennedy Boulevard. Brandywine announced another new lab building at 31st and Market Streets in November 2020.[1]

To the west of the Drexel Campus, Wexford (the bulk of whose life science and medical real estate assets were acquired by the Chicago-based real estate investment trust Ventas in 2016) was building as well. Its first project, a fourteen-floor high rise, which replaced a parking garage at 3675 Market Street, opened in November 2018. This development furnishes a new headquarters for the University City Science Center's administrative offices and coworking and business incubation space managed by the Cambridge Innovation Center.[2] One uCity Square, a 400,000-square-foot lab building that broke ground in January 2020 before pausing in March with the lockdown of the pandemic, resumed construction in January 2021 on the strength of lease agreements with three life sciences companies. Drexel nursing and medical school facilities are moving from elsewhere in the city to occupy a new "Academic Tower" at 36th and Filbert Streets, adjacent to the K-8 public school that Drexel began leasing at nominal cost to the Philadelphia School

District in fall 2021. Finally, GMH Communities opened a six-story market-rate apartment building at 3700 Lancaster Avenue in August 2021. Called uCity Square ANOVA, the development features a resort-style swimming pool, a fitness center, a coffee and beer bar, and a pet wash spa among other amenities.

The effects of the COVID-19 pandemic and accompanying economic downturn make the future of these projects somewhat uncertain. The value of office buildings—the "fixed capital" of greatest importance to cities where services supplanted manufacturing as the primary economic driver in the second half of the twentieth century—is in question in the aftermath of a period when many became habituated to working from home.[3] It remains unclear what will happen in the 2020s to demand for Philadelphia's existing office inventory, let alone for the millions of new square feet envisioned at Schuylkill Yards and uCity Square. At the same time, University City's specializations in education, healthcare, and the life sciences may be an exception; it is difficult to connect with students, do bench research, or prototype a new therapeutic from a home office. An expansion of health-related technology companies and lab-reliant life science firms could put West Philadelphia's purpose-built innovation districts in a favorable position to attract tenant firms going forward. Further, the partners undertaking innovation-centered development in West Philadelphia are striving to create new residential neighborhoods: environments whose exceptional qualities (walkability, accessibility to transit, cultural vibrancy) set in motion a virtuous circle of job growth, population growth, and revenue growth for the city. The possibility of a decline in the commercial property market challenges this vision, but it does not foreclose it.

Recent anxieties about a shift in demand for offices nevertheless lay bare the extent to which the "triple helix"—as scholars call the economic development partnership among higher education, government, and high-tech companies—is permeated by the classic, property-based urban growth coalition. As shown in recent work by Jennifer Clark and Sharon Zukin, real estate firms are as deeply imbricated with the triple helix today as software and media startups, life sciences enterprises, or advanced manufacturers.[4] Innovation districts and knowledge neighborhoods are, first and foremost, real estate investment vehicles. As such, the land price dynamics they trigger are knowable in advance. Because all who live and work in a polity require physical space at a cost that falls within their means, property-led economic development in the absence of complementary interventions to de-commodify land and housing (or vastly increase the means of incumbent residents) visits collateral effects on marginal enterprises and households. Thus, despite Drexel's investments in education, job training, and public health, in spite of the Promise Zone and Promise Neighborhood, in spite of the $9.3 million to be delivered to local organizations over twelve years by the Schuylkill Yards Community Benefits Agreement, the residents of Mantua and other low-wealth portions of the Lower Lancaster Corridor have reason to be concerned for the longevity of the neighborhoods they know.

Does innovation-led development inevitably lead to deeply uneven outcomes and loss of place? Critical urban theory implies a resounding yes. From the perspective of much contemporary critical scholarship, innovation district initiatives (and their close relative, policies centered on the attraction of the creative class) amount to little more than contemporary iterations of the entrepreneurial mode of urban governance first excoriated by David Harvey in 1989.[5] In this narrative, having accepted a framing of economic development dominated by the idea of inter-urban competition for global capital, planners condemn themselves to "the speculative construction of place" on behalf of investors.[6] But it is difficult for people who work on the ground in Philadelphia to dismiss the potential of the twenty-first-century knowledge economy as a source of broad-based city revitalization. Philadelphia's poverty rate stood at 23 percent prior to the pandemic.[7] While it has gained population every year since 2006, and employment every year since 2010, it has 200,000 fewer jobs and 365,000 fewer residents than it had in the early years of the University City Science Center. In part because Philadelphia is the same physical city it was five decades ago—but with older infrastructure—balancing the city's budget is an agonizing annual task. Applying public sector resources to the reduction of operating costs for biotechnology firms and other cutting-edge enterprises may generate revenues that enable the city to address more of the needs of its most vulnerable residents.[8] The same logic is at work well beyond Philadelphia, as innovation district development and related initiatives proceed in Detroit, St. Louis, Baltimore, and many other cities.

Very little positive change is possible, however, unless planners and decision-makers in the public sector shift from a mitigative to a reparative stance as they contemplate low-wealth neighborhoods at the edges of innovation development. This involves recognizing the impacts and ongoing legacy of territorial stigmatization, from the workings of the real estate color line that helped produce the dilapidated "slum" conditions of the Black Bottom, to the workings of the liberal governing coalition that rationalized the displacement of thousands of households from that "slum," to the workings of a contemporary discourse that casts the neighborhoods that survived urban renewal but continue to struggle as "blots on the map," teeming with dysfunction.[9] Throwing off this tendency to stigmatize could lead officials to treat land in these neighborhoods differently.

If they want to promote development without displacement in the neighborhoods adjacent to innovation districts, planners need to focus on holding property markets at bay in these neighborhoods to the greatest extent possible. In an article about the Atlanta Beltline project, Dan Immergluck and Tharunya Balan state this precept clearly:

> Communities considering large-scale . . . projects that generate environmental amenities should begin by recognizing that the benefits of these projects to surrounding neighborhoods are rapidly capitalized into housing values, and thus will spur higher housing costs very quickly. Planners who seek to avoid large-scale gentrification, or at least seek to further "development without displacement" and to maintain some minimum level of economic diversity in the nearby areas, must recognize that addressing housing affordability should be an early-stage, central component of planning for such projects. It is not enough to plan for trickle-down affordable housing development down the road after the project gets up a head of steam.[10]

In Philadelphia, officials are taking some action to support affordability in the Lower Lancaster neighborhoods. They are prioritizing property tax relief for households with low or fixed incomes that have seen their property tax assessments rise in the past several years as previously disinvested neighborhoods experience spikes in growth. But this may not be enough. In Mantua, many owner-occupiers with rising tax bills are also behind on mortgage and utility payments. The City of Philadelphia and State of Pennsylvania should thus consider creating a trust fund that would stabilize vulnerable homeowners, helping them become current on payments and attending to deferred maintenance on their homes, in exchange for a claim on a portion of the sales price when the property is eventually sold. Alternatively, or additionally, a land trust entity (such as that currently under development at the Mount Vernon Manor Community Development Corporation) could acquire the homes with the city's help, transferring the buildings back to their owners on a limited-equity basis and maintaining the property itself as permanently affordable housing in the neighborhood. The city should also consider instituting rent regulation and eviction protections for apartments currently renting for $1,000 or less per month, adjusting increases through an adjudicated process similar to the one used for rent-stabilized housing in New York City. Finally, city officials, possibly in collaboration with the Mantua-Powelton Alliance (the group that negotiated the Schuylkill Yards Community Benefits Agreement), should do all they can to convey the remaining publicly owned land in Mantua to organizations dedicated to housing families for whom market-rate shelter is out of reach. For example, the city could use its Land Bank to divert properties from the sheriff's sale process and convey them to mission-driven entities.[11] Only with aggressive interventions that remove at least some land and housing from the specula-tive marketplace will it be possible for the new K-8 school at uCity Square, Powel/SLAMS, to remain accessible to a mix of children.

University City's experience is relevant to any city where large-scale public/private investment is exerting influence on property values in nearby neighborhoods. It is particularly relevant in cities in which "eds and meds" are significant elements of a revitalization formula. The literature on eds and meds, often called anchor institutions, demonstrates the ways in which they boost wealth in their immediate neighborhoods while supporting mu-nicipal and regional economies.[12] It also documents the benefits they gener-ate in the more disadvantaged neighborhoods near their campuses, through partnerships that faculty, students, and administrators forge with govern-ment agencies, school districts, and community-based organizations.[13] And yet, as David Perry and Wim Wiewel observe, "Nowhere is the complex, of-ten conflicted nature of the university as an urban institution more evident than in its real estate development practices."[14] The historical and current phenomena that I unpack in this book bear out this assertion.

In their preface to the 2010 report *The Road Half Traveled*, Ted Howard and Gar Alperovitz argue that "benefiting low-income residents . . . often is at best a secondary motive" of anchor institutions' neighborhood redevelop-ment strategies, because these institutions are concerned foremost with the desirability of the environments they are creating for university-affiliated in-dividuals.[15] This is understandable given the universities' institutional incen-tives, but it does not undo the fact that university-sponsored place-making often leads to physical and cultural displacement when the public sector is neither providing adequate social housing nor exerting control over land prices. The work that Drexel University and its partner, the University City

District, are doing to center the economic advancement of disadvantaged job seekers in West Philadelphia has a great deal of merit. But residential instability may partially undermine these efforts, given the rapidity with which land prices are rising in the areas surrounding the uCity Square and Schuylkill Yards innovation districts. This pattern is bound to repeat near other innovation district developments. While academic institutions are not uniquely responsible for property market dynamics near campuses, they can use their influence in government to press for the intensification of existing anti-displacement policies and the initiation of new ones.

Rethinking Investment

The Young Great Society and Mantua Community Planners were born from their leaders' determination to create belonging and opportunity for groups that were thoroughly marginalized from the mainstream economy in the mid-twentieth century. Their efforts in the 1960s and 1970s did not reverse the forces acting on their community. They did not make Mantua a prosperous middle-class neighborhood. They did launch many individuals—including the founding executive director of the Mount Vernon Manor Community Development Corporation—onto paths that led to economic success in adulthood. Recollections of YGS and MCP also became part of the groundwork for renewed community engagement that occurred in Mantua in the 2010s. The residents who volunteered their time to produce the 2013 Mantua Transformation Plan made plain their connection to the neighborhood's history and their desire to preserve it as a new wave of university-led development arrived. The Mantua Transformation Plan, as well as the "Funeral for a Home" project the next year, demonstrated community members' conviction that the time, care, and energy that people invest in their daily environments—and in one another—are precious, despite their negligible worth in real estate terms. While economic development officials focused on dollars of capital pledged and square feet to be constructed and leased, activists conceived of investment in ways it was not possible to denominate in dollars or property values.[16]

To this day, the Mantua Civic Association and the Mount Vernon Manor Community Development Corporation continue to advance heterodox definitions of investment. In some cases, city, university, and corporate representatives have validated these definitions. Brandywine Investment

Trust's support for local workforce development and capital access programs can be seen through this lens, as can the fact that in 2018, Drexel sheltered a community-serving resource from market forces by acquiring the West Philadelphia Community Center, a recreation facility that had been created through the Mantua Community Planners' efforts.[17] In October 2020, the Philadelphia Parks and Recreation Department announced a significant renovation plan for a 2.5-acre playground that bears the name of Young Great Society member Miles Mack, a former youth worker and basketball coach in the Mantua neighborhood.[18]

But everyone hoping to honor what the market does not validate in University City is nevertheless working under urban entrepreneurialism's rules. The emerging Village Square development at 36th Street and Haverford Avenue provides a poignant example of this: the land on which the Village Square development is now being constructed includes several parcels acquired by the Philadelphia Redevelopment Authority (PRA) in conjunction with the 1969 Urban Renewal Plan that the Mantua Community Planners organization helped to formulate. In 2006, after leaving it vacant for several decades, the PRA began working to combine the urban renewal land with adjacent parcels; the agency's goal was to sell the resulting assemblage to a developer who intended to site a much-desired supermarket there.[19] But a celebrated local visual artist, James Dupree, fought the acquisition in court, because the proposed project would have meant the seizure and demolition of his studio by the Redevelopment Authority.[20] PRA abandoned this effort in 2014 after years of litigation,[21] and released a new Request for Proposals in 2017; this time, all proposals were required to feature designs that allowed for the preservation of Dupree's studio. In 2018, PRA selected a development partnership that includes Black-owned Lomax Real Estate Partners and the Mount Vernon Manor Community Development Corporation; the project features a 15,000-square-foot grocery store, a coffee shop, and the headquarters of the Black-owned talk radio station WURD. The centerpiece of the development is 166 densely constructed homes: a five-story apartment building and attached four-family row houses.[22]

Village Square brings a food amenity that Mantua residents have long clamored for. It also brings significant market-rate development to the center of the neighborhood. The Mantua Civic Association, with the strong support of the Redevelopment Authority and the local councilmember,[23] negotiated hard to achieve a modest amount of affordable housing as part of the plan. Though a total of thirty-two units will rent to households earning below the Area Median Income, just five of them will be affordable to households whose incomes approximate those of the typical Mantua household currently.[24] Citing fiscal needs, redevelopment officials did not feel they could part with the land for the project at a cost to Lomax of less than $1 million, which, together with the developer's threshold rate of return, set a limit on the affordability of the housing.[25] In an interview with a reporter from Philadelphia's public radio station, James Dupree, the artist whose legal action had thwarted the earlier development, "lamented what he views as the impending and inevitable gentrification of Mantua and said he was ambivalent about the new development that will rise around his studio."[26] Dupree said he might leave the neighborhood.

Thanks to the Schuylkill Yards Community Benefits Agreement, the members of the Mantua-Powelton Alliance have a chance to inject their own funds into Mantua's development market. As of fall 2020, the group was working on a strategic plan to determine how to deploy the $650,000 that Brandywine will provide on an annual basis through 2032. There is robust discussion about how the funds should be split between Powelton and Mantua, whether they should be spent down or invested in an endowment that produces interest in perpetuity, and what proportion of them should be dedicated to property-related activity as opposed to education, workforce training, and civic capacity-building. The choices are not straightforward. The fact that community representatives have a chance to make them at all is a testament to the tenacity of civic and community development organizations in insisting on being part of conversations about publicly subsidized, university-led development. But the resources that community organizations have available to them for the next twelve years will have an impact in the land market only if the groups receive the endorsement and material support of public sector agencies intent on preserving both deeply affordable rental housing and affordable home-ownership opportunities in Powelton and Mantua. Official recognition of nonfinancial assets built up over time by local residents would be welcome in this situation.

Rethinking Innovation

In recent years, innovation-themed urban development has proliferated quickly. As noted in the Introduction, Kayanan, Drucker, and Renski identify over fifty innovation districts in existence in the U.S. in 2020.[27] The economic rationale for this phenomenon is that "start-up activity has shifted back to dense cities and urban areas, which have the talent and diversity to generate them."[28] But it is not always easy to connect the dots between economic theories of innovation and the policies and strategies conceived to support contemporary urban innovation districts. Knowledge spillovers among firms can contribute to the concentration and growth of local economic activity, as can professional and personal networks among entrepreneurs. But the relationship between the proximity of talent and the commercialization of ideas is not linear, and the success of public policy in encouraging these spillovers and networks is highly context-dependent.[29] What is clear is that the power exerted by real estate in urban politics contributes to uncritical acceptance of the idea that newly built space is the crucial turnkey for innovation's emergence. Thus, property development incentives predominate in the innovation district policy model.

Reliance on real estate return as the animating force behind innovation-led economic development confines planners to the belief that only by attracting new residents and employees to newly constructed neighborhoods can cities generate vibrancy and prosperity. But ingenuity and vitality need not be the exclusive province of social elites.[30] All people are searching, in the words of Amartya Sen, for the means to live lives that they have reason to value.[31] While innovation districts may offer particularly favorable environments to enterprises seeded by university-derived medical and engineering discoveries, older neighborhoods whose existence preceded the new districts are sites of potential too. One need search no further for evidence of innovation, in fact, than the ideas for systems reform in youth services articulated by the Mantua Civic Association member quoted in Chapter 4. The political will and financial resources to organize and implement an integrated re-entry experience for young people returning from juvenile detention would be difficult to muster, but not for lack of innovative ideas. A successful such program would likely be enormously beneficial economically to individuals and families, as well as to the public sector in the form of reduced re-incarceration costs.

Even as they boost industrial innovation as conventionally conceived, public and academic institutions can design more economically inclusive policies. In her recent book *Putting Skill to Work*, Nichola Lowe examines dozens of place-based workforce institutions whose keen insight into the dynamics of skill and productivity expands the prospects of innovation sector employees without college degrees.[32] One of the places in which this inclusive innovation model has thrived is North Carolina's biotechnology sector, where intermediaries have "pulled down the career ladder" and provided employment and career advancement opportunities to non-college-educated job seekers. A key participant in this effort is a network of public community colleges that offer a certification called BioWork. The BioWork program trains and certifies about 750 people per year for employment in biopharmaceutical production and testing facilities. This program—which has enabled firms across the region to integrate biotechnology research with biomanufacturing—has contributed to the healthy growth of North Carolina's life sciences cluster. As Drexel, Brandywine, and the University City District have already shown, effective entrepreneurship development and workforce pipeline initiatives need not be philanthropic afterthoughts or concessionary social services programs. They can also be sources of cost-effectiveness and improved performance for employers.

Moving Toward Repair

Mantua and Powelton residents' mobilization in the 2010s—their strong determination to shape the terms on which innovation districts would come into being around them—demonstrates that past activism can be a source of inspiration and energy for civil society organizations. Even after the concept of "equitable development" had become commonplace, advocates still operated in a milieu where much of the political discourse reinforced the belief that low educational attainment, economic vulnerability, and encounters with the criminal justice system (i.e., life circumstances that prevented full participation in the innovation economy) were functions primarily of the limitations or pathology of those experiencing them.[33] A sense of community history was a crucial ingredient in counteracting these perceptions. Creating space to understand the historical antecedents of persistent social and economic distress in the neighborhoods adjacent to Schuylkill Yards and uCity Square lent efficacy to the struggle to win policies that would help avoid a soft version of the direct displacement that had occurred in the 1960s.

Scholars and commentators increasingly regard the historical record as a starting point for discussions about how to meet the challenges facing economically insecure communities of color in contemporary cities and regions.[34] But although they recognize the injustices committed during the urban renewal era, universities often do not reference the enduring impacts of history when discussing contemporary development projects in the neighborhoods adjacent to their campuses. The community benefits negotiation that enabled the Philadelphia City Council's passage of the Schuylkill Yards land use approvals in 2017 hewed to an ahistorical "mitigation" logic, confining discussion largely to measures that reduced or compensated for direct negative effects. While activists connected the dots between current and past development, their counterparties in the local political arena did not.

In negotiating the Schuylkill Yards Community Benefits Agreement, members of the Mantua-Powelton Alliance stayed, of necessity, within the narrow bounds of a mitigative logic. But the fact that a particular venue proved inhospitable to a broader conversation does not mean that a reparative planning approach—one that takes history more fully into account—is indefinitely out of reach. Public officials and university administrators have acknowledged that legal and social norms contributed to the political and economic marginalization of people of color during past waves of redevelopment; they also can come to recognize how current norms uphold that marginality, and how these norms discount longtime residents' investment in and attachment to places. In forcing such a recognition, activist planners can plant the seeds for changes to both academic discourse and public policy, such that nonfinancial investments in place come to count for more.

A NOTE ON SOURCES

As a faculty member at the University of Pennsylvania from 2008–2014, I taught the course "Introduction to Community and Economic Development." That course is what first brought me into contact with the neighborhoods that became the focal point of this book.

Embarrassingly, given my teaching specialization, I was not (and am not) a Philadelphian. For six years I commuted there from my home in Brooklyn, New York, riding an Amtrak train into the city several times a week and typically spending one or two nights in the home of a generous colleague. My Penn colleagues also educated me on Philadelphia politics and on the complicated ecosystems of community, civic, and social services organizations operating in the city's neighborhoods. The knowledge and contacts I gained through them enabled me to embed the teaching of community development research and practice within Philadelphia's specific local context.

After some false starts, I settled on a format for the introductory course that involved a series of exercises along an eleven-block stretch of Lancaster Avenue, a struggling commercial corridor about a mile to the north of Penn's campus. The first assignment asked students—master's degree candidates in City and Regional Planning—to describe a walk westward from 34th to 45th Street along the avenue, a diagonal thoroughfare that long predates the current street grid (originally a Native American trail, Lancaster became the state of Pennsylvania's first turnpike in 1795; the streetcar suburb that emerged in West Philadelphia in the mid-nineteenth century grew up around it). Later assignments entailed a retail market assessment, a housing market analysis for the neighborhoods surrounding the corridor, and a proposal for a public space intervention. Readings and guest speakers exposed the students to the institutions that had shaped the Lower Lancaster neighborhoods—West Powelton, Saunders Park, Belmont, Mantua, and Powelton Village—over time. These included government agencies, philanthropies, churches, community groups, associations of merchants, artists, and urban gardeners, and the two major universities that had given University City its name—the University of Pennsylvania and Drexel University.

In these years, I became aware of imminent changes in this section of West Philadelphia, catalyzed primarily by partnerships being initiated by Drexel, which seemed determined to match the luster and economic impact of its Ivy League neighbor. Under a dynamic new president, Drexel was engaging in strategic visioning for its campus, conducting outreach with nearby organizations, and crafting transformative development projects. At the same time, civic and community organizations along the corridor were also using planning to stake claims to neighborhood space. The Lower Lancaster neighborhoods lay outside the coverage area of the well-known West Philadelphia Initiatives undertaken by the University of Pennsylvania in the late 1990s and early 2000s, but it was clear that they stood to be profoundly affected by Drexel's adaptation of this model. Plans for innovation-driven development on both the eastern and the western edges of Drexel's campus prompted reflection on the continuities between twenty-first–century university-community politics and their mid-twentieth-century antecedents. The 2013 closure of the University City High School and its subsequent demolition to make way for a live/work/play innovation neighborhood called uCity Square riveted my attention, as did Drexel's announcement that it intended to redevelop its corner of University City in a manner consistent with equity and inclusion. The Obama administration's designation of a federal Promise Zone in neighborhoods along the corridor in 2014 sparked curiosity about the numerous overlapping zones and districts that university and government officials were now overlaying on neighborhoods where boundaries—between "safe" and "unsafe" areas, between town and gown, between the turfs of rival gangs—had long shaped community life.

The formal research for the book took place after I left Penn's faculty. In 2015, as a visiting researcher at the Center for Urban Research at the City University of New York Graduate Center, I obtained Internal Review Board (IRB) approval for a protocol entitled "Attitudes toward redevelopment in Philadelphia's Lower Lancaster corridor" and began key-informant interviews with university and government officials and neighborhood-based stakeholders. The interviews were structured around informants' thoughts about, opinions of, and aspirations for the uCity Square and Schuylkill Yards developments. To quote the script I used when I contacted potential interviewees, "my research is concerned with affected individuals' sense of their own capacity and power in the process of neighborhood change; with the demands they make on themselves and others in the context of that change; and, in this particular case, with their conceptions of what is possible for Lower Lancaster neighborhoods and their residents in the immediate future." I conducted the bulk of the interview research in the summer and fall of 2016, with a few additional interviews taking place in the spring of 2017. I returned to several of the original interviewees for follow-up conversations after the passage of the Schuylkill Yards Community Benefits Agreement in June of that year. Throughout, I was interested in what (if anything) interviewees thought residents of the neighborhoods closest to Drexel's innovation-themed redevelopment projects should be entitled to expect from them.

Over time, the importance of the Mantua and Powelton Village neighborhoods came into clearer focus, as did the key role of history. As a result of the latter, I included archival research as one of my methods, working both in the University of Pennsylvania's archives and in the Urban Archives at Temple University, which included the papers of the West Philadelphia Corporation as well as the clippings and photograph collections of the now-defunct *Philadelphia Evening Bulletin*. As noted in Chapter 4, the research process also involved attending meetings of the Mantua Civic Association between October 2015 and September 2017. Online searches of contemporary media coverage yielded other important details included in that chapter.

The historical sections of this book rely on rich, easily accessible, and expertly maintained document, media, and photo collections at the Penn and Temple Archives. Work that draws from these archives has been equally important to this non-historian—particularly John Puckett and Mark Frazier Lloyd's *Becoming Penn: The Pragmatic American University, 1950–2000* (2015); Richardson Dilworth and Scott Gabriel Knowles's edited volume *Building Drexel: The University and Its City, 1891–2016* (2017); Matthew Countryman's *Up South: Civil Rights and Black Power in Philadelphia* (2006); Guian McKee's *The Problem of Jobs: Liberalism, Race, and Deindustrialization in Philadelphia* (2008); and Thomas Sugrue's *Sweet Land of Liberty: The Forgotten Struggle for Civil Rights in the North* (2008). Ryan Good's work on the 2013 Philadelphia school closure debate was also very helpful, as were Edward Epstein's 2020 doctoral dissertation on Penn's work with West Philadelphia elementary and secondary schools in the 1960s and 1970s and Eve L. Ewing's *Ghosts in the Schoolyard: Racism and School Closings on Chicago's South Side* (2020). A late stage read of Michael Burawoy's essay on the ethnographic revisit helped me put a name to my methodological approach. Finally, the meaningful work of the many research assistants listed in the acknowledgments section helped make this book a reality.

Most of the people I interviewed for this book will recognize themselves within these pages, though confidentiality agreements prevent me from naming them in most cases. To all of you: I am very grateful for the time you spent with me, for your thoughts and insights, and for your dedication to the honoring of history and the maintenance of neighborhood identity and diversity in the Lower Lancaster corridor. Among people who I am able to identify, I would like to specially thank Pearl Battle Simpson, Walter Palmer, and A. J. Schiera.

At a meeting of the Mantua Civic Association on February 18, 2016, Mantua Community Planners founder Andrew Jenkins gave a presentation about the organization in which he asserted that "White people write too much of Black history." He reported having told one academic historian that "the history you have on our neighborhood is read by people like you—higher educators." The history he hoped to create, in contrast, would be accessible "for this neighborhood, in years to come, when it's a totally different-looking Mantua."

I have brought biases to this research both as a white person and as a representative of academia. I apologize for the errors of interpretation that have inevitably resulted. I admire the efforts of the Mantua Community Planners, the Mantua Civic Association, the Mount Vernon Manor Community Development Corporation, and the Powelton Village Civic Association to elevate and preserve the history and ongoing survival of their extraordinary neighborhoods.

NOTES

Introduction

1. The title of this introduction is borrowed from Lawrence Vale's *Purging the Poorest: Public Housing and the Design Politics of Twice-Cleared Communities* (Chicago, IL: University of Chicago Press, 2013).

2. "Analysis of Current and Anticipated Tax Yield to the City of Philadelphia from the University City Research and Development Center" (Philadelphia, PA: West Philadelphia Corporation, May 27, 1963), Box 11, Folder 12, West Philadelphia Corporation Records, Acc. 350, 701, Special Collections Research Center, Temple University Libraries, Philadelphia, PA.

3. "Statement on Renewal Plan for Unit III," Box 11 Folder 10, West Philadelphia Corporation Records, Acc. 350, 701, Special Collections Research Center, Temple University Libraries, Philadelphia, PA.

4. *West Philadelphia Corporation Fifth Annual Report* (Philadelphia, PA: West Philadelphia Corporation, February 1965), Box 1, Folder 5, West Philadelphia Corporation Records, Acc. 350, 701, Special Collections Research Center, Temple University Libraries, Philadelphia, PA.

5. See Margaret Pugh O'Mara, *Cities of Knowledge: Cold War Science and the Search for the Next Silicon Valley* (Princeton, NJ: Princeton University Press, 2015).

6. Drexel purchased the University City High School property in June 2014, a year after the school closed. Jenny DeHuff, "Drexel buys University City High School," *Philadelphia Inquirer*, June 17, 2014, https://www.inquirer.com/philly/business/20140617_Drexel_buys _University_City_High_School.html.

7. James Jennings, "Hip to Be uCity Square: Science Center Unveils New Vision, New Name," *Philadelphia Magazine*, September 16, 2015, https://www.phillymag.com/property /2015/09/16/hip-to-be-ucity-square-science-center-unveils-vision-new-name/.

8. Jerry Sweeney of Brandywine Realty Trust, quoted in Michael Tanenbaum, "Drexel Square officially opens at Schuylkill Yards in West Philly," *PhillyVoice*, June 11, 2019, https:// www.phillyvoice.com/drexel-square-opens-schuylkill-yards-west-philly-brandywine-realty -trust/.

9. According to one estimate, 70 and 80 percent of the people displaced by urban renewal projects nationwide were African American. See Robert Halpern, *Rebuilding the Inner City: A History of Neighborhood Initiatives to Address Poverty in the United States* (New York: Columbia University Press, 1995); Wendell E. Pritchett, "The 'Public' Menace of Blight: Urban Renewal and the Private Uses of Eminent Domain," *Yale Law and Policy Review* 21, no. 1 (2003), https://digitalcommons.law.yale.edu/ylpr/vol21/iss1/2; and Raymond A. Mohl, "The Second Ghetto and the 'Infiltration Theory' in Urban Real Estate," in *Urban Planning and the*

African American Community: In the Shadows, ed. June Manning Thomas and Marsha Ritz-dorf (Thousand Oaks, CA: Sage Publications, 1997), 58–74.

10. Martin E. Gold and Lynne B. Sagalyn, "The Use and Abuse of Blight in Eminent Do-main," *Fordham Urban Law Journal* 38, no. 4 (2011): 1119–73, https://ir.lawnet.fordham.edu/ulj/vol38/iss4/5/.

11. George Lipsitz, "Living Downstream: The Fair Housing Act at 50," in *The Fight for Fair Housing,* ed. Gregory D. Squires (New York: Routledge, 2017), 266–90; Devah Pager, Bart Bonikowski, and Bruce Western, "Discrimination in a Low-Wage Labor Market," *American Sociological Review* 74, no. 5 (2009): 777–99; Keeanga-Yamahtta Taylor, *Race for Profit: How Banks and the Real Estate Industry Undermined Black Homeownership* (Chapel Hill: Univer-sity of North Carolina Press, 2021).

12. Eugenie L. Birch, "From Science Parks to Innovation Districts: Research Facility De-velopment in Legacy Cities on the Northeast Corridor" (Philadelphia, PA: Penn Institute for Urban Research, 2015), 9, https://penniur.upenn.edu/uploads/media/20150730_From _Science_Parks_to_Innovation_Districts2.pdf. See also Bruce Katz and Julie Wagner, "The Rise of Innovation Districts: A New Geography of Innovation in America" (Washington, DC: Metropolitan Policy Program at Brookings, 2014), 1, https://www.brookings.edu/essay/rise -of-innovation-districts/; Richard Florida, "The Creative Class and Economic Develop-ment," *Economic Development Quarterly* 28, no. 3 (2014): 196–205; Battelle Technology Partnership Practice, "Driving Regional Innovation and Growth" (Association of Univer-sity Research Parks, August 2012), https://aurp.memberclicks.net/assets/documents/aurp _batelllereportv2.pdf.

13. Interview with author #6, July 14, 2016. In her book about the politics of eminent do-main in Philadelphia, Becher defines investment in property as "sacrifice of value of any kind—money, time, labor, love, or relationships," asserting that "Residents who demand a say in how a neighborhood will change and whether particular changes will enhance or detract from the community's value justify this demand through their past sacrifices to the commu-nity." Deborah Lynn Becher, *Private Property and Public Power: Eminent Domain in Phila-delphia* (Oxford: Oxford University Press, 2014), 8. Unless otherwise noted, all interviews were conducted in confidentiality, and the names of interviewees are withheld by mutual agreement.

14. See "Funeral for a Home" project, Temple University, Tyler School of Art and Archi-tecture. https://tyler.temple.edu/funeral-home.

15. See Samuel Stein, *Capital City: Gentrification and the Real Estate State* (London: Verso, 2019); Laura Wolf-Powers, "Understanding Community Development in a 'Theory of Action' Framework," *Readings in Planning Theory* (June 2015): 324–47, https://doi.org/10.1002 /9781119084679.ch16.

16. Lucy Kerman, "How Schuylkill Yards could change West Philly," *Radio Times,* WHYY, March 28, 2016, https://whyy.org/episodes/how-schuylkill-yards-could-change-west -philly-2/.

17. Interview with author #1, June 7, 2016.

18. Elizabeth Hinton, *From the War on Poverty to the War on Crime: The Making of Mass Incarceration in America* (Cambridge: Harvard University Press, 2016).

19. John Puckett and Mark Frazier Lloyd, *Becoming Penn: The Pragmatic American Uni-versity, 1950–2000* (Philadelphia: University of Pennsylvania Press, 2015), 254–56.

20. Puckett and Lloyd, *Becoming Penn,* 138.

21. The Kelo case turned on the question of whether it is constitutional for a government to condemn privately owned land and transfer it to another private owner for economic development purposes. While the court decided the case in favor of the City of New London, many state governments responded with laws and regulations making this type of property condemnation more difficult. See Gold and Sagalyn, "The Use and Abuse."

22. See Kelly L. Patterson and Robert Mark Silverman, "Institutions and the New Normal for Community Development," in *Schools and Urban Revitalization*, ed. Kelly L. Patterson and Robert Mark Silverman (New York: Routledge, 2014), 3–14.

23. John A. Fry, "Remarks by President John A. Fry" (Philadelphia, PA: Anthony J. Drexel Society Gala, November 17, 2012), https://drexel.edu/president/messages/speeches/2012/November/gala-2012/.

24. Jim Saksa, "With New Schuylkill Yards, Drexel and Brandywine Promise Development without Displacement," PlanPhilly, WHYY, March 8, 2016, https://whyy.org/articles/with-new-schuylkill-yards-drexel-and-brandywine-promise-development-without-displacement/.

25. Brentin Mock, "Urban Planners May Have Finally Found How to Get to Sesame Street," Grist, February 13, 2015, https://grist.org/cities/urban-planners-may-have-finally-found-how-to-get-to-sesame-street/amp/.

26. Loïc Wacquant, Tom Slater, and Virgílio Borges Pereira, "Territorial Stigmatization in Action," *Environment and Planning A: Economy and Space* 46, no. 6 (January 2014): 1270–80. The authors argue that "neighborhood taint is a new and distinctive phenomenon that crystallized at century's end, along with the sudden breakdown or gradual dissolution of the districts of relegation emblematic of the Fordist–Keynesian phase of industrial capitalism" (1273). I disagree; neighborhood taint has, in my view, been baked into the sociodynamics of urban real estate markets for as long as modern cities have existed. A particularly vicious brand of it exists with respect to majority-Black neighborhoods.

27. Hamish Kallin and Tom Slater, "Activating Territorial Stigma: Gentrifying Marginality on Edinburgh's Periphery," *Environment and Planning A: Economy and Space* 46, no. 6 (January 2014): 1351–68. See also Edward Glenn Goetz, *Clearing the Way: Deconcentrating the Poor in Urban America* (Washington, DC: Urban Institute Press, 2003).

28. Imogen Tyler, "Resituating Erving Goffman: From Stigma Power to Black Power," *Sociological Review* 66, no. 4 (December 2018): 744–65.

29. Martine August, "Challenging the Rhetoric of Stigmatization: The Benefits of Concentrated Poverty in Toronto's Regent Park," *Environment and Planning A: Economy and Space* 46, no. 6 (January 2014): 1317–33; Susan Clampet-Lundquist, "Moving over or Moving up? Short-Term Gains and Losses for Relocated HOPE VI Families," *Cityscape: A Journal of Policy Development and Research* 7, no. 1 (January 2004): 57–80.

30. Dr. Pearl Battle Simpson, interview with author, March 22, 2019. Dr. Simpson directed me to the 1967 film *In the Heat of the Night* for an example of a "Bottoms" neighborhood.

31. Hinton, *From the War on Poverty to the War on Crime.*

32. See Eddie S. Glaude, *Democracy in Black: How Race Still Enslaves the American Soul* (New York: Broadway Books, 2017). In an interview about the book published in *The Baffler*, Glaude states, "We've got to move from this philanthropic model, where racial equality is a loose expression of charitable enterprise, to actual racial justice.... That means a society built upon non-domination." Lindsay Gilbert, "When All Boats Aren't Lifted: Q & A with

Eddie Glaude," *The Baffler*, October 18, 2016, https://thebaffler.com/latest/interview-eddie
-glaude.

33. See Alexander Ferrer, "It's Time to Ditch the Stakeholder Discourse," Progressive City,
April 13, 2021, https://www.progressivecity.net/single-post/it-s-time-to-ditch-the-stakeholder
-discourse.

34. Michael Burawoy, *The Extended Case Method: Four Countries, Four Decades, Four
Great Transformations, and One Theoretical Tradition* (Berkeley: University of California
Press, 2009), 75.

35. Mary E. Pattillo, *Black on the Block: The Politics of Race and Class in the City* (Chicago: University of Chicago Press, 2007).

36. Burawoy, *Extended Case*, 131. Per Burawoy, this "archaeological" version of the ethnographic revisit lends historical depth to ethnography where there is no reference study.

Chapter 1

1. "400 Sleep in College Hall to Protest UCSC Policies College Hall Sit-in Extends into
Second Day," *Daily Pennsylvanian*, February 19, 1969, 1, 5.

2. Judith Ann Fowler, "Six Days in College Hall—'A Strange War in Which All Sides
Won,'" *Pennsylvania Gazette*, March 1969, 6–15.

3. "400 Sleep in College Hall," *Daily Pennsylvanian*.

4. "College Hall Sit-in Ends; Community Committee Forms," *Daily Pennsylvanian*, February 24, 1969, 1, 5.

5. "College Hall Sit-in Ends," *Daily Pennsylvanian*.

6. Berl Schwartz, "Sit-In Ends; Penn Students Claim Victory," *Philadelphia Evening Bulletin*, February 24, 1969. The remark that "nothing was destroyed" referred to the contrast
between the College Hall sit-in and student protests at other universities, notably Columbia.
Fowler's portrait in the *Gazette* emphasized courtesy and order: "No buildings were barricaded,
no offices broken into . . . no classes were dismissed or facilities smashed" (6–7). "Demonstrator
clean-up crews collected garbage and swept out classrooms, halls, and bathrooms daily. Their
sandwiches, oranges, coffee, and occasional homemade stew were shared with security
guards protecting files in the building" (8).

7. Fowler, "Six Days," 11.

8. Interview with author #40, October 20, 2016.

9. John Puckett and Mark Frazier Lloyd, *Becoming Penn: The Pragmatic American University, 1950–2000* (Philadelphia: University of Pennsylvania Press, 2015), 102. The connections binding the university, the Science Center, and the city included Penn Fine Arts
Dean G. Holmes Perkins, who chaired the Philadelphia City Planning Commission from
1958 to 1968; Penn Trustee Gustave Amsterdam, who chaired the Redevelopment Authority
from 1961 to 1968; and Penn Trustee Paul J. Cupp, Chairman of the Board of the Science Center from its inception in 1963 into the mid-1970s.

10. The history and racial politics of University City's development are also recounted by
Margaret Pugh O'Mara in Chapter 4 of *Cities of Knowledge: Cold War Science and the Search
for the Next Silicon Valley* (Princeton, NJ: Princeton University Press, 2015).

11. MacKenzie Carlson, "History of the University City Science Center," University Archives and Records Center, September 6, 2018, https://archives.upenn.edu/exhibits/penn
-history/science-center. The Philadelphia City Planning Commission designated the University
Redevelopment Area in 1948. Puckett and Lloyd note that starting in the late 1940s, Planning

Commission documents concerning West Philadelphia align with the university's campus development plans (Puckett and Lloyd, *Becoming Penn*, 33).

12. Carlson, "History." According to this official history of the University City Science Center, "Units 1 and 2 . . . were developed by Penn and Drexel in the late 1950s and early 1960s; the University City Science Center . . . was the primary redeveloper of Unit 3; Penn and Drexel continued to expand their campuses in Units 4 and 5, respectively."

13. John H. Mollenkopf, *The Contested City* (Princeton, NJ: Princeton University Press, 1988); Guian A. McKee, *The Problem of Jobs: Liberalism, Race, and Deindustrialization in Philadelphia* (Chicago: University of Chicago Press, 2019).

14. Edmund Bacon, the executive director of the City Planning Commission in this era, is still revered for his political deftness in using federal dollars to transform Center City Philadelphia.

15. McKee, *The Problem of Jobs*; Deborah Lynn Becher, *Private Property and Public Power: Eminent Domain in Philadelphia* (Oxford: Oxford University Press, 2014). A 1963 analysis cited by Becher found that in the 1950s, urban renewal projects in Philadelphia had demolished 6,200 housing units and constructed just 3,400.

16. McKee, *The Problem of Jobs*, 24–32.

17. Mollenkopf, *The Contested City*.

18. Puckett and Lloyd, *Becoming Penn*, 60–65.

19. *West Philadelphia Corporation First Annual Report* (Philadelphia, PA: West Philadelphia Corporation, December 1960), Box 1, Folder 3, West Philadelphia Corporation Records, Acc. 350, 701, Special Collections Research Center, Temple University Libraries, Philadelphia, PA.

20. *West Philadelphia Corporation Second Annual Report* (Philadelphia, PA: West Philadelphia Corporation, October 1961), Box 1, Folder 2, West Philadelphia Corporation Records, Acc. 350, 701, Special Collections Research Center, Temple University Libraries, Philadelphia, PA.

21. Puckett and Lloyd, *Becoming Penn*, 101.

22. Two entities were incorporated: the University City Science Center Corporation and the University City Science Institute. Other than Penn, the governing institutions for these entities were the Drexel Institute of Technology, the Philadelphia College of Pharmacy and Science, Presbyterian Hospital, and Temple University (Carlson, "History").

23. "University City Plans Development of Science Center for Research," *Daily Pennsylvanian*, October 29, 1963, 1–5.

24. Margaret Pugh O'Mara, *Cities of Knowledge: Cold War Science and the Search for the Next Silicon Valley* (Princeton, NJ: Princeton University Press, 2015).

25. "West Philadelphia Corporation" (Philadelphia, PA: West Philadelphia Corporation, undated brochure from late 1962 or early 1963), Box 1, Folder 2, West Philadelphia Corporation Records, Acc. 350, 701, Special Collections Research Center, Temple University Libraries, Philadelphia, PA.

26. Puckett and Lloyd, *Becoming Penn*, 92.

27. See also Eric C. Schneider, *The Ecology of Homicide: Race, Place, and Space in Postwar Philadelphia* (Philadelphia: University of Pennsylvania Press, 2020).

28. Meyerson left Penn in 1957 for a post at Harvard, returning to the university as its president in 1970. Eugenie L. Birch, "Reviving the Art of Biography," *Journal of Planning History* 10, no. 3 (2011): 175–79.

29. Puckett and Lloyd, *Becoming Penn*, 93–96. As Puckett and Lloyd show, the cases of Morningside Heights, Inc., in the Columbia University-adjacent neighborhoods of Upper Manhattan, and the Southeast Chicago Commission in the Kenwood-Hyde Park area abutting the University of Chicago were similarly effective efforts by universities to exert leverage over the machinery of urban renewal.

30. In addition to Puckett and Lloyd, see Mike Lyons, "Remembering a Murder That Changed West Philadelphia Forever and the Forgiveness That Followed," West Philly Local, July 27, 2016, https://www.westphillylocal.com/2016/07/27/remembering-a-murder-that -changed-west-philadelphia-forever-and-the-forgiveness-that-followed/ and "Powelton Village: University Expansion Destroyed a Community," Philadelphia Neighborhoods, December 4, 2012, https://philadelphianeighborhoods.com/2012/12/04/powelton-village-university -expansion-destroys-a-community/.

31. University of Pennsylvania, Drexel Institute of Technology, Presbyterian Hospital, Philadelphia College of Pharmacy and Science, and the Philadelphia College of Osteopathy.

32. "Developments in Our Institutional Area" (Philadelphia, PA: West Philadelphia Corporation, June 1958), Box 4, Folder 39, West Philadelphia Corporation Records, Acc. 350, 701, Special Collections Research Center, Temple University Libraries, Philadelphia, PA.

33. Leo Molinaro, letter to G. Holmes Perkins, January 20, 1961. Box 11, Folder 6, West Philadelphia Corporation Records, Acc. 350, 701, Special Collections Research Center, Temple University Libraries, Philadelphia, PA.

34. Stefan M. Bradley, *Upending the Ivy Tower: Civil Rights, Black Power and the Ivy League* (New York: New York University Press, 2021); Matt Delmont, "Making Philadelphia Safe for 'WFIL-Adelphia,'" *Journal of Urban History* 38, no. 1 (2012): 89–113; O'Mara, *Cities of Knowledge*, 190–91.

35. N. D. B. Connolly, *A World More Concrete: Real Estate and the Remaking of Jim Crow South Florida* (Chicago: University of Chicago Press, 2016); Beryl Satter, *Family Properties: How the Struggle over Race and Real Estate Transformed Chicago and Urban America* (New York: Henry Holt & Co., 2010). Akira Drake Rodriguez, *Diverging Spaces for Deviants: The Politics of Atlanta's Public Housing* (Athens: University of Georgia Press, 2021).

36. Raymond A. Mohl, "The Second Ghetto and the 'Infiltration Theory' in Urban Real Estate, 1940–1960," in *Urban Planning and the African American Community: In the Shadows*, ed. June Manning Thomas and Marsha Ritzdorf (Thousand Oaks, CA: Sage Publications, 1997), 58–75.

37. Thomas J. Sugrue, *Sweet Land of Liberty: The Forgotten Struggle for Civil Rights in the North* (New York: Random House, 2008); Matthew Countryman, *Up South: Civil Rights and Black Power in Philadelphia* (Philadelphia: University of Pennsylvania Press, 2007).

38. See McKee, *The Problem of Jobs*; Thomas J. Sugrue, *The Origins of the Urban Crisis: Race and Inequality in Postwar Detroit* (Princeton, NJ: Princeton University Press, 2005); James Wolfinger, *Philadelphia Divided: Race and Politics in the City of Brotherly Love* (Chapel Hill: University of North Carolina Press, 2007).

39. "Contract between the Redevelopment Authority of the City of Philadelphia and the West Philadelphia Corporation" (Philadelphia, PA: West Philadelphia Corporation, November 8, 1961), Box 1, Folder 89, West Philadelphia Corporation Records, Acc. 350, 701, Special Collections Research Center, Temple University Libraries, Philadelphia, PA.

40. West Philadelphia Corporation, *Second Annual Report*.

41. "West Philadelphia Corporation," Undated brochure.

42. *1962 Annual Report* (Philadelphia, PA: Philadelphia Redevelopment Authority, 1962), Box A-571, Redevelopment Authority Annual Reports, 1947–1970, Acc. 161.2, Philadelphia City Archives.

43. "Excerpt from 1960 Census Figures" (Philadelphia, PA: West Philadelphia Corporation, undated), Box 11, Folder 12, West Philadelphia Corporation Records, Acc. 350, 701, Special Collections Research Center, Temple University Libraries, Philadelphia, PA. These figures are also cited in a memo from West Philadelphia Corporation Executive Vice President Leo Molinaro to the WPC Board of Directors on March 20, 1963. These figures are slightly lower than those quoted in Chapter 1, which come from a different WPC memo produced in 1963 to estimate the gain in real estate value assessable for tax purposes that the Science Center and related development would produce.

44. "Analysis of Current and Anticipated Tax Yield to the City of Philadelphia From the University City Research and Development Center" (Philadelphia, PA: West Philadelphia Corporation, May 27, 1963), Box 11, Folder 12, West Philadelphia Corporation Records, Acc. 350, 701, Special Collections Research Center, Temple University Libraries, Philadelphia, PA.

45. Per the site www.theblackbottom.wordpress.com, the neighborhood "was framed by 33rd and 40th Streets on the east and west, and Lancaster/Powelton and Curie Boulevard (University Avenue) on the north and south." See also Pearl Battle Simpson, "The Black Bottom," in *The Black Bottom Picnic: A Collection of Essays, Poems and Other Musings* (Philadelphia, PA: self-published, 2005).

46. Countryman, *Up South.*

47. Dr. Pearl Battle Simpson, interview with author, March 22, 2019. Puckett and Lloyd also note the harmful influence of mass-transit improvements on the predominantly African American blocks surrounding Market Street in this area in the late 1940s (*Becoming Penn*).

48. Puckett and Lloyd, *Becoming Penn*, 103–7. Puckett and Lloyd conclude that the lack of mention of the Black Bottom in West Philadelphia Corporation or University of Pennsylvania planning documents suggests either that the term was "an African American cultural construction to which white elites, prior to the clearances, were not privy" or that the idea of the community acquired inflated significance in retrospect, due to a "halo effect" and sensationalized media coverage. My conjecture based on archival research is that officials deliberately chose not to use the name, both out of distaste and because it would have had a legitimating effect. They were certainly aware of the residents' level of organization and their interest in remaining in the neighborhood.

49. "'University City' Granted $317,500; Relocatees Promised 'Safe, Decent Quarters,'" *Philadelphia Tribune*, December 30, 1961.

50. Per the second working paper, "Through the use of social work skills social welfare needs can be uncovered as early as possible so that public and private resources can be brought to bear on the needs so rehabilitation might be extended and physical relocation can be a new start for a new person." The papers' tone alternated between the language of citizen empowerment (the first referred to the "grass roots" and to the "development of indigenous leadership") and that of ministerial condescension: "Based on the needs of those to be relocated an education program can be designed which should be of some help to those who are presently functioning at a low level of individual and social responsibility. A model apartment can be helpful in teaching home making skills, including budgeting, and a wide variety of helpful devices for better housekeeping can be built into the program." "Working Paper #1, Procedure in Relocation" (June 1962) and "Working Paper #2: Early Phases of Urban Renewal,

University City III—A Pilot Project" (November 15, 1962), Box 11, Folder 28, West Philadelphia Corporation Records, Acc. 350, 701, Special Collections Research Center, Temple University Libraries, Philadelphia, PA.

51. Puckett and Lloyd, *Becoming Penn*, 108. See also "Walk-Out Ends 'University City' Meeting; Redevelopment Official Unable to Say Which Homes in West Philadelphia Area Will Be Affected," *Philadelphia Tribune*, February 20, 1962.

52. Troy L. Chapman, memo to Richard J. Watson (Philadelphia, PA, February 1962), Box 11, Folder 28, West Philadelphia Corporation Records, Acc. 350, 701, Special Collections Research Center, Temple University Libraries, Philadelphia, PA.

Watson was the RDA's director of community relations. There are no archival records of the Citizens Committee for University City Urban Renewal Area Unit 3. Limited documentation of the committee's formation and activities exists in contemporary media accounts and in the files of the West Philadelphia Corporation, whose staff apparently took an interest in the group's activities and obtained their materials from the Redevelopment Authority.

53. Troy L. Chapman, memo to Richard J. Watson (Philadelphia, PA, April 12, 1962), Box 11, Folder 28, West Philadelphia Corporation Records, Acc. 350, 701, Special Collections Research Center, Temple University Libraries, Philadelphia, PA.

54. "Statement on Renewal Plan for Unit III," Box 11, Folder 10, West Philadelphia Corporation Records, Acc. 350, 701, Special Collections Research Center, Temple University Libraries, Philadelphia, PA.

This undated statement was appended to a 1965 letter written by a Citizens Committee member to Housing and Homes Finance Agency administrator Robert Weaver. I am conjecturing that it is a copy of the policy statement mentioned by Chapman. The policy statement supports the inference that the Citizens Committee's core membership consisted of homeowners in the eastern part of Unit 3 north of Filbert Street.

55. "City Appeases 2nd Sit-In Group in Housing Row," *Philadelphia Inquirer*, May 17, 1963. According to the article, the mayor sent the Redevelopment Authority's executive board a telegram stating: "Must respectfully insist that you convene the membership of the city's Redevelopment Authority at once in order to give immediate attention to complaints made by citizens from University City Unit 3, which I understand is under consideration by the Redevelopment Authority . . . I must insist that the authority take action on this either by way of withdrawing the plan or clarifying this situation with the people affected."

56. "City Appeases," *Philadelphia Inquirer*. Notably, that day's *Inquirer* also reported on backlash by union members against Mayor Tate's decision the previous day to a halt a city construction project in response to a May 14 sit-in by would-be Black tradespeople protesting effective whites-only employment at city construction sites. NAACP President and civil rights firebrand Cecil B. Moore, who was at the center of the demonstrations against discrimination by construction unions, also participated in the Citizens' Committee sit-in, and in the negotiation with Redevelopment Authority figures. The exclusion of Blacks from unionized construction employment continues to be a contentious issue in Philadelphia politics (see Chapter 4).

57. "City Appeases," *Philadelphia Inquirer*.

58. Richard A. Keiser, *Subordination or Empowerment?: African-American Leadership and the Struggle for Urban Political Power* (New York: Oxford University Press, 1997).

59. Leo Molinaro, memo to West Philadelphia Corporation executive board members (Philadelphia, PA: November 20, 1963), Box 11, Folder 12, West Philadelphia Corporation

Records, Acc. 350, 701, Special Collections Research Center, Temple University Libraries, Philadelphia, PA.

60. The hospital expansion site extended from Powelton Avenue on the north to Market Street on the south, and between 38th Street on the east and 40th Street on the west.

61. Molinaro, memo, November 20, 1963. Apparently the RDA's "compromise proposal" was equally unsatisfying to the Citizens Committee.

62. "Background on Controversial Seven Acre Parcel," (Philadelphia, PA: West Philadelphia Corporation, Summer 1966), Box 11, Folder 10, West Philadelphia Corporation Records, Acc. 350, 701, Special Collections Research Center, Temple University Libraries, Philadelphia, PA.

63. A history of the University City High School project, in both concept and execution, can be found in Edward M. Epstein, "Race, Real Estate and Education: The University of Pennsylvania's Interventions in West Philadelphia, 1960–1980" (dissertation, University of Pennsylvania, 2020). Per Epstein, the West Philadelphia Corporation's advocacy for the high school was one element of the Universities-Related Schools program, a broad-based effort it pursued to enrich the curricula of West Philadelphia's K-12 schools and "increase college access for their graduates" (8).

64. "Comments on University City Urban Renewal Area Unit #3 Prepared for the Redevelopment Authority of Philadelphia" (Philadelphia, PA: West Philadelphia Corporation, March 19, 1963), Box 11, Folder 11, West Philadelphia Corporation Records, Acc. 350, 701, Special Collections Research Center, Temple University Libraries, Philadelphia, PA.

65. Leo Molinaro, letter to Francis Lammer (Philadelphia, PA, December 1, 1963). Box 11, Folder 9, West Philadelphia Corporation Records, Acc. 350, 701, Special Collections Research Center, Temple University Libraries, Philadelphia, PA.

66. "Agreement between the School District of Philadelphia and the West Philadelphia Corporation," Box 4, Folder 85, West Philadelphia Corporation Records, Acc. 350, 701, Special Collections Research Center, Temple University Libraries, Philadelphia, PA.

67. Leo Molinaro, memo to WPC Board of Directors (Philadelphia, PA: May 20, 1963), Box 11, Folder 13, West Philadelphia Corporation Records, Acc. 350, 701, Special Collections Research Center, Temple University Libraries, Philadelphia, PA.

68. Epstein, "Race, Real Estate and Education," 252.

69. The circumstances under which incumbent Unit 3 residents would have been able to afford redeveloped housing on the controversial seven acres are disputed. WPC board and staff members claimed that the housing in Clay's proposal would be unaffordable to the existing residents, using this as a rationale for the argument that the RDA should abandon housing as a goal. RDA records suggest that there were several scenarios under which incumbent Unit 3 residents might have been able to afford new or rehabilitated housing. A federal program to provide rent subsidy to households dislocated by urban renewal was proposed in 1965, and was mentioned by Francis Lammer as a potential tool, but this program ultimately was not included in the U.S. Senate's 1965 housing legislation. See Francis J. Lammer, memo to Redevelopment Authority Senior Staff (Philadelphia, PA: June 4, 1965), Box 11, Folder 12, West Philadelphia Corporation Records, Acc. 350, 701, Special Collections Research Center, Temple University Libraries, Philadelphia, PA. On the fate of the rental subsidy program, see Wendell E. Pritchett, *Robert Clifton Weaver and the American City: The Life and Times of an Urban Reformer* (Chicago: University of Chicago Press, 2014), 257–59.

70. Puckett and Lloyd's account of this saga amply characterizes Unit 3 residents' fate as an injustice. However, it portrays Clay's redevelopment proposal as a single unsatisfactory option that the RDA had no choice but to reject. It does not address the likelihood that with the WPC's cooperation, a solution could have been found that enabled organized Black Bottom homeowners to remain in the part of the neighborhood that University City High School ultimately occupied.

71. Weaver received an emotional appeal from UCCDC Vice President (and Unit 3 resident) Franny Robinson in October 1965 ("Letter to Robert Weaver from Franny Robinson, October 7, 1965," Box 11, Folder 10, "Unit 3, Clay Group Lawsuit," West Philadelphia Corporation Records, Acc. 350, 701, Special Collections Research Center, Temple University Libraries, Philadelphia, PA). Although President Johnson had signed legislation creating the Department of Housing and Urban Development in September 1965, it would be several more months before he named Weaver its first secretary. See Pritchett, *Robert Clifton Weaver and the American City*, 262–75.

72. The following year, another, civic association, Powelton Village Neighbors, prevailed in a similar conflict with Drexel University by petitioning HUD to the effect that the university's redevelopment plans failed to comply with Title I of the 1949 Housing Act. This type of claim, rather than a civil rights argument, may have been a better legal strategy for UCCDC. See "Powelton Village Neighbors Petition to Robert Weaver and Warren Phelan," Box 11, Folder 10, West Philadelphia Corporation Records, Acc. 350, 701, Special Collections Research Center, Temple University Libraries, Philadelphia, PA.

73. Leo Molinaro, memo to developers in University City Unit #3 (Philadelphia, PA: August 5, 1966), Box 11, Folder 12, West Philadelphia Corporation Records, Acc. 350, 701, Special Collections Research Center, Temple University Libraries, Philadelphia, PA.

74. Richardson Dilworth, letter to Gustave Amsterdam (Philadelphia, PA: October 17, 1966), Box 11, Folder 15, West Philadelphia Corporation Records, Acc. 350, 701, Special Collections Research Center, Temple University Libraries, Philadelphia, PA.

75. *West Philadelphia Corporation Seventh Annual Report* (Philadelphia, PA: West Philadelphia Corporation, February 1967), Box 1, Folder 7, 12–14, West Philadelphia Corporation Records, Acc. 350, 701, Special Collections Research Center, Temple University Libraries, Philadelphia, PA. The report announced that Unit 3 clearance had been greenlighted for a variety of uses including "renovated and new housing units for those homeowners currently living in the area." New moderate-income housing was not built in the Unit 3 footprint until the 1980s, however.

76. "1000 Families to Lose Homes if Education Board Builds University City Science School: Area 3 Citizens Up in Arms Over the 'Settlement,'" *Philadelphia Tribune*, October 22, 1966. This article details an early October delegation to HUD's office in Washington, DC, led by Philadelphia NAACP and CORE chapter officials, aimed at persuading Secretary Weaver to reverse course and enjoin the Redevelopment Authority from selling the disputed land to the School District.

77. "A Special Report to the Friends of University City," (Philadelphia, PA: West Philadelphia Corporation, September 1968), Box 1, Folder 8, "Eighth Annual Report," West Philadelphia Corporation Records, Acc. 350, 701, Special Collections Research Center, Temple University Libraries, Philadelphia, PA.

78. Volunteer Community Resources Center, "Unit 3, Clay Group Lawsuit," (Philadelphia, PA: West Philadelphia Corporation, May 1968), Box 11, Folder 10, West Philadelphia

Corporation Records, Acc. 350, 701, Special Collections Research Center, Temple University Libraries, Philadelphia, PA.

79. Iris Marion Young, *Inclusion and Democracy* (Oxford: Oxford University Press, 2010), 57.

80. "West Philadelphia Corporation" brochure, 1963; "Special Report," 1968.

81. Kirk R. Petshek, *The Challenge of Urban Reform: Policies & Programs in Philadelphia* (Philadelphia, PA: Temple University Press, 1973), 247.

82. Paul Lyons, *The People of This Generation the Rise and Fall of the New Left in Philadelphia* (Philadelphia: University of Pennsylvania Press, 2003); Fowler, "Six Days."

83. Historian Wayne Glasker also credits the sit-in with prompting administrators to admit more Black students from a wider variety of economic backgrounds to Penn. Wayne Glasker, *Black Students in the Ivory Tower African American Student Activism at the University of Pennsylvania, 1967–1990* (Amherst: University of Massachusetts Press, 2009), 26.

84. For example, Clark and Dilworth aggressively implemented civil service standards that produced significant gains in Black municipal employment and supervised a new Commission on Human Relations charged with responding to employment and housing discrimination. Keiser, *Subordination or Empowerment?*; Countryman, *Up South*; Wolfinger, *Philadelphia Divided*. McKee, *The Problem of Jobs*, highlights the city's proactive stance toward deindustrialization and structural unemployment. For more on Bacon's achievements, see Gregory L. Heller, *Ed Bacon: Planning, Politics, and the Building of Modern Philadelphia* (Philadelphia: University of Pennsylvania Press, 2016); and Scott Gabriel Knowles, ed., *Imagining Philadelphia: Edmund Bacon and the Future of the City* (Philadelphia: University of Pennsylvania Press, 2009).

85. McKee, *The Problem of Jobs*, 10. See also Countryman, *Up South*; Sugrue, *Sweet Land*; Wolfinger, *Philadelphia Divided*.

86. Petshek, *The Challenge*, 253.

87. G. Holmes Perkins, interview with Walter Phillips (1976), *Walter Massey Phillips Oral Histories*, Special Collections Research Center, Temple University Libraries, Philadelphia, PA. Phillips was himself an icon of midcentury Philadelphia liberalism who spent hundreds of hours of his retirement recording interviews with his former contemporaries in government and civic association circles. As noted above, he ran unsuccessfully as a reform Democrat against incumbent Mayor James Tate in 1963.

88. See Danielle Allen, *Talking to Strangers: Anxieties of Citizenship Since Brown vs. Board of Education* (Chicago: University of Chicago Press, 2004).

89. Walter Palmer, interview with author, September 21, 2016.

Chapter 2

1. "Statement of the Board of Trustees" (Philadelphia, PA: University of Pennsylvania Board of Trustees, February 23, 1969), Box 188, University Archives and Records Center, University of Pennsylvania. The agreement stated that Renewal Housing Inc., the community nonprofit tapped to rehabilitate housing in Unit 3, would designate five members of the commission, with student members designated by the "community of demonstrators" and faculty members designated by the University's Faculty Senate. Five seats were to be filled by university trustees.

2. "Statement of the Board of Trustees."

3. "Statement of the Board of Trustees."

4. Cathy Barlow, "Minutes of the First Meeting of the Commission on University-Community Development, March 10" (Philadelphia, PA: 1969), Box 188, University Archives and Records Center, University of Pennsylvania.

5. At the March 24 meeting, for example, Andrew Jenkins of Mantua Community Planners presented a proposal on behalf of his organization's gang-control work. See Lillian G. Burns, "Quadripartite Commission, March 24, 1969" (Philadelphia, PA, 1969), Box 188, University Archives and Records Center, University of Pennsylvania.

6. John Eckman, letter to John Ames Ballard, Esq, December 15, 1969, Box 188, University Archives and Records Center, University of Pennsylvania.

7. John C. Hetherston, "Commission on University-Community Development, Meeting Minutes" (Philadelphia, PA, March 17, 1969), Box 188, University Archives and Records Center, University of Pennsylvania.

8. "Resolution of April 28" (Philadelphia, PA, Commission on University-Community Development, 1969), Box 188, University Archives and Records Center, University of Pennsylvania.

9. Meeting minutes also report recurrent conflict about whether the commission's meetings should be open to members of the press (namely, the student newspaper, the *Daily Pennsylvanian*).

10. Martin Meyerson, letter to Professor Howard J. Lesnick, February 8, 1971, Box 188, University Archives and Records Center, University of Pennsylvania.

11. "'We Are Mantua!' Mantua Transformation Plan" (Philadelphia, PA: Kitchen & Associates on behalf of Mt. Vernon Manor Inc., 2013), 24. http://www.mvmcdc.org/wp-content/uploads/2015/11/mantua-transformation-plan.pdf.

12. Hank Resnik, *Turning on the System: War in the Philadelphia Public Schools* (New York: Pantheon Books, 1970). According to the Powelton Village Civic Association, Powelton Village was created in 1852 through the subdivision of the Samuel Powel estate.

13. "'We Are Mantua!,'" 24; Puckett and Lloyd, *Becoming Penn*, 92.

14. John Puckett, "Mantua Hall: From Tower to Square," West Philadelphia Collaborative History, accessed March 19, 2020, https://collaborativehistory.gse.upenn.edu/stories/mantua-hall-tower-square; John F. Bauman, *Public Housing, Race, and Renewal: Urban Planning in Philadelphia, 1920–1974* (Philadelphia, PA: Temple University Press, 1987).

15. Countryman, *Up South*, 191, Epstein, "Race, Real Estate and Education," 39. Epstein, drawing on the work of geographer Katherine McKittrick, asserts that gang territory represented Black communal space. See Katherine McKittrick, "On Plantations, Prisons, and a Black Sense of Place," *Social & Cultural Geography* 12, no. 8 (2011): 947–63.

16. Among three Black men of that generation that I interviewed, all spoke proudly of the fierceness of the gangs they had associated with and of injuries they had sustained or narrowly avoided.

17. After finishing high school, Jenkins had been stationed in Germany while in the military and had then played professional basketball in Italy for two years before returning to Philadelphia.

18. John Puckett, "Mantua Against Drugs," West Philadelphia Collaborative History, accessed May 21, 2021, https://collaborativehistory.gse.upenn.edu/stories/mantua-against-drugs.

19. One Powelton Village interviewee for this study had worked for YGS in 1969 as part of her orientation to a master's degree program in education, organizing arts activities, games,

and tutoring on special traffic-free play streets. Interview with author #7, August 8, 2016, Philadelphia, PA.

20. Joseph R. Daughen, "Youths Found 'People Who Cared,' Tell of W. Phila Gang Reformation," *Philadelphia Evening Bulletin*, April 8, 1966; "W. Philadelphia Unit Praised for Self-Improvement Plan," *Philadelphia Evening Bulletin*, October 29, 1966; Nancy Burden, "Jean Wrice Pitches In To Help Teen Girls," *Philadelphia Evening Bulletin*, June 26, 1968; Nicholas W. Stroh, "West Phila. Poverty Council Put in Shade by 2 Community Groups," *Philadelphia Evening Bulletin*, June 26, 1968; Desmond Ryan, "'Young Greats' Sponsor W. Phila Pallet Repair Shop," *Philadelphia Evening Bulletin*, December 1, 1968.

21. Claude Lewis, "Bored W. Phila. Boy Leads a Gang To Escape a Tedious, Crowded Life," *Philadelphia Evening Bulletin*, February 26, 1968.

22. Interview with author #1, June 7, 2016, Philadelphia, PA.

23. Resnik, *Turning on the System*, 162–63.

24. Paul Davidoff's well-known article "Advocacy and Pluralism in Planning" had created a stir in the profession in 1965 with its exhortation to planners to assist local groups whose disenfranchisement from the political process left them vulnerable to the whims and designs of bureaucrats and property investors. I could find no evidence, however, that Davidoff worked with Mantua organizations while serving on the planning faculty of the University of Pennsylvania from 1958 to 1965.

25. Nancy Burden, "Amazing Mrs. Hamilton Gives Mantua a Boost," *Philadelphia Evening Bulletin*, June 16, 1968.

26. "Mantua Group Lists Redevelopment Goals, Hemphill Joins Talks," *Philadelphia Inquirer*, February 7, 1967. Hemphill was Alexander Hemphill, who ran unsuccessfully against incumbent James Tate in the Democratic mayoral primary the following June.

27. McKee, *The Problem of Jobs*, 119–24. The selective patronage movement achieved visible victories at companies such as Tasty Baking, local Pepsi Cola bottling companies, and the oil refineries that lined the Lower Schuylkill River.

28. See McKee, *The Problem of Jobs*, 182–210.

29. Thomas J. Sugrue, "Affirmative Action from below: Civil Rights, the Building Trades, and the Politics of Racial Equality in the Urban North, 1945–1969," *Journal of American History* 91, no. 1 (January 2004): 145–73. As noted in Chapter 1, the high point of the Citizens Committee of University City Redevelopment Area Unit 3's campaign to save homes in the Black Bottom—a May 16, 1963, sit-in at the office of Mayor James Tate—occurred just two days after demonstrators occupied his office protesting his failure to enforce Philadelphia's construction industry antidiscrimination policy.

30. Countryman, *Up South*, 185; 214.

31. Countryman, *Up South*, 261–71.

32. Sigmund C. Shipp, "The Road Not Taken: Alternative Strategies for Black Economic Development in the United States," *Journal of Economic Issues* 30, no. 1 (1996): 79–95. Shipp argues that Washington, and later the Community Development Corporation movement, had favored accommodation and appeasement, while Garvey and Du Bois advocated self-sufficiency through freestanding intra-racial economic cooperation. This second path is "the road not taken" in community development policy. See also Laura Warren Hill and Julia Rabig, "Toward a History of the Business of Black Power," in *The Business of Black Power: Community Development, Capitalism and Corporate Responsibility in Postwar America*, ed. Laura Warren Hill and Julia Rabig (Rochester, NY: University of Rochester Press, 2012).

33. See Countryman, *Up South*; McKee, *The Problem of Jobs*.

34. Paul Grimes, "Penn Extends a Hand to Mantua, but Ghetto Blacks Are Suspicious," *Philadelphia Evening Bulletin*, February 9, 1969.

35. Russell L. Ackoff, "A Black Ghetto's Research on a University," *Operations Research* 18, no. 5 (1970): 761–71.

36. Ackoff, "A Black Ghetto's Research on a University."

37. Paul Grimes, "Mantua Revisited: Still Blighted but Self-Help Is Paying Dividends," *Philadelphia Evening Bulletin*, February 12, 1969; Albert V. Gaudiosi, "All 'Reneged' on Pledges to Poor, Wrice Charges," *Philadelphia Evening Bulletin*, June 24, 1969; William Thompson, "Young Great Society Is Hoping for a Miracle," *Philadelphia Evening Bulletin*, March 9, 1979.

38. Kos Semonski, "Phila. Trims Model City Plan by a Third," *Philadelphia Evening Bulletin*, January 15, 1968.

39. Robert Rafsky, "Manta Mini School is Disbanding; Staff Now Proposes 'Street Schools,'" *Philadelphia Evening Bulletin*, June 28, 1970; Resnik, *Turning on the System*, 161–87. Despite the disorganization reported by official sources, community-based interviewees five decades later testified to the school's effectiveness: "We were able to reach these kids and have them really learn where they were not learning in their regular schools . . . the attendance was much greater, and they were proud to be going to their own school." "All the schools loved us because they gave us all their worst kids . . . gave us all the kids with the worst problems. We had the best couple of years in that building—those kids learned more and did more. We made the school district look so bad, they cut the program." Interview with author #1, June 7, 2016, Philadelphia, PA.

40. Peter Binzen, "'Grantsmanship' Hampers Mantua Ties, Penn Official Says," *Philadelphia Evening Bulletin*, November 9, 1972.

41. Ackoff, "Black Ghetto," 769.

42. "Black capitalism: a study of struggle," *Business Week*, January 16, 1971.

43. "Mantua: Self-Help Theory," *Philadelphia Evening Bulletin*, November 28, 1969.

44. Peter Binzen, "U.S. Delays Mantua Renewal Plan In Dispute Over Role of Community," *Philadelphia Evening Bulletin*, February 19, 1970.

45. See Stephen Hess, *The Professor and the President: Daniel Patrick Moynihan in the Nixon White House* (Washington, DC: Brookings Institution Press, 2015).

46. Bayard Brunt and Albert V. Gaudiosi, "Wrice Blasts E. Powelton Group in Power Struggle," *Philadelphia Evening Bulletin*, January 24, 1971.

47. Harry G. Toland, "For a meaningful '76, Black Help," *Philadelphia Evening Bulletin*, September 29, 1969. See also Scott Gabriel Knowles, "Staying Too Long at the Fair: Philadelphia Planning and the Debacle of 1976," in *Imagining Philadelphia: Edmund Bacon and the Future of the City*, ed. Scott Gabriel Knowles (Philadelphia: University of Pennsylvania Press, 2009), 78–111.

48. PAAC, administered by concert promoter and operative Sam Evans, was known as an arm of the city's Democratic patronage machine under Mayor Tate. See Countryman, *Up South*, 296–300; Keiser, *Subordination or Empowerment?*, 99.

49. "'We Are Mantua!,'" 4.

50. A 1975 article profiling a children's book about Wrice written by author Jean Horton Berg stated, "He has assisted big industry in race relations, helped end the Watts (Calif.) riots, given counsel to [Pennsylvania] Gov. Shapp, and worked with the Episcopal Diocece of

Philadelphia, among other groups . . . Miss Berg was an eyewitness when Mr. Wrice aided during the unrest at her alma mater, the University of Pennsylvania, several years ago. 'When other black groups were handing out literature trying to stir people up, Herman calmed them down and got the whites and blacks to talk to one another.'" Eleanor Eby, "Children's Reading Round Table Book for October Salutes a Healer of Local Gang Wounds," *Philadelphia Inquirer*, October 19, 1975.

51. Alfonso Brown Jr., "One-Time Gang Leader in Phila. Now Helping Youths in Iowa," *Philadelphia Evening Bulletin*, February 22, 1978; Bill Gaither, "Herman Wrice 1939–2000," *Powelton Post*, May 2000. The motivation for Wrice's Iowa move is unclear. Gaither's obituary attributed it to Wrice's disappointment and frustration in the aftermath of an unsuccessful challenge to 3rd District City Council Member Lucien Blackwell.

52. Alfonso Brown Jr., "Ex-Leader Won't Return to Help W. Phila. Group," *Philadelphia Evening Bulletin*, September 18, 1978.

53. "Mantua: Self-Help Theory," *Philadelphia Evening Bulletin*, November 28, 1969.

54. Agis Sapulkas, "Moratorium on Housing Subsidy Spells Hardship for Thousands," *New York Times*, April 16, 1973.

55. These are not Rizzo's words but a retrospective characterization of his message by liberal Republican politician Thacher Longstreth. Countryman, *Up South*, 313.

56. Elizabeth Hinton, *From the War on Poverty to the War on Crime: The Making of Mass Incarceration in America* (Cambridge, MA: Harvard University Press, 2016).

57. Timothy J. Lombardo, *Blue-Collar Conservatism: Frank Rizzo's Philadelphia and Populist Politics* (Philadelphia: University of Pennsylvania Press, 2018).

58. Rizzo's endorsement of President Nixon's reelection bid in 1972 also left Philadelphia well-positioned with respect to federal urban funding.

59. Walter Naedele, "28-Home Renewal in Mantua Gets Tentative OK for U.S. Funds," *Philadelphia Evening Bulletin*, January 27, 1974; Laura Murray, "Planners OK Home Units in W. Phila.," *Philadelphia Evening Bulletin*, July 17, 1974. Buildings in the Section 236 program were expected to house a combination of tenants paying market and below-market rent.

60. Alfonso Brown Jr., "Project in Mantua Revived," *Philadelphia Evening Bulletin*, January 19, 1978.

61. Funding also came through from the U.S. Economic Development Administration for a multipurpose recreation center and library at 34th and Haverford Streets. This facility, completed in 1978, was also part of the Mantua Community Planners' original design for the neighborhood.

62. Clifton O. Lee, "W. Phila. Neighborhood is rising from ashes of the past," *Philadelphia Evening Bulletin*, July 8, 1979.

63. Epstein, "Race, Real Estate and Education," 9. Epstein's sympathetic yet critical evaluation of the Universities-Related Schools initiative concludes that its sponsors at the West Philadelphia Corporation "tended to put public relations ahead of real change in the schools."

64. A less charitable interpretation of the facts is that the WPC had no interest in supporting an innovative curriculum for what would clearly be a predominantly Black student body whose parents were unaffiliated with the neighborhood's universities.

65. Epstein, "Race, Real Estate and Education," 269.

66. Jessica Lee Oliff, "University City High School: An Experiment in Innovative Education, 1959–1972" (Thesis, University of Pennsylvania, 2000), 109–10.

67. Scott Gabriel Knowles, Jason Ludwig, and Nathaniel Stanton, "The Promise of a New Century: Drexel and the City Since the 1970s," in *Building Drexel: The University and Its City, 1891–2016*, ed. Richardson Dilworth and Scott Gabriel Knowles (Philadelphia, PA: Temple University Press, 2017), 371–98. Mantua is also assumed to be the model for "Northton" (and Powelton Village for the "Village") in Elijah Anderson's 1990 book *Streetwise* (Chicago: University of Chicago Press), which investigates the relationships between middle-class and "underclass" residents of two adjacent neighborhoods.

68. Gaither, *Herman Wrice*; Kendall Wilson, "Dr. Herman Wrice, 61, was dedicated and fearless," *Philadelphia Tribune*, March 14, 2000. Gaither's obituary asserts that Wrice returned to Mantua at the urging of Russell Ackoff, the Wharton professor who authored the *Operations Research* article cited earlier in this chapter.

69. Yvonne Latty, "Mantua Drug Warrier Dies—Herman Wrice Stricken in Fla. Before March," *Philadelphia Inquirer*, March 11, 2000; Glenn A. McCurdy, "Activism of Herman Wrice Touched Hundreds of Lives," *Philadelphia New Observer*, February 14, 2001.

70. Walter Palmer, interview with author, September 21, 2016.

71. The record should reflect, however, that the organizations were masculinist; women tended not to have a path to leadership within them. Relatedly, interviewees mentioned that while many YGS and MCP alumni had "made good," others had died violent deaths or spent decades in prison.

Chapter 3

1. John A. Fry, "Keynote Address," *Economy League of Greater Philadelphia: Leadership Exchange*, October 25, 2013, https://drexel.edu/president/messages/speeches/2013/October/economy-league/.

2. James Simmie, "Critical Surveys Edited by Stephen Roper Innovation and Space: A Critical Review of the Literature," *Regional Studies* 39, no. 6 (2005): 789–804.

3. European Commission, *Dgs XIII and XVI RITTS and RIS Guidebook* (Brussels, BE: Regional Actions for Innovation, 1996).

4. Joseph A. Schumpeter, *Business Cycles: A Theoretical, Historical, and Statistical Analysis of the Capitalist Process* (New York: McGraw-Hill, 1939).

5. Alfred Marshall, *Principles of Economics* (London: Macmillan, 1890).

6. Jane Jacobs, *The Economy of Cities* (London: Weidenfeld, 1968).

7. Henry Etzkowitz and Loet Leydesdorff, "The Dynamics of Innovation: From National Systems and 'Mode 2' to a Triple Helix of University–Industry–Government Relations," *Research Policy* 29, no. 2 (2000): 109–23. See also D. B. Audretsch and M. P. Feldman, "R&D Spillovers and the Geography of Innovation and Production," *American Economic Review* 86, no. 3 (1996): 630–40.

8. O'Mara, *Cities of Knowledge*; Ann Markusen et al., *The Rise of the Gunbelt: The Military Remapping of Industrial America* (New York: Oxford University Press, 1991).

9. See Susan Christopherson and Jennifer Clark, *Remaking Regional Economies: Power, Labor, and Firm Strategies in the Knowledge Economy* (London: Routledge, 2016); J. Clark, H.-I Huang, and J. P. Walsh, "A Typology of 'Innovation Districts': What It Means for Regional Resilience," *Cambridge Journal of Regions, Economy and Society* 3, no. 1 (2010): 121–37; AnnaLee Saxenian, *Regional Advantage: Culture and Competition in Silicon Valley and Route 128* (New York: ACLS History E-Book Project, 2005).

10. Bruce Katz and Julie Wagner, "The Rise of Innovation Districts: A New Geography of Innovation in America" (Washington, DC: Metropolitan Policy Program at Brookings, 2014), 1, https://www.brookings.edu/essay/rise-of-innovation-districts/.

11. James Jennings, "Hip to be uCity Square: Science Center Unveils Vision, New Name," *Philadelphia Magazine*, September 16, 2015, https://www.phillymag.com/property/2015/09/16/hip-to-be-ucity-square-science-center-unveils-vision-new-name/.

12. Dustin C. Read, "Case Studies in Innovation District Planning and Development" (Herndon, VA: NAIOP Research Foundation, 2016), 21, https://www.naiop.org/en/Research-and-Publications/Reports/Case-Studies-in-Innovation-District-Planning-and-Development.

13. Dustin Read and Drew Sanderford, "Innovation Districts at the Cross Road of the Entrepreneurial City and the Sustainable City," *Journal of Sustainable Real Estate* 9, no. 1 (January 2017): 131–52.

14. Read and Sanderford, "Innovation Districts," 136.

15. Read and Sanderford, "Innovation Districts," 142.

16. Eugenie L. Birch, "From Science Parks to Innovation Districts: Research Facility Development in Legacy Cities on the Northeast Corridor" (Philadelphia, PA: Penn Institute for Urban Research, 2015), https://penniur.upenn.edu/uploads/media/20150730_From_Science_Parks_to_Innovation_Districts2.pdf.

17. See also Jennifer Clark, *Uneven Innovation: The Work of Smart Cities* (New York: Columbia University Press, 2020), 95–123.

18. uCity Square and Schuylkill Yards both required significant changes to the Philadelphia zoning code, for example, which the City Planning Commission orchestrated in collaboration with local city council member Jannie Blackwell. Just before Blackwell left office, in December 2019, she brought legislation to the council that would have made it much more difficult to operate food trucks around the Drexel campus. She withdrew the proposal after an outcry of protest from vendors and the public.

19. For example, the financing plan for the Cortex Innovation Community in St. Louis, Missouri (associated with Washington University, the University of Missouri St. Louis, and St. Louis University), relies on concessionary rents in city-owned buildings, federal New Markets and historic tax credits, a $12 million state tax credit for land assembly, and a $168 million city TIF bond. The city of Scottsdale issued $81 million in municipal debt to acquire land for the Arizona State-affiliated SkySong development (Read, "Case Studies," 14–21).

20. Harley F. Etienne, *Pushing Back the Gates: Neighborhood Perspectives on University-Driven Revitalization in West Philadelphia* (Philadelphia: Temple University Press, 2013), 17.

21. Richardson Dilworth, "Drexel, Philadelphia, and the Urban Ecology of Higher Education," in *Building Drexel: The University and Its City, 1891–2016*, ed. Richardson Dilworth and Scott Gabriel Knowles (Philadelphia: Temple University Press, 2017), 7–25. Dilworth compares Drexel with New York City's Cooper Union and Pratt Institute, and with the school that would become Philadelphia's University of the Arts.

22. Dilworth, "Drexel," 15.

23. Brown and Keener Urban Design, "Powelton Village Directions 2011 Neighborhood Plan" (Philadelphia, PA: Powelton Village Civic Association, 2011), 16.

24. Dilworth, "Drexel," 21; Knowles, Ludwig, and Stanton, "The Promise," 371–98.

25. Brown and Keener, "Powelton Village," 16.

26. Knowles, Ludwig, and Stanton, "The Promise," 387.

27. John Kromer and Lucy Kerman, *West Philadelphia Initiatives: A Case Study in Urban Revitalization* (Philadelphia: University of Pennsylvania Office of the President and Fels Institute of Government, 2015).

28. Kromer and Kerman, *West Philadelphia Initiatives*, 44–46.

29. Meagan M. Ehlenz, "Neighborhood Revitalization and the Anchor Institution: Assessing the Impact of the University of Pennsylvania's West Philadelphia Initiatives on University City," *Urban Affairs Review* 52, no. 5 (2016): 714–50.

30. Etienne, *Pushing Back*, 31. In addition to Etienne (2013), Puckett and Lloyd (2012), and Kromer and Kerman (2015), see Judith Rodin, *The University and Urban Revival: Out of the Ivory Tower and into the Streets* (Philadelphia: University of Pennsylvania Press, 2007).

31. Puckett and Lloyd, *Becoming Penn*, 340.

32. John Fry, as quoted in Knowles, "The Promise," 396.

33. *Drexel Institute of Technology: A Look at Tomorrow* (Philadelphia, PA, 1964), Campus Expansion Program Records, Collection UR.10.011, Drexel University Archives.

34. Jeannine Keefer, "The End of Urban Renewal: Area V and Drexel's Expansion into Powelton Village," in *Building Drexel: The University and Its City, 1891–2016*, ed. Richardson Dilworth and Scott Gabriel Knowles (Philadelphia: Temple University Press, 2017), 218–32.

35. James Wolfinger, "Drexel, Urban Renewal, and Civil Rights," in *Building Drexel: The University and Its City, 1891–2016*, ed. Richardson Dilworth and Scott Gabriel Knowles (Philadelphia: Temple University Press, 2017), 202–15.

36. Keefer details bitter conflict *among* civic organizations in Powelton Village during the 1960s and 1970s, with some groups favoring conciliation with Drexel and others determined to oppose all campus expansion. Powelton Neighbors and the Powelton Village Civic Homeowners Association (from which today's Powelton Village Civic Association is descended) focused on the integrity of the neighborhood's built environment. East Powelton Concerned Residents, a more politically radical and tactically confrontational group, had an agenda that encompassed structural social issues.

37. Brown and Keener, "Powelton Village," ix.

38. Brown and Keener, "Powelton Village," 16.

39. Powelton Village Civic Association, "Constitution and Bylaws" (Philadelphia: Powelton Village Civic Association, revised 2018), https://pvca1.files.wordpress.com/2018/08/pvca-constitutionbylaws-1806.pdf.

40. Powelton residents often associate their mission to preserve architecture and promote owner-occupancy with an attachment to the neighborhood's progressive past. As described in Chapter 2, the community was well-known in the 1960s and 1970s as an enclave of the New Left; it was home to founders of the antiwar group the Philadelphia Resistance as well as several key members of the white antiracist organization People for Human Rights. Housing co-operatives and intentional communities, including Quaker-affiliated homes that served as havens for men who had resisted the Vietnam War draft, numbered among its stately Victorian residences. An interviewee who had moved to the neighborhood in the 1990s remarked, "I really love this neighborhood. . . . The idea that Powelton Village was an enclave that was progressive, inclusive, diverse—I think that's the community a lot of us came to." Interview with author, June 5, 2016, Swarthmore, PA.

41. Brown and Keener, "Powelton Village," 61.

42. Interview with author, June 5, 2016, Swarthmore, PA.

43. Knowles, Ludwig, and Stanton, "The Promise," 375.

44. "'We Are Mantua!,'" 27.

45. 3rd District City Council representative Jannie Blackwell was a central figure in the neighborhood's inter-organizational disputes. Conflict between Blackwell and the leadership of the Mantua Community Planners dated to Herman Wrice's challenge of her husband Lucien Blackwell in the city council election of 1976. Long-standing contention erupted into litigation in 2011, after a representative of Philadelphia's Department of Parks and Recreation, allegedly at Blackwell's behest, disposed of the contents of an office that Mantua Community Planners had used at the James L. Wright recreation center. Blackwell's loyalties lay with a competing organization, the Mantua Community Improvement Coalition. Animosity between Blackwell and Jenkins persisted but became less significant as the Mantua Civic Association evolved as the successor to MCP.

46. The business model for a HUD Section 236 project involves a mix of tenants, some paying subsidized rent using federal Section 8 vouchers and some paying market rent. By 2010, Mount Vernon Manor had no market-rate tenants; although the rents were fairly low by Philadelphia standards, the development could not attract people whose incomes enabled them to exercise a choice about where to live.

47. Diamond earned a joint degree in law and city planning from Penn in 1979. He describes Jenkins as having been a "mythic figure" in West Philadelphia at the time.

48. Enmities and burned bridges that had dogged Jenkins from his days at the Redevelopment Authority, combined with the widespread perception that he and other board members had neglected the well-being of Mount Vernon Manor's tenants, prompted Philadelphia city officials to insist on a replacement board. The financial and physical deterioration of the complex was, in this author's judgment, the product of many factors, including poor-quality original construction; the complexities of HUD Section 236's arcane subsidy structure; a lack of on-site social services for a struggling tenant population; and the ill-preparedness of Jenkins and the other directors for the difficult and often tedious work involved in supervising government-subsidized housing.

49. Choice Neighborhoods was the Obama Administration's answer to the HOPE VI program for severely distressed government-subsidized housing.

50. Interview with author #29, July 7, 2016.

51. Kitchen & Associates, *Mantua Transformation Plan Community Input Report* (Philadelphia, December 2011).

52. Interview with author #6, July 14, 2016; interview with author #31, August 16, 2016. Another interviewee referred to needing representation from "all corners . . . because we had six gangs here." Interview with author #10, September 16, 2016.

53. LISC also facilitated capacity-building and strategic planning for the boards of the Mount Vernon Manor LLC and the Mantua Civic Association.

54. Interview with author #31, August 16, 2016.

55. The renovation's first stage involved a tax credit equity allocation from the Pennsylvania Housing Finance Authority and City of Philadelphia Neighborhood Stabilization Program funds (dedicated to revitalizing neighborhoods in the wake of the 2008 financial crisis). The Mount Vernon Manor LLC later became the Mount Vernon Manor Community Development Corporation, a nonprofit, and in 2017 obtained financing for Phase II of the complex's rehabilitation.

56. This included a Byrne Criminal Justice Innovation Grant (2012) a federal Promise Zone designation (2013), and a U.S. Department of Education Promise Neighborhoods grant (2016).

57. One community leader had reportedly likened the groups in Mantua in the early 2000s to "crabs in a bucket." Interview with author #9, September 16, 2016. The "We Are Mantua!" process was widely acknowledged to have created neutral ground on which they could articulate common goals and pursue common interests.

58. Interview with author #5, July 8, 2016.

59. "'We Are Mantua!,'" 84.

60. Office of the President of Drexel University, *Transforming the Modern Urban University: Drexel University Campus Master Plan* (Philadelphia, PA: Drexel University, 2011), 1.

61. Office of the President of Drexel University, *Transforming*, 10.

62. Inga Saffron, "Changing Skyline: Drexel's Big Plans," *Philadelphia Inquirer*, September 8, 2012, https://www.inquirer.com/philly/home/20120907_Changing_Skyline__Drexel_s_big_plans.html.

63. In 2012, these lots were being used for parking, athletics, and urban agriculture. Behind the Science Center buildings that fronted on Market Street, they had the appearance of desolate, mostly unused space.

64. John A. Fry, "Remarks by President John A. Fry" (Philadelphia, PA: Anthony J. Drexel Society Gala, November 17, 2012), https://drexel.edu/president/messages/speeches/2012/November/gala-2012/.

65. Ryan M. Good, "Neighborhood Schools and Community Development: Revealing the Intersections through the Philadelphia School Closure Debate," *Journal of Planning Education and Research*, February 2019, https://doi.org/10.1177/0739456x19839769.

66. See Ryan M. Good and Katharine L. Nelson, "With a Little Help from Our Friends: Private Fundraising and Public Schools in Philadelphia," *Journal of Education Policy* 36, no. 4 (2020): 480–503.

67. An interviewee who graduated from the school in the 1990s said: "My mother actually cried because she didn't want me to go to UC High School—but all the other high schools were full and UC was kind of the dumping ground high school. And it was very much that kind of experience. My friends and I joke that it was like being in [the movie] *Lean on Me*—a cross between *Lean on Me* and *Sister Act* because I had music—I was a musician—we had a very strong music program. But that's all we had. There wasn't a lot of classes, there wasn't a lot of discipline." Interview with author #21, March 16, 2017.

68. Kati Stratos, Tonya Wolford, and Adrienne Reitano, "Philadelphia's Renaissance Schools Initiative after Four Years," *Perspectives on Urban Education* 12, no. 1 (2015), https://www.urbanedjournal.org/archive/volume-12-issue-1-spring-2015/philadelphia%e2%80%99s-renaissance-schools-initiative-after-four-years/; Dale Mezzacapa, "What Went Wrong with Promise Academies?" The Notebook, April 1, 2015, https://thenotebook.org/articles/2015/04/01/what-went-wrong-with-promise-academies/. The school had also entered into a partnership with the Netter Center for Community Partnerships at the University of Pennsylvania that focused on post-secondary planning.

69. "Schools recommended for closure were identified based on four school-specific metrics: academic performance, building utilization, building condition, and cost savings. Local groups analyzing the recommendations found that poor and African American

students stood to be disproportionately affected by the restructuring" (Good, "Neighborhood Schools," 4).

70. "UNIFIED: University City High School's Fight to Keep its Community Together" (video), https://www.uchstimecapsule.com/the-fight-13.html.

71. Interview with author #13, October 19, 2016.

72. Ryan M. Good, "Invoking Landscapes of Spatialized Inequality: Race, Class, and Place in Philadelphia's School Closure Debate," *Journal of Urban Affairs* 39, no. 3 (2016): 358–80. For work on Chicago's parallel experience, see Eve L. Ewing, *Ghosts in the Schoolyard: Racism and School Closings on Chicago's South Side* (Chicago: University of Chicago Press, 2020).

73. In an interview, Schiera noted a divide among advocates about what, exactly, it was important to preserve. Alumni and longtime community members who remembered the razing of homes and businesses in the Black Bottom to construct the school were attached to the building and site. Students, who were more attached to one another and their teachers, focused on persuading School District administrators to move their school community intact to a new location if the school building could not be saved. In Schiera's view, this tension complicated advocacy efforts.

74. Interview with author, June 21, 2016.

75. See, for example, Natalie Kostelni, "$1B plan to transform University City site," *Philadelphia Business Journal*, June 12, 2015, https://www.bizjournals.com/philadelphia/morning_roundup/2015/06/wexford-university-city-hs-powelton-village.html.

76. "Homepage," Wexford Science & Technology, May 9, 2021, https://wexfordscitech.com/.

77. Natalie Kostelni, "uCity Square: Science Center, Wexford's vision for West Philly innovation hub," *Philadelphia Business Journal*, September 16, 2015, https://www.bizjournals.com/philadelphia/blog/natalie-kostelni/2015/09/ucity-square-science-center-wexford-west-philly.html. Four acres—those occupied by the University City High School building itself—remained "a reserved spot for the possibility of constructing another public school." Jenny DeHuff, "Drexel bounds closer to buying UCHS," *Philadelphia Inquirer*, June 13, 2014, https://www.inquirer.com/philly/news/politics/20140613_Drexel_bounds_closer_to_buying_UCHS.html.

78. Jennings, "Hip to be uCity Square."

79. "Drexel and Brandywine Trust Partner on 'Schuylkill Yards' Innovation Development" (Philadelpha, PA: Office of University Communications, Drexel University, March 2, 2016).

80. Natalie Kostelni, "Drexel, Brandywine to develop new $3.5B neighborhood called Schuylkill Yards," *Philadelphia Business Journal*, March 2, 2016, https://www.bizjournals.com/philadelphia/morning_roundup/2016/03/drexel-brandywine-schuylkill-yards-university-city.html. See also Melissa Romero, "Drexel University Unveils Massive $3.5B Schuylkill Yards Development Plans," *Curbed Philly*, March 2, 2016, https://philly.curbed.com/2016/3/2/11147980/drexel-unveils-schuylkill-yards-renderings.

81. The uCity Square and Schuylkill Yards projects are sometimes referred to as components of a University City innovation district and sometimes as separate innovation neighborhoods, innovation communities, or innovation ecosystems. A 2017 Brookings Institute monograph identifies a "University City-Center City innovation district" that encompasses a

1.5-square-mile area beginning at 17th Street in downtown Philadelphia. See Scott Andes, Jason Hachadorian, Bruce Katz, and Jennifer S. Vey, *Connect to Compete: How the University City-Center City Innovation District can help Philadelphia excel globally and serve locally* (Washington, DC: Brookings Institute, May 2017).

82. "Redevelopment Assistance Capital Program - Grant Releases 1986 through 5/1/20," State of Pennsylvania Office of the Budget, 2021, https://www.budget.pa.gov/Programs/RACP /Pages/Main%20Page.aspx.

83. See "Leverage Your Location," uCity Square, 2021, https://ucitysquare.com/tax-incentives/.

84. Raymond A. Mohl, "Planned Destruction: The Interstates and Central City Housing," in *From Tenements to the Taylor Homes: In Search of an Urban Housing Policy in Twentieth-Century America*, ed. Kristin M. Szylvian, Roger Biles, and John F. Bauman (University Park: Pennsylvania State University Press, 2000), 226–45; Wendell Pritchett, "The 'Public' Menace of Blight: Urban Renewal and the Private Uses of Eminent Domain," *Yale Law & Policy Review* 21, no. 1 (2003), 1–52.

85. Keeanga-Yamahtta Taylor, *Race for Profit: How Banks and the Real Estate Industry Undermined Black Homeownership* (Chapel Hill: University of North Carolina Press, 2019); June Manning Thomas, *Redevelopment and Race: Planning a Finer City in Postwar Detroit* (Detroit: Wayne State University Press, 2013).

86. John Pløger, "Millennium Urbanism - Discursive Planning," *European Urban and Regional Studies* 8, no. 1 (2001): 63–72. See also Raphael Fischler, "Strategy and History in Professional Practice: Planning as World-Making," in *Spatial Practices*, eds. Helen Liggett and David C. Perry (London: Sage, 1996), 13–59.

87. "With the positive re-evaluation of the 'neighborhood' in urban planning and politics, many groups have gained an interest in claiming to represent a neighborhood community. They will utilize symbolic politics in order to prove their claims. Sometimes . . . a community is built, in part, as a result of such actions." Philip Kasinitz, "The Gentrification of 'Boerum Hill': Neighborhood Change and Conflicts over Definitions," *Qualitative Sociology* 11, no. 3 (1988): 163–82.

Chapter 4

1. The amendments converted several industrial parcels along John F. Kennedy Boulevard and Market Streets near 30th Street to a CMX-5 zoning designation permitting high-density mixed-use development.

2. Jim Saksa, "Planning Commission Hears Community Concerns, Supports Rezoning for First Phase of Schuylkill Yards," Plan Philly, WHYY, January 18, 2017, https://whyy.org /articles/planning-commission-hears-community-concerns-supports-rezoning-for-first -phase-of-schuylkill-yards/.

3. In Philadelphia, a tradition of "councilmanic prerogative" dictates that land use and development approvals move forward in the city's legislative body at the behest of the council member representing the district in which the development is proposed.

4. Saksa, "Planning Commission."

5. John A. Fry, "Schuylkill Yards Announcement," Presidential Speeches, Drexel University Office of the President, March 2, 2016, https://drexel.edu/president/messages/speeches /2016/March/2016-schuylkill-yards/.

6. Lindy also endowed the Lindy Center for Civic Engagement, which coordinates service learning and community volunteering for Drexel students.

7. Dan Eldridge, "Drexel Will Share Its Expertise with the Community at New Dorn-sife Center," Flying Kite Media, June 24, 2014, http://www.flyingkitemedia.com/devnews /dornsifecenter062414.aspx.

8. "Home," Dornsife Center for Neighborhood Partnerships, accessed June 16, 2021, https://drexel.edu/dornsifecenter/.

9. "At Drexel, Community Comes Together as Dragons Stay Apart," Dornsife Center for Neighborhood Partnerships, April 8, 2020, https://drexel.edu/dornsifecenter/news/news -archive/2020/April/At-Drexel-Community-Comes-Together-as-Dragons-Stay-Apart/.

10. Interview with author #36, September 15, 2016.

11. Founded in 1997, the UCD is a special services district whose approximately $15 mil-lion in annual revenue comes primarily from the institutional and corporate members of its board. While it incorporates many West Philadelphia institutions and businesses into its gov-ernance structure, UCD was closely identified at its founding with Penn's West Philadelphia Initiatives. Kromer and Kerman, *West Philadelphia Initiatives*.

12. See Paige Gross, "Science Center Is Hosting Its First Cohort of Free STEM Workforce Development Training," Technical.ly Philly, Technically Media, June 17, 2020, https:// technical.ly/philly/2020/06/17/science-center-bulb-first-cohort-free-stem-workforce -development-training/.

13. In 2018, 72 percent of WPSI program participants completed their programs, and 91 percent of these graduates were placed in jobs. The average wage at placement was $14.54 per hour, and 6- and 12-month retention rates were greater than 80 percent. The program significantly outperforms government-funded workforce initiatives. See Bruce Katz and Me-gan Humes, *West Philadelphia Skills Initiative: A Model for Urban Workforce Development* (Philadelphia, PA: Nowak Metro Finance Lab, Drexel University, 2019).

14. "West Philadelphia Public School Initiative," Community Outreach, Drexel Univer-sity School of Education, accessed July 20, 2020, https://drexel.edu/soe/partners/community/.

15. "Science Leadership Academy Middle School Opens in Powelton; Opening Cele-bration Sept 20," West Philly Local, September 16, 2016, http://www.westphillylocal.com/2016 /09/16/science-leadership-academy-middle-school-opens-in-powelton-opening-celebration -sept-20/. SLAMS later moved to a second temporary location in the University City Science Center.

16. Bill Hangley, "Powel-SLAMS Construction Project Finally Breaks Ground," Chalk-beat Philadelphia, December 9, 2019, https://philadelphia.chalkbeat.org/2019/12/9/22186570 /powel-slams-construction-project-finally-breaks-ground.

17. Philadelphia Industrial Development Corporation President John Grady, as quoted in Hangley above. At the end of 2019, Grady left this quasi-public entity to become the head of Northeast U.S. operations for Wexford Science + Technology LLC.

18. Brown and Keener, "Powelton Village," 3.

19. Educational politics in Mantua and Powelton are vexingly complicated. The catch-ment for Powel School and the Science Leadership Academy begins at Spring Garden Street, the border of Powelton Village. Children in Mantua are assigned to the Morton McMichael School on Fairmount Avenue in the northern part of the neighborhood. Both Powel and SLAMS currently have spaces for "out-of-catchment" students that are available to Mantua parents, and the new school would offer more such spaces. Mantua activists, however, fought hard in 2012 and 2013 to save the McMichael School—their neighborhood school—from closure, and many are fiercely determined that their children succeed there. The effort to

preserve and improve McMichael is a gesture of racial solidarity (and McMichael is, like Powel/SLAMS, a Drexel-assisted school), but one outcome of loyalty to McMichael is the reduced likelihood that Mantua-based children will attend the new school at uCity Square.

20. Interview with author #5, July 7, 2016; interview with author #9, September 16, 2016; interview with author #13, October 20, 2016.

21. Meagan M. Ehlenz, "Neighborhood Revitalization and the Anchor Institution: Assessing the Impact of the University of Pennsylvania's West Philadelphia Initiatives on University City," *Urban Affairs Review* 52, no. 5 (March 2016): 714–50; Samantha Melamed, "The Penn Alexander Effect: Is There Any Room Left for Low-Income Residents in University City?" *Philadelphia Inquirer*, November 1, 2018, https://www.inquirer.com/philly/news/penn -alexander-university-city-west-philly-low-income-affordable-housing-20181101.html. Melamed notes that between the school's opening and the 2017–18 school year, Black students went from making up 57 percent of Penn Alexander's student body to 21 percent; students qualifying for free meals declined 9 percentage points, from 51 percent to 42 percent, between 2012 to 2013 and 2017 to 2018.

22. Lynda Rubin, "Finance and Facilities Committee Report: June 13, 2019," Alliance for Philadelphia Public Schools, June 20, 2019, https://appsphilly.net/2019/06/20/finance-and -facilities-committee-report-june-13-2019/.

23. Interview with author #4, July 8, 2016.

24. Interface Studio, V. Lamar Wilson Associates & Community Design Collaborative, *University City High School/Drew School Site Reuse: Community Input and Design Workshop* (Philadelphia, PA: People's Emergency Center, March 2014), 5.

25. Interview with author #13, October 20, 2016. "When the District closed the school, we knew the School District was going to sell the site, but we had no idea that Drexel was going to try to purchase the site—or we knew that they were going to try, but what were they looking for? They made us think that there was no plan . . . and that doesn't work. That doesn't ensure that the community interest will be as supported as it should be."

26. Philadelphia City Council, *An ordinance to amend the Philadelphia Zoning Maps by changing the zoning designations of certain areas of land located within an area bounded by Powelton Avenue, Lancaster Avenue, 37th Street, Warren Street, 36th Street, Filbert Street and 38th Street, and by revising use and dimensional regulations in that area of the City, under certain terms and conditions,* Bill No. 140437-A, introduced in Council May 15, 2014, 16.

27. "To the extent the Owner develops the Site to have greater than 2.7 million gross square feet of building space (the 'Additional Space'), the Owner shall make a contribution to a fund for the benefit of the Powel School, the McMichael School and any district public school on the Site, to be shared equally among those schools (the 'Contribution'). Owner's Contribution shall be made following the expiration of 60 days from the issuance of a final Occupancy Permit for any building(s) that contains the Additional Space. The amount of the Contribution shall be calculated on the following formula: an amount equal to 1% of the hard core and shell costs of the Additional Space."

28. Philadelphia City Council, Bill No. 140437-A, 14.

29. Interview with author #4, July 8, 2016.

30. Interview with author #5, July 8, 2016.

31. It was explained to me that alternation between meeting locations was deliberate. It helped to identify the organization with all of Mantua, not with one or another of its historically antagonistic subsections.

32. The February 18, 2016, meeting of the Mantua Civic Association featured a Mantua history presentation and gospel performance by Jenkins in honor of Black History Month.

33. Author's notes, May 19, 2016.

34. See Countryman, *Up South*, 74–177.

35. Spencer was a professional artist and member of the Mantua Community Planners organization who led a successful youth mentoring program, the Philadelphia Anti-Graffiti Network (PAGN), under Mayor Wilson Goode in the 1980s. The Philadelphia Mural Arts Project, now an independent organization, was originally an arm of PAGN. Some Mantua Civic Association members were resentful of the Philadelphia Mural Arts Project, arguing that Spencer had not received sufficient credit for its inception.

36. Mike Lyons, "As Developers (and Students) Descend on Mantua, Residents Look to Rezone," West Philly Local, May 4, 2016, http://www.westphillylocal.com/2016/05/03/as -developers-and-students-descend-on-mantua-residents-look-to-rezone/.

37. Jake Blumgart, "Mantua Residents Want to Downzone Their Neighborhood. Does Their Councilwoman?" PlanPhilly, WHYY, June 8, 2016, https://theasthmafiles.org/sites /default/files/artifacts/media/pdf/planphilly_mantua_residents_want_to_rezone_their _neighborhood._does_their_.pdf.

38. Blackwell explained that she had reservations about restricting owners' ability to sub-divide their own homes. Others pointed to the councilwoman's close relationships with some of the developers who were acquiring property in Mantua.

39. Jake Blumgart, "Why Does Philadelphia Love Downzoning So Much?" PlanPhilly, WHYY, November 2, 2017, https://whyy.org/articles/why-does-philadelphia-love-downzoning -so-much/.

40. Blumgart, "Why Does Philadelphia Love Downzoning So Much?"

41. "'We Are Mantua!,'" 29.

42. From 2001 through 2010, the median annual number of sheriff sale transactions in Ward 24, which coincides with Mantua and Powelton Village, was 75.5. From 2011 through 2019, the corresponding number was 123, a 63 percent increase as compared with a 23 percent increase citywide over the same timeframe (City of Philadelphia Department of Records).

43. The project was sponsored by Temple University's Tyler School of Art through a grant from the Pew Charitable Trusts.

44. "'We Are Mantua!,'" 29.

45. The Philadelphia Land Bank became operational in 2015. By 2019, it held 2,200 parcels formerly owned by other public agencies (the Department of Public Property, the Housing Authority, and the Redevelopment Authority) and had acquired 463 formerly privately owned properties by purchasing them through a foreclosure sales process. It had disposed of 132 properties. See "Strategic Plan & Performance Report 2019" (Philadelphia, PA: Philadel-phia Land Bank, 2019), https://secureservercdn.net/104.238.71.140/k05.f3c.myftpupload.com /wp-content/uploads/2019/07/2019_StrategicPlan_DRAFTREPORT_PublicRelease_060519 _PRINT-6.5.19-REDUCED.pdf.

46. Author's notes, May 19, 2016.

47. Countryman, *Up South*, 144–48; Sugrue, "Affirmative Action."

48. David Hamilton Golland, *Constructing Affirmative Action: The Struggle for Equal Employment Opportunity* (Lexington: University Press of Kentucky, 2011).

49. Tom Ferrick, "Despite Pledges to Diversify, Building Trades Still Mostly White Males," AxisPhilly, June 10, 2013, http://web.archive.org/web/20170222134309/http://axisphilly.org

/article/despite-pledges-to-change-phillys-building-trades-still-dominated-by-white-males/. If members of the city's majority-minority laborers' union were removed, whites comprised 81 percent. AxisPhilly was a public service news website housed in Temple University's Center for Public Interest Journalism. While the site won awards for its coverage, Temple discontinued it in 2014, after two years of operation.

50. Malcolm Burnley, "In 2017, Is White Supremacy Still Alive and Well in This Philadelphia Building Trades Union?" WHYY, July 25, 2017, https://whyy.org/articles/in-2017-is-white-supremacy-still-alive-and-well-in-this-philadelphia-building-trades-union/.

51. One interviewee recalled a meeting with University of Pennsylvania officials in the early 1970s at which he had taken officials to task for the underrepresentation of Blacks on University City construction projects. Interview with author #10, September 16, 2016.

52. Sugrue, "Affirmative Action," 173.

53. Sugrue, "Affirmative Action," 173.

54. Michael B. Katz, "Why Don't American Cities Burn Very Often?" *Journal of Urban History* 34, no. 2 (2008): 185–208.

55. For a recent example, see Mayor's Advisory Commission on Construction Industry Diversity, "Report and Recommendations" (Philadelphia, PA, 2009), http://www.econsult.com/wp-content/uploads/2014/09/031609_MACCID_Full_Report-1.pdf. Since 2006, the city's Office of Economic Opportunity has also published an annual disparity study analyzing the availability and utilization of minority-, women-, and disabled-owned enterprises (M/W/DSBEs) on city and quasi-public contracts as well as reporting on the utilization of minority construction workers on projects requiring Economic Opportunity Plans.

56. City of Philadelphia, Bill No. 140437-A, 8.

57. According to the 2019 disparity study, the utilization rate for minority workers on projects with Economic Opportunity Plans was 34 percent (compared with an "availability" of 45 percent). The utilization rate for Black workers was 18 percent, as against an "availability" of 27 percent. Office of Economic Opportunity, "Annual Disparity Study Fiscal Year 2019" (City of Philadelphia Department of Commerce, 2020), https://www.phila.gov/media/20200826084552/OEO-FY19-Disparity-Study.pdf.

58. The goals stated in the Economic Opportunity Plan were reproduced in the text of the June 14, 2014, community benefits agreement:

> The following construction contract goals have been set for the project: Local Residents: 50%. Drexel University in a joint venture with Wexford Science and Technology agrees to exhaust Best and Good Faith Efforts to employ minority persons and females in its workforce of apprentices and journeymen at the following levels: Minority Journeymen—32% of all journey hours worked across all trades; Female Journeypersons—2% of all hours worked across all trades; Minority Apprentices: 50% of all hours worked by all apprentices; Female Apprentices: 7% of all hours worked by all apprentices. (City of Philadelphia, Bill No. 140437-A, 8)

Another section of the plan articulated similar goals related to the issuance of construction and professional services contracts to minority- and female-owned businesses.

59. Holly Otterbein, "Can Kenney Make White-Dominated Building Trades More Diverse?" *Philadelphia Magazine*, January 12, 2016, https://www.phillymag.com/citified/2016/01/12/jim-kenney-john-dougherty-building-trades/; The Editorial Board, "Minority Firms Face

Too Little Progress: Editorial," *Philadelphia Inquirer,* June 10, 2019, https://www.inquirer.com/opinion/editorials/philly-report-minority-share-city-contracts-20190610.html.

60. Interview with author #13, October 20, 2016.

61. Interview with author #6, July 14, 2016.

62. Interview with author #6, July 14, 2016.

63. Interview with author #6, July 14, 2016.

64. Jacob Adelman, "Drexel Outlines Ambitious Plans to Build Business-Residential Enclave," *Philadelphia Inquirer,* March 2, 2016, https://www.inquirer.com/philly/business/20160303_Drexel_chooses_developer_for_massive_project.html. The University of Pennsylvania was also developing Pennovation, a complex of offices, labs, and studios at a former industrial site south of its campus on the west side of the Schuylkill.

65. Glenn Blumenfeld, "Why Philadelphia's Central Business District May End up in University City," *Philadelphia Business Journal,* January 26, 2016, https://www.bizjournals.com/philadelphia/morning_roundup/2016/01/why-philadelphias-central-business-district-may.html; Jacob Adelman, "Aramark Moving Schuylkill-Side as Downtown Office District Shifts West," *Philadelphia Inquirer,* September 12, 2016, https://www.inquirer.com/philly/business/real_estate/commercial/aramark-pmc-market-schuylkill-west-office-center-city.html.

66. Stephen Stofka, "Sizing Up Schuylkill Yards," Hidden City Philadelphia, March 30, 2016, https://hiddencityphila.org/2016/03/sizing-up-schuylkill-yards/.

67. Sarah Reckhow, "Cities for Sale: Subsidies and Side Payments in Urban Development," 2019 Annual Conference of the American Political Science Association, August 30, 2019.

68. John E. Balzarini and Anne B. Shlay, "Gentrification and the Right to the City: Community Conflict and Casinos," *Journal of Urban Affairs* 38, no. 4 (2016): 503–17.

69. Interview with author #56, August 21, 2019.

70. Young was a controversial figure who had lost political credibility in 2013 when it came to light that in addition to being the founder and head of a nonprofit group in Mantua, he also stood to realize significant gains as a property owner and developer on a site that the Philadelphia Redevelopment Authority planned to acquire for a revitalization project. See Ryan Briggs, "Mantua Civic Leader Pushing Supermarket Also Is a Developer on the Project," My City Paper, Philadelphia City Paper, November 21, 2013, https://mycitypaper.com/article.php?A-Double-Role-16940. The example of Young, in addition to demonstrating how fraught the question of "community representation" can be in the context of a CBA process, also reveals a double standard. The prominent representation of real estate executives in the ranks of organizations structured around growth-boosterism and development lobbying does not draw opprobrium; Young's conflict of interest was costly to him, while more genteel (if more attenuated) instances of self-dealing read as unobjectionable, perhaps because their protagonists occupy a higher place in the social hierarchy.

71. Interview with author #56, August 21, 2019.

72. Said one Powelton interviewee as the Schuylkill Yards negotiation was beginning, "We've been in solidarity with Mantua and West Powelton on those economic issues and they've been in solidarity with us on the physical development issues. Solidarity has gone a long way toward developing an agenda in common." Interview with author #2, July 5, 2016.

73. Seventy-two million dollars represents approximately two percent of the $3.5 billion estimated development budget of Schuylkill Yards.

74. "'We Are Mantua!,'" 84.

75. Brandywine also created a program to introduce tenants in Schuylkill Yards and its other developments to local vendors, and to extend financial incentives to tenants who contracted with such vendors.

76. Interview with author #56, August 21, 2019.

77. "Councilman Bill Greenlee, chairman of the committee that considered the bill Tuesday, said that after more than a year of negotiations Blackwell believed it was time to 'start to move on.' A lawyer for Brandywine said Blackwell has asked the developers and the civic associations to reach an agreement before the legislation comes up for a final vote, which could be as early as June 22. After Tuesday's hearing, staff from Council President Darrell L. Clarke's office were attempting to mediate those negotiations." Tricia L. Nadolny, "Schuylkill Yards First Phase Gets Council Committee Approval, despite Neighbors' Unrest," *Philadelphia Inquirer*, June 13, 2017, https://www.inquirer.com/philly/news/politics /schuylkill-yards-first-phase-gets-council-committee-approval-despite-neighbors-unrest -20170613.html.

78. The CBA signed in 2017 covered Phase 1 of the Schuylkill Yards development, as did the zoning approval that the CBA facilitated. The Mantua-Powelton Alliance intended to negotiate for a larger share of the development budget in subsequent bargaining connected to later land use approvals. However, community groups ultimately agreed simply to extend the five-year contribution specified in 2017 for an additional ten years. Brandywine will thus contribute $620,000 annually to the Community Fund through 2032. This total amount represents 0.05 percent of the Schuylkill Yards development budget (and far less in present value terms).

79. Harold Meyerson, "No Justice, No Growth," *American Prospect*, October 22, 2006, https://prospect.org/special-report/justice-growth/.

80. See reference in Chapter 3 to Walter Phillips interview with G. Holmes Perkins. Digital Collection, Walter Massey Phillips Oral Histories, Special Collections Research Center, Temple University Libraries. Philadelphia, PA.

81. See Ta-Nehisi Coates, "The Case for Reparations," *Atlantic*, May 14, 2021, https:// www.theatlantic.com/magazine/archive/2014/06/the-case-for-reparations/361631/; Edward G. Goetz, Rashad A. Williams, and Anthony Damiano, "Whiteness and Urban Planning," *Journal of the American Planning Association* 86, no. 2 (June 2020): 142–56; A. Kirsten Mullen and William Darity, *From Here to Equality: Reparations for Black Americans in the Twenty-First Century* (Chapel Hill: University of North Carolina Press, 2020).

82. Laura Wolf-Powers, "Community Benefits Agreements in a Value Capture Context," in *Land Policy Series: Value Capture and Land Policies*, ed. Gregory K. Ingram and Yu-Hung Hong (Lincoln Institute of Land Policy, 2012), 217–28.

83. Gentrification and displacement are beginning in some places to be considered as impacts of development, thus fitting anti-displacement measures within the rubric of mitigation. See Miriam Zuk and Karen Chapple, "Case Studies on Gentrification and Displacement in the San Francisco Bay Area" (Berkeley, CA: Center for Community Innovation, 2015), https://www.urbandisplacement.org/sites/default/files/images/case_studies_on _gentrification_and_displacement-_full_report.pdf.

84. Interview with author #4, July 8, 2016.

85. Interview with author #5, July 8, 2016.

86. Interview with author #1, June 7, 2016.

87. Hilary Silver, "National Urban Policy in the Age of Obama," in *Urban Policy in the Time of Obama*, ed. James DeFilippis (Minneapolis: University of Minnesota Press, 2016), 11–44. Obama's timid attempts to achieve tax exemptions for businesses that located or invested in his 22 Promise Zones nationwide met with no success in Congress.

88. Stephen J. McGovern, "Analyzing Urban Politics: A Mobilization-Governance Framework," *Urban Affairs Review* 56, no. 42020: 1011–52, 1039.

Conclusion

1. Melissa Romero, "$3.5 Billion Schuylkill Yards Breaks Ground on Future Park," *Curbed Philly*, November 8, 2017, https://philly.curbed.com/2017/11/8/16622906/schuylkill -yards-groundbreaking; Inga Saffron, "Don't Count out Office Buildings Yet. Philly Developers Push Ahead with New, Pandemic-Resistant Designs," *Philadelphia Inquirer*, November 17, 2020, https://www.inquirer.com/real-estate/inga-saffron/schuylkill-yards-ucity-square -innovation-district-west-philadelphia-brandywine-wexford-labs-life-science-20201117 .html.

2. Michelle Caffrey, "University City Science Center Celebrates Grand Opening of 3675 Market St.," *Philadelphia Business Journal*, November 15, 2018, https://www.bizjournals.com /philadelphia/news/2018/11/15/photos-university-city-science-center-celebrates.html.

3. Sharon Zukin, "Planetary Silicon Valley: Deconstructing New York's Innovation Complex," *Urban Studies* 58, no. 1 (March 2020): 3–35.

4. Jennifer Clark, *Uneven Innovation: The Work of Smart Cities* (New York: Columbia University Press, 2020); Sharon Zukin, *The Innovation Complex: Cities, Tech, and the New Economy* (New York: Oxford University Press, 2020).

5. See Jamie Peck, "Struggling with the Creative Class," *International Journal of Urban and Regional Research* 29, no. 4 (2005): 740–70.

6. David Harvey, "From Managerialism to Entrepreneurialism: The Transformation in Urban Governance in Late Capitalism," *Geografiska Annaler. Series B, Human Geography* 71, no. 1 (1989): 3–17.

7. The Pew Charitable Trusts, Philadelphia 2021: The State of the City, April 2021, https:// www.pewtrusts.org/-/media/assets/2021/04/philadelphia-2021-state-of-the-city.pdf.

8. It was suggested to me that the public subsidy to office development might be passed on to tenants in the form of below-market rents, giving the innovation districts an advantage over other locations in the metropolitan region. However, inherent pressure to maximize return to shareholders of the real estate investment trusts who are party to the uCity Square and Schuylkill Yards developments makes this unlikely. Operating cost savings for tenants of the new complexes will come in the form of abatement of sales taxes, corporate income taxes, and personal income taxes for partners in limited liability corporations.

9. See John Marchese, "West Philadelphia, Reborn and Razed," *POLITICO Magazine*, July 13, 2014, https://www.politico.com/magazine/story/2014/07/philadelphia-drexel-john-fry -108819/. Marchese's article, a profile of Drexel President John Fry, asserted:

> High-tone name notwithstanding (the original Mantua was the home of the
> Roman poet Virgil), the area of trash-strewn empty lots and rundown brick houses
> has long been an unsolvable blot on the Philadelphia map. . . . Long ago carved out
> of what had once been part of the estate of one of the country's first federal judges,
> Mantua by the mid-20th century had become a stable home for working-class

homeowners when white flight and urban decay turned it into a center of black poverty. By 1970, the area was almost completely African American, and most of its residents made half as much money each year as the average Philadelphian. By the '80s and '90s, Mantua was besieged by drug dealers, gangs and the crime that accompanied them. Those who could get out, did; over the last several decades, Mantua's population declined by 50 percent. . . . Enter John Fry, who, almost from the day he assumed the presidency of nearby Drexel University in 2010, has made it his mission, and the mission of the school's 26,000 students, to be what he called "the most civically engaged university in the nation." And that very much involves the audacious task of reinventing Mantua, whose sketchy row houses and abandoned storefronts lie just minutes from the university's compact urban campus.

10. Dan Immergluck and Tharunya Balan, "Sustainable for Whom? Green Urban Development, Environmental Gentrification, and the Atlanta Beltline," *Urban Geography* 39, no. 4 (April 2017): 546–62.

11. A deep examination of our country's current affordable housing finance system is beyond the scope of this analysis. But it is extremely difficult for a city, acting unilaterally, to catalyze the production of deeply affordable housing. If the City of Philadelphia is to realize the full potential of recommendations made here, changes are necessary that free resources for social housing at the state and federal levels of government.

12. Strong surveys of the "anchors" literature can be found in Meagan M. Ehlenz, "Gown, Town, and Neighborhood Change: An Examination of Urban Neighborhoods with University Revitalization Efforts," *Journal of Planning Education and Research* 39, no. 3 (August 2017): 285–99; and Meagan M. Ehlenz, "Neighborhood Revitalization and the Anchor Institution," *Urban Affairs Review* 52, no. 5 (March 2016): 714–50.

13. Research documenting many of these efforts can be found through the websites of the Coalition of Urban and Metropolitan Universities (http://www.cumuonline.org/) and the Democracy Collaborative (https://democracycollaborative.org/). See also John L. Puckett and Ira Harkavy, "The Role of Mediating Structures in University and Community Revitalization: The University of Pennsylvania and West Philadelphia as a Case Study," *Journal of Research and Development in Education* 25 (1991): 10–25.

14. David C. Perry and Wim Wiewel, *The University as Urban Developer: Case Studies and Analysis* (London: Routledge, 2005), 2.

15. Rita Axelroth Hodges and Steve Dubb, "Preface," in *The Road Half Traveled: University Engagement at a Crossroads* (East Lansing: Michigan State University Press, 2012), x. See also Davarian L. Baldwin, *In the Shadow of the Ivory Tower: How Universities Are Plundering Our Cities* (New York: Bold Type Books, 2021).

16. It is also possible to view this dilemma through the lens of cost. Legal scholar Sheila Foster has pointed out that land use regulation in the United States does not grapple with costs imposed when social networks in geographically defined communities deteriorate as a result of land use and development decisions. Foster argues for neighborhood social capital as "a common resource that deserves protection." Sheila Foster, "The City as an Ecological Space: Social Capital and Urban Land Use," *Notre Dame Law Review* 82, no. 2 (December 2006): 527–83.

17. "Drexel to Expand Dornsife Center, Seeking Community Input," West Philly Local, September 24, 2018, http://www.westphillylocal.com/2018/09/24/drexel-to-expand-dornsife -center-seeking-community-input/. Reportedly, the nonprofit organization that owned the center would otherwise have sold the building to a developer of student housing. The building is now operating as a satellite facility for Drexel's Dornsife Center for Neighborhood Partnerships.

18. Jim Brown, "Mayor Kenney and Others Show Unity in Rebuilding City Playgrounds," *Philadelphia Sunday Sun*, October 30, 2020, https://www.philasun.com/local/mayor-kenney -and-others-show-unity-in-rebuilding-city-playgrounds/. Mack was killed by gunfire while handing out basketball trophies in 2008.

19. See Chapter 4, note 65.

20. Dupree told a reporter in 2019 that he had moved to Mantua in the 1970s "with hopes of revitalizing the area through a grassroots artistic movement." Ryan Briggs, "Met Fresh Supermarket, 166 Homes and WURD Radio Are Moving to Mantua," *Philadelphia Tribune*, November 19, 2019, https://www.phillytrib.com/metros/met-fresh-supermarket-166-homes -and-wurd-radio-are-moving-to-mantua/article_860a69ce-656f-5dd5-af19-668b56c1bee4 .html.

21. Dan McQuade, "James Dupree Will Get to Keep his Mantua Art Studio," *Philadelphia Magazine*, December 11, 2014, https://www.phillymag.com/news/2014/12/11/james-dupree -will-get-keep-mantua-art-studio/.

22. Inga Saffron, "Mantua artist's resistance pushes Philly to build a better grocery store," *Philadelphia Inquirer*, January 19, 2018, https://www.inquirer.com/philly/columnists/inga _saffron/mantua-artists-resistance-pushes-philly-to-build-a-better-grocery-store-20180119 .html?mobi=true.

23. In 2017, urban planner and nonprofit executive Jamie Gauthier defeated incumbent Jannie Blackwell for the city council seat in Philadelphia's 3rd District. Blackwell had held the seat since 1992, when she took it over from her husband, Lucien Blackwell, who had held it since 1974.

24. One hundred and twelve of the units will be priced at market rate. Eighteen will be priced as "workforce housing" for homebuyers. Twenty-seven will rent to households earning 50 to 60 percent of Philadelphia's Area Median Income (AMI). Five will rent to households earning less than 20 percent of the AMI.

25. In a classic density/affordability tradeoff, potential affordability was also foreclosed by Mantua Civic Association members' resistance to a project that was significantly out of scale with the surrounding neighborhood. Lomax's initial proposal was for two hundred units of housing and a seven-story structure.

26. Briggs, "Met Fresh Supermarket."

27. Carla Maria Kayanan, Joshua Drucker, and Henry Renski, "Are Innovation Districts an Effective Strategy for Community Economic Development?" presented at the Association of Collegiate Schools of Planning Annual Conference, November 6, 2020.

28. Richard Florida, Patrick Adler, and Charlotta Mellander, "The City as Innovation Machine," *Regional Studies* 51, no. 1 (2016): 86–96. Florida, Adler, and Mellander assert that "place has come to replace the industrial corporation as the key economic and social organizing unit in the modern-day knowledge economy," 91.

29. Kayanan, Drucker, and Renski, "Innovation Districts."

30. Zitcer, Hawkins, and Vakharia rely on data from the Lower Lancaster Corridor to make a similar point about arts and cultural development. Andrew Zitcer, Julie Hawkins, and Neville Vakharia, "A Capabilities Approach to Arts and Culture? Theorizing Community Development in West Philadelphia," *Planning Theory & Practice* 17, no. 1 (2015): 35–51.

31. Amartya K. Sen, *Development as Freedom* (Oxford: Oxford University Press, 1999).

32. Nichola Lowe, *Putting Skill to Work: How to Create Good Jobs in Uncertain Times* (Cambridge, MA: The MIT Press, 2021). See also Nichola J. Lowe and Laura Wolf-Powers, "Who Works in a Working Region? Inclusive Innovation in the New Manufacturing Economy," *Regional Studies* 52, no. 6 (2017): 828–39.

33. See Marchese, "Reborn and Razed."

34. Goetz, Williams, and Damiano, "Whiteness and Urban Planning"; Coates, "The Case for Reparations"; Ewing, *Ghosts in the Schoolyard*; Katherine Franke, *Repair: Redeeming the Promise of Abolition* (Chicago: Haymarket Books, 2021); Ezra Klein, "Bryan Stevenson on How America Can Heal," *Vox*, July 20, 2020, https://www.vox.com/21327742/bryan-stevenson-the-ezra-klein-show-america-slavery-healing-racism-george-floyd-protests.

INDEX

ACKNOWLEDGMENTS

I have many people to thank. My wonderful parents, Charles W. Powers and Barbara Ley Toffler and Elizabeth and David Champney, have offered unstinting support, as have the beloved members of my nuclear family, Josh and Sasha Wolf-Powers. I owe each of these people deep gratitude for believing that I could complete a book manuscript and for allowing me the time and space to do so. Thank you for the last-minute copy edit, Josh. Also crucial were my sister, Catherine Powers, and my father-in-law, Frank Wolf, and his partner, Steven Abel, who welcomed me to their home on Fire Island for a writing retreat in October 2020.

Many academic allies have contributed to this book. Colleagues at the University of Pennsylvania's School of Design, especially Amy Hillier and Randall Mason, welcomed me generously when I arrived at Penn and have remained dear friends. My current friends and colleagues in Hunter College's Department of Urban Policy and Planning under the leadership of Joseph Viteritti helped carry me through the pandemic and have enabled me to remain optimistic about the future of planning and urban studies education. My students at Hunter are a continual inspiration and reminder of what academic research is for.

Numerous friends have discussed or read parts of this book in various stages of its development and offered invaluable contributions. They include Bob Beauregard, James DeFilippis, Marc Doussard, Akira Drake-Rodriguez, Ryan Good, Bob Lake, Nichola Lowe, Sigmund Shipp, Elaine Simon, Ken Steif, Peter Wissoker, James Wright, and Andrew Zitcer. In a more general sense, the community I have found with Jennifer Clark, Marc Doussard, Bill Lester, Nichola Lowe, and Greg Schrock has been a touchstone over many years. John Mollenkopf, who took me on as a research fellow at the Center for Urban Research at the CUNY Graduate Center at a key moment, deserves special appreciation. John is also my fellow editor at *Metropolitics*, an online journal of public scholarship about cities and urban politics, where I have had the privilege of working with a brilliant group of peers since 2014. I would also like to thank Daniel Kirk-Davidoff, Todd Krichmar, Cristina Mathews, Marla Nelson, Kim Robinson, Lisa Sitkin, Laura Solitare, Kio Stark, and Rachel Weber for their friendship and inspiration, and my Rutgers University graduate advisers—Dorothy Sue Cobble, Susan S, Fainstein, and Ann Markusen—for theirs. In a very real way, this journey began in my undergraduate American Studies major, where Michael Denning and Ann Fabian were important influences. Before that, Mrs. Deanna Miller shaped my early interest in history and politics as my teacher at Western High School in Baltimore, Maryland.

Special thanks go to the Penn Press team—Mary Francis, Robert Lockhart, Lily Palladino—and to the research assistants who helped with this book: Vincent DeCesare, Jonathan Goins, Diana Lu, Josefina Peralta, Sophia Reuss, and most especially Lizzie Hessek (aka Elizabeth Rose), who is responsible for many of the visual images, including beautiful cartography. Thank you also to the dozens of people who gave their time to share insights, perspectives, memories, and analysis about the complex and ever-intriguing development politics of University City and Greater Philadelphia (see also "A Note on Sources" pages 151–154).